SEGMENTS
of
SOUTHERN THOUGHT

BY

Edd Winfield Parks

1938

COPYRIGHT, 1938

THE UNIVERSITY OF GEORGIA PRESS

ATHENS

COMPOSED AND PRINTED AT THE
WAVERLY PRESS, INC.
BALTIMORE, U. S. A.

To
MY FATHER AND MOTHER

Preface

IN RECENT years, the South has received its full share of attention. Many distinguished studies have appeared, ranging in nature from closely detailed monographs to broad interpretative surveys. Some of these works have approached definitiveness; more of them have indicated that we have only begun to investigate the complexity and many-sidedness of the region. Our recent industry has not compensated for the neglect of decades; and our interests have necessarily gone beyond those of research and of writing. At a time when we have as a section just been labelled "Economic Problem number 1," we may be on the point of receiving more than adequate attention, especially if this intense planning concerns itself with knowing the present and future only.

The informal studies presented here are tentative; they are intended to be suggestive, not final. They treat certain phases of Southern life and literature from a point of view, not overly popular at the present time, which is best described as distributist-agrarian; although I have made no attempt to impose this point of view upon a particular subject, I find it impossible to write without attempting also to interpret according to my own beliefs. It is only fair to note that some of these essays have a few times been called partisan, and they may be: the first essay may stand as invitation or as warning. The consistency in philosophical outlook may give some unification to the diverse matters which I have written about; I have also attempted to impose some order and sense of development through the arrangement, and through some revision; but the essays remain occasional pieces, written for specific reasons, and not prepared as a unit. Most of them have been printed before (I have inserted a record of first publication, to acknowledge my indebtedness to various magazines, books, and editors); two were presented as speeches before the Modern Language Association and the Southern Historical Association. The marks of origin are perhaps over-strong in places; and some duplication was inevitable, though I fear that I must ask the indulgence of readers for some repetition that was not as necessary as it once seemed.

I have no desire to claim Eugene O'Neill or George Borrow as Southern. In a sense, the inclusion of articles about them belies the title of this book, but I have properly segregated them. It may be that my approach, being in these instances so distinctly regional, will justify the inclusion; otherwise, it is traceable only to the author's whim.

The invitation to help in launching a University of Georgia Press, which would naturally be interested in regional matters, has seemed to me an extremely high compliment; for it, I am grateful to the Officials of the University and of the Press. Mrs. Malcolm H. Bryan helped to plan the book and was from the first its enthusiastic champion; Mr. Frazier Moore has given me many valuable suggestions, has read the proofs, and has aided greatly in the arduous labor of seeing the book through the press. Other publishers have been exceedingly gracious: The American Book Company has allowed me to reprint the Introduction to *Southern Poets*, which appeared in their American Writers Series under the general editorship of Harry Hayden Clark; Mr. W. T. Couch of the University of North Carolina Press has granted me the use of one chapter from the symposium, *Culture in the South*, which he edited; and Mr. Norman Forgue of The Black Cat Press has permitted the use of material which first appeared as an Introduction to *Sut Lovingood Travels with Old Abe Lincoln*. For help given in many ways, directly and indirectly, I am indebted to

John Donald Wade, Donald Davidson, Frank Owsley, Roosevelt Walker, and John Crowe Ransom; I hope that the use I have made of their wit and knowledge will reflect on them in a way not unworthy. Always, in the writing, the proof-reading, and the indexing, I have had the constant and perceptive help of my wife, Aileen Wells Parks.

E. W. P.

Athens, Georgia
September 20, 1938.

Contents

PART ONE

PART TWO

PART THREE

Part One

I

On Banishing Nonsense

I AM twenty-seven. It is an excellent time to make a personal inventory. The time has arrived, intellectually, for coming of age; for the setting, not the taking in, of sail. A friend who has almost reached the sail-gathering stage warns me that now is the time to banish nonsense from mind and life.

Yet the putting away of childish things calls, inevitably, for more stable and reliable things to put in their place. I am not ready to surrender such foibles as I possess until I can find equally attractive tenets and beliefs that seem to possess more validity. I want to have some vague understanding of my ship and its destination before I fret myself too much over sail and speed. The advice of Mr. Charles Edison, recently given to his employees, was: "Buy something. . . . It does not matter what you do—but get going and keep going. This old world is going to move." Such advice seems to touch the nadir of infantilism. It places all virtue in activity, in empty movement; it matters not whether we advance backward or forward, so long as we preserve the illusion of advancement.

We arrive at maturity, personally and nationally, by moulting just such illusions. The witches in *Macbeth* chant that they must *do and do and do*; our modern business men and their bridge-playing wives, many even of our most noted thinkers, seem to attach an equal importance merely to *doing*, without any regard for results. I have no desire to worship *that* ascendant god, however powerful he may seem at the moment; there are older, and I think better, gods not yet ready to be cast away. Surely, even in this

3

rapid age, there remains some place for reflection, though that particular god is in little demand just now. This seems to me unfortunate, for I see too many persons who set out blindly to achieve some good, and who, in the achieving, seem only to mar all that they touch.

I met a perfect example of this type recently. He had achieved some measure of fame, or at least of national reputation through, I suppose, the ability to write platitudes convincingly. The editor of a woman's magazine had commissioned him to spend a few days in the college halls, in order to discover what students were thinking. He flew from New York to Nashville, lingered on the Vanderbilt campus for less than twenty-four hours, and departed with a clear-cut conception of what Southern college students were about.

I for one do not know quite what students are thinking, though I have taught them for five years; I doubt if very many of them could give a lucid, reasoned statement of beliefs or principles. Such an article, if it embraced the views of many students, would require careful shading of expression and infinite subtlety of thought, and it would still be inadequate. Yet this man who surveyed the whole of college life in a few days will write dogmatically on the subject, telling the world what he thought should have been said; he will be read and believed by two million women, devoted lovers of platitudes, and these women will in turn pound his mis-statements into the heads of two million men; and we, in some new day, will reap the whirlwind whose seeds he has so blithely and thoughtlessly sown.

He had one particularly fine phrase: "We moderns need to think with our eyes." As nearly as I could gather, this came down to accepting as "progress" all the developments that are most conspicuous on the landscape, and being prepared to go forward, unquestioning, to greater and more rapid progress. As an example, he cited the great strides made by the world under the guidance of modern science.

I appreciate the comforts that science has bestowed upon us, but I realize only too well how dearly we have paid for such physical comforts. Science has done amazing things for the body, but it seems to have made little progress with either mind or spirit. And when science becomes theoretical, with regard to the universe, it becomes absurd. We may yet recognize that when men scrapped the mediaeval conception of the universe, with its idea of an all-inclusive ethic, then we gave up a system far more valuable than can be found in all the laws and theories of science. But these had moved the world, until the world was sadly out of joint and crying for any panaceas; and science had replaced old fable with doubtful fact, therefore science must, in all its phases, be good. Progress, to him also, meant movement.

And he talked at great length of one thing that education must do: the colleges must tear down the walls and let the world in.

Such a statement simply went far toward proving that, for all his survey of student life, he knew almost nothing of our colleges. Here the world is with us always, and the student rarely escapes it for longer than one hour at a time, in the occasional classes that are handled in formally scholastic fashion. The student has made of college a world in miniature, with extra-curricular activities as the primary and essential part of education; he must attend the movies, the dances, the games, the club meetings, even—by virtue of efficient supervision taken over from the time-clock system of business—his classes. He has so many things to attend that he has no chance to think about any one of them. Not only has the student no time to stand and stare; he has neither the desire nor the ability.   Always there are activities *to go out for*, with tangible letters and keys and insignia to prove his proficiency; always on the go, with as little thought about the desirability of his ultimate destination as any modern industrialist can have.   He thinks, even now, only with his eyes, and he rarely suspects that once walls existed around buildings no longer cloistered.

There are many definitions of education, and many conflicting ideas of how education can best be handed out, or acquired.   But, for my purpose, all these shades of meanings can be gathered roughly into two definitions.   The new idea—certainly one of the most forcefully applied new ideas—is that boys and girls can be taken, given certain information, molded to a certain pattern, and then turned out to save the world.   We are training leaders who cannot lead, thinkers who cannot think, for the sole emphasis is placed upon results: in this case, to secure and to retain facts, and to learn, preferably through extra-curricular activities, how to get ahead in the world.   Through a magic formula, graduation from college enables more men to become millionaires, to make high salaries, and to get in *Who's Who.*   So, at least, the colleges advertise.   Advocates of this type of education tend to believe that the greatest problems facing modern education are: first, to get more students into the colleges, and then for the teachers to learn how to handle large and ever larger classes effectively.

Queerly enough, I have noticed that the strongest exponents of industrialism and the strongest exponents of Communism are allied in this matter—and they receive great support from the quacks who preside in teachers' colleges. Education under their guidance, with a liberal dosage of intelligence tests, credit requirements, and propaganda, tends to become utterly mechanical and utilitarian.   Under this theory, no class can be good unless it contains hundreds

of students, no college can be considered important unless its enrolment runs into thousands. The personal equation is forgotten under the pressure of mass education.

But there exist, also, a few remaining persons who feel that the only real value of education lies in that neglected personal equation. Chiefly, it must be confessed, these persons tend to follow, though not with equanimity, the fallen lords of our civilization—the humanities, the classics, the culture that, according to communistic critics, leads nowhere—and they are slightly bewildered at the quick allegiance a majority of students pay to the up-and-pushing lords of economics and commerce and modernity. But it may be that in some dim tomorrow we may again have our day; and we can never get out of our heads the old and apparently forgotten truth that the real test of any civilization is the individuals who are produced in it. We do not prate much of *culture*, since that word has fallen into evil days, and we tend to shy away from the equally obnoxious word *gentleman* . . . but we are really intent on making students value culture not as knowledge alone, but as the distillation of sensitivity that remains after facts are forgotten, and equally intent on making them value men as individual persons, not as symbols of wealth, or of classes (proletariat or other), or of races. In an age when individualism has been almost totally submerged, we continue to talk only of individual values.

I know that I, for one, am doomed to continue talking of such values until they are not only submerged, but have completely ceased to exist. It may seem to be nonsense to follow this fallen lord, but I am not yet ready to forsake him.

II

But I have neglected too long the magazine writer who represents, as far as I am concerned, most of the things that

I consider evil. That same evening we talked of Communism, and he was as strongly for it as I am against it. But he spoke of it mainly, and most enthusiastically, as a *practical religion*, the greatest and most inspiring practical religion that the world has ever known. Shades of Christian Science! Cannot we have one thing of beauty or mysticism upon this earth, without some practical and very tangible matter being hitched to it? A practical religion is a paradox, an anomaly—something that has neither rhyme nor reason, nor excuse for being. We have come to the point that we cannot treasure intangibles, but must make a religion of work, or of play, or of a five-year plan ... and in the process become as brutish as the beasts in the slaughter-pen.

Later that same evening I talked with a deeply religious man from the little town that I continue to call home, and he began in a fashion that I find equally disconcerting. His church, he said, had never neglected, as so many churches have done, to perfect a plan for salvation. In a sense, this too is a practical religion, with some hope of reward in a not-too-distant day. But any plan of salvation must necessarily be imperfect, when measured by perfection, and I am content to believe that any God who may exist will be unable to see the creed for looking at the man.

Although I believe as little in the perfect creed as I do in the practical religion of Communism, I am not, and have never been, self-sufficient, and I feel the need of solace and comfort here on earth. Religion is neither entirely a matter of adequate clothes and food and dollars, nor entirely a fear of hell. Whatever it may be, the church does not offer it to me. Mysticism has gone out, and dignity, and grandeur in the nobler sense, and for replacement the church has provided campaigns against evolution or liquor or birth-

control. It has ceased to represent any world save the one
we know too well, and it has shown a marvelous genius for
taking the wrong side in any temporal quarrel.

Perhaps this discontent can be explained most concretely
by a description of my grandfather's funeral. That gentleman had been an Elder in the Presbyterian Church for over
fifty years, but his funeral service was conducted by a
young and enthusiastic preacher. The ceremony, at first,
was dignified and appropriate. Then, after a few well-
deserved remarks about the dead, the preacher launched
forth into a sermon to save souls and to reform the world—
for, after all, the man before us was gone, and nothing could
be done for him, but he could yet be used as an example of
what we, eventually, must come to.

Nothing could be done for him, it was true, save those last
rites and ceremonies, but something could have been done
for us. We had known and loved him, and we wanted to
feel that this man in the coffin had been, somehow and in
some indefinable manner, something more than flesh and
blood, that with him something had gone from the world
that could never, quite, be replaced. I wanted to feel that
human life was of greater dignity than the human body.
Instead, I felt cheapened, as I felt that he had been cheapened, and that the church through its representative had
failed us.

And the church, as I know it, has continued to fail most of
us. For the church, too, must be up-and-doing, with a
thousand meaningless campaigns and activities. As I write
this, every State that has voted on the liquor question has
voted for repeal, yet the church continues to organize the
prohibition forces, in a desperate effort to force men to be
good, through the domination of a small minority. This
seems to me a flat contradiction of any ethical principles that

may exist in the world, but I have long since ceased to expect a high code of ethics from any organization, and least of all from that body which prates most about goodness. The church is busy to save the heathen, but itself it cannot save. It is active always, and it too has no time for reflection. I once heard a preacher explain that these activities, and others like them, kept the minds of people from turning to evil thoughts, but it seems inevitable that this must also keep their minds from turning, in any larger sense, to good. Sterility is not merely negative, but positive—and is itself evil.

Jesus continues to live in the world not as my communistic friend said, because he drove the money-changers from the temple, or even because he advocated socialism; He continues because people are weak, and need comfort, and demand explanations of life that can never be proved by any laws of logic. All the rest seems to me nonsense, and I grow sick of it.

III

Let me try to make my point of view clearer by providing some personal details. I was born in a small town in the South, of a family that had been, in the main, farmers and planters since the days in the eighteenth century when a Scottish rebellion had made Scotland untenable for them. In many ways the family retains today something of a clannish feeling, and it retains as well a long, straight, rather large nose that gives the males a distinct resemblance to each other. As a result of this feeling of clan loyalty, perhaps, I believe that heredity influences and largely governs the total person as much as it does his features. Such a statement is unfashionable, today, and the most advanced thinker on our campus states dogmatically that people can, and must, be changed completely by the new ideals of education and of life. But I find little that is attractive in these new ideals, and I am more hopeful than he, for I think that the word *well-born* will continue for many generations to be used in praise, and not in blame, of an individual.

Ownership of land was in my father's blood. In his subconscious mind—which is to say, *really*—he has never felt that stocks and bonds possess tangible value. In one sense, I think that he is right. I do not suppose that he has clipped a coupon in his life. But hogs and cattle, horses and mules, corn, wheat, hay, and cotton are honest products, in which a man can take honest pride, and broad acres have not only a tangible bodily value, but an added non-monetary quality that carries an inflation of spirit. Of ownership in this sense, no amount of paper securities can ever mean anything. But he likes to walk or ride through fields of growing grain, to call hogs, and to supervise the multifarious farm duties.

Yet he has never been, in the strict sense, a dirt farmer; that is, one who does his own plowing and attends to most farm work personally. He has, however, a direct sense of pride and achievement and responsibility in the ownership of land that I have never quite known. In most of the days that I can remember, a farm has been a liability, with a disproportionate money tax upon it, and with an exceedingly uncertain financial return. I lack also his direct dependence on the land, as a source of spiritual strength as well as of financial security—recent years have sadly shaken his faith in that second item—but I know also that any philosophy I may ever have will be tempered and largely controlled by a similar faith.

In the last ten years I have lived for the most part in three large cities: Los Angeles, Boston, and Nashville. In all that time I have never once thought of myself as a city man, a cosmopolite and sophisticate. Always, behind each decision and each judgment, there has been a clear, if often unrecognized, background of small-town life. It has come, then, as something of a shock to realize that the word *city*, when used as an adjective, means all that is fine and desirable, *country* all that is backward and crude. This is an overturning of tradition and also, I believe, of fact: my experience has been precisely the opposite, that cities and city people are in general less considerate, more hurried, more ill-mannered, and possess fewer of the elements of culture (not, in my opinion, to be confused with literacy), than the country and its people.

A friend of mine, who came from Kansas and has travelled widely, recently told me that he regarded small-town life as the worst possible background for a child. In a city he would have the benefits of boy scout troops, libraries, and various activities ... he would have the benefit of directed and organized play. I know few men whom I like or admire more, but this attitude amazed me. It is one of the anomalies of American life that we must be taught to play. Even for children, there can be no such thing as spontaneous pleasure. The regimen of getting a group of children into bathing suits, in one teacher's college that I know, has all the formality of a Prussian military drill. Lift the left leg, put it through the suit, lift the right leg, et cetera, until the children are mere automatons capable only of following directions and, at nine, have less initiative than a West Point graduate. It is all a part of American efficiency, of the doctrine of work hard while you work and play hard, so as to get the most out of it, while you play.

Unfortunately, I do not believe in the doctrine, just as I do not believe that the small town is bad for the child. For him in particular, it seems the best of all possible worlds. I can watch my own nine-year-old brother, and I notice that he is never bored, that he cannot, in fact, make the day stretch sufficiently to encompass all that he desires to do. He can hunt, swim, fish, ride a pony, drive cattle, play baseball and a hundred other games, keep a miniature and constantly changing zoo, visit with his friends, white and black, and get into and out of mischief with amazing facility. Always, when not in school, he is occupied with spontaneous play. And he enjoys school. The teacher may lack certain qualities and the school certain equipment, but the relationship remains at all times human. Efficiency has not mechanized any phase of his training. Whatever defects may exist can be corrected by the family.

In his day he will read a ton of trash, but that will do him far less harm than reading for a purpose. Enough that he enjoys reading, enjoys being read to, and has good books constantly around him, that will be commented on in his presence and that may attract him. With the uncritical enthusiasm of youth he will sample many things, but of this I am certain: his reading will never be guided in such a way that he will realize that it is being *directed for him*. If he has not native wit enough to enjoy the better books, and to grow beyond a liking for merely popular literature, then may Zane Grey and his fellows always be a comfort to him, as the Catholic Church has comforted in another way equally unintellectual people. Enough also that he enjoys small-town life. Now in New Mexico, he writes me that he is living mainly to return home in order to buy himself a goat. I too once owned a goat and wagon, until pride of ownership and pleasure in riding ceased to be novelties, but in that period, I remember well, were several adventurous wrecks and countless unkind remarks about the odor clinging to my person. But he will have his goat, and the family will suffer until he tires of it, and he will be the better for the experience. It will be worth more to him than ten years of organized play.

IV

In the same conversation this man added that for him the ideal life would be to have an apartment in midtown New York, near the theatre district, and money enough to go to Europe once or twice a year. I am not trying here to set up a man of straw, in order to have a target that can easily be knocked down, for I realize only too well that in the eyes of most people such an existence is greatly to be prized. Yet to me it seems singularly unattractive.

One must have roots somewhere. I do not go as far as the old lady who said, "Where the roots are set, the plant ought to grow." But I do believe that one must have a sense of permanence, a feeling of belonging, that can never be reached by an apartment-dweller in any large city. I remember that some years back, in a more prosperous day, almost every house in Los Angeles had a *For Sale* sign on the lawn—which helps to explain much of the shoddy cheapness of that and of many another city. For men are not like articles in a store, and a rapid turnover of residential inhabitants signifies invariably that something is wrong with the city, the people, or both. That statement does not accord with American life, I know, for our most valid tradition has been one of *change*. In a sense, this shifting population is a distinct outgrowth of the frontier, with its pattern that moved, with amazing rapidity, ever westward, then turned about on itself and made of our cities a final frontier. But it has been in every case a physical movement; our philosophical content with life has lagged in inverse ratio to the rapidity of our material advances. For my part, I am ready to dig in, to try to assay the profits and losses of the action and of the movement that seems to have bewildered all of us.

I am of Tennessee. It may be that the civilization of England or of Virginia or even—though God knows I do not believe it—of New York is better than the one in which I grew up. But I have no desire to transplant myself. When I graduated from the oldest college in the country, I toyed for many days with the idea of newspaper or magazine work in Boston or New York . . . work that I had previously done in various large cities. That was in a day when such jobs could be found, and I secured one offer that seemed eminently satisfactory. Yet, in the end, I gave it up, to return to meagre opportunities in the section that I prefer to regard as home. A few times, when overwhelmed by petty discontents, I have regretted that day, and regretted similar opportunities that I have let slip through somewhat reluctant fingers.

But I know that is is better so. I never felt at home in Boston or New York or Los Angeles: they were pleasant towns to visit, but none of them could ever be satisfactory to live in. I prefer a more leisurely way of life, in a place where at least the surface amenities and decencies are preserved, and where men even yet tend to value another man for what he *is*, rather than what he *has*, or what he *has done*. I need to feel that I have roots somewhere, and permanence. The city as a collective whole has a massive stability, but no single part and most certainly no person in it has. It is a confused flux and blur of change, and that change, to my mind, has rarely been for good.

The entire process has made for the standardization and mechanization of mankind. Personal values are lost in a collective virtue, until men, too often, are known by the organizations they keep up. Men come to look upon other men as so many robots, to be shouldered aside without any sense of personal obligation for the other person. Indeed, life has become too complex, too highly competitive, for any man to worry over ethical problems, or personal obligations, or even common decency.

But this complexity seems artificially constructed, by men who have no philosophy of life save that of material progress. When an important manufacturer can announce that automobiles are too well-made and last too long, when great bankers can juggle without scruple with other men's money, when newspapers and magazines print shoddy half-truths and false advertisements deliberately, when every decent idea seems to be used only as a hypocritical gloss to cover lack of personal or organized integrity, it seems time to call a halt. Men cheapened by prosperity have not become ennobled through adversity. The world continues to hunt, and be hunted, in packs, and woe to him that fails. Our greatest economic fallacy, perhaps the root of the many fallacious economic ideas, was that any great or permanent good could ever come through tremendous organizations and through the centralization of wealth. Once again the personal equation has been forgotten: a manufacturer recently explained to me that he felt no compunctions about turning out shoddy goods, since he did not know any of the people who bought his product. I have stated baldly what he phrased most delicately, and I have seen and checked hundreds of other delicately phrased statements that come to the same unadorned truth when stripped of verbiage.

The net result of our intricate and interrelated business system has been to relieve every person of direct responsibility. I do not pretend to understand the vast system that has grown up, but it requires only the faintest glimmer of comprehension to realize that much of it is bad. I do not expect to do anything about it; I do not pretend to know what should be done, in many cases. But I have a firm conviction that wealth must again be decentralized, that small and local industries must replace the great chains, and that we must once more realize that basically the city is only a clearing-house for the country. If that day ever comes, we may again have a sane national life, we may cease to be a nation of salesmen trying to stimulate artificial demands for articles that are useless and unnecessary, and we may again have business men who feel that personal integrity is not too dear a luxury, and honest craftsmanship is an obligation to oneself as well as to one's customer. In other words, we may abolish the cant of service and restore the idea of honest workmanship.

But that day seems far off, and almost unattainable. In a civilization that seems headed for Communism, and that is already experimenting with Socialism, that worships at the shrine of the abstract billion-dollar corporation and the high-pressure salesman, it seems absurdly futile to talk of the direct values, both tangible and intangible, of localism and of agrarianism, of the small but independent business and the small but independent man. For that lord, too, has fallen, and he may never rise again. But if there is one thing of value in the semi-feudal system that we are rapidly scrapping, if there is one thing of value or dignity in the Southern tradition, it is precisely to be found in this value set upon the individual. I know that it is rank and quixotic nonsense not to join the great bandwagon of industrialism, not to substitute prosperity for all those matters so closely entwined with localism and tradition that I consider most valuable, and not to be an ardent liberal in a land that damns the conservative. But I can place little faith in social planning that attempts to deal only with a mechanistic civilization, or with social reforms that reduce all human beings to an exact standard and neglect all the imponderables of life.

Men who believe implicitly in the value of the *idea*—it does not matter much what that idea may be—who dedicate themselves to acquiring a position of power, or of reforming the world, or even of securing for themselves some recognition by posterity, will undoubtedly accomplish much in this world. But that accomplishment, too often, has made for evil rather than for good—especially when men have attempted to reduce individuals to mathematical or social abstractions, in order to make them accord with some preconceived idea. It may be that we need to think more of the present and less of the future, more of making ourselves decent persons and less of reforming others, and that, above all, we need to set more value on *being* and less on *doing*. By too great a widening of horizons we may lose everything save perspective; by narrowing the horizon, we may intensify not only thought, but emotion. For some years it has been the fashion to talk of the moral obligation to be intelligent; it seems even more true that a man is under a moral obligation to be pleasant, and, if he has wit enough, to be amusing. At least by this process we set the primary value upon the person, though we may waste a certain amount of time that would help us onward in the world, and we do not attempt to over-simplify life by discarding those human elements which will not fit neatly into our theories.

Only through human relationships can men understand those uncertainties and those imponderables that endure always, and that make me, for one, doubtful of simple and clear-cut schemes to save mankind. I find it difficult to forget, also, that flood and rain and storm have never yet been harnessed by clerks in an office, and that no scientist has yet devised an asbestos jacket for a sun that is lavishly wasteful of heat and energy.

Until that day shall come, or at least until the way of life that I prize has been irrevocably doomed, I expect to neglect the two broad and easy roads open to the modern—that of enthusiasm for centralized industrialism or Fascism on the right, and for Communism or something similar on the left— for the narrow and rutty lane of localism and individualism. Since I am no romantic, I know full well that what I shall have to say will be of slight avail, and may be of little worth, but I can at least retain an honest skepticism about the infallible virtues of progress, in a civilization that is going too fast, and without direction; and I can hint softly, from time to time, that leisure also has its worth, and that the normal pace of society is slow.

II

The Background of Southern Thought

WHEN Captain John Smith arrived in Jamestown in 1607, he brought with him an English attitude which distrusted all things foreign to his own race and tradition. He noted with a curious eye the customs of the Indians, who seemed to him and to his successors heathen savages, either to be exterminated, or Christianized and made into peaceful servants. Whatever culture these Indians had made no impression upon the doughty captain, who had a neat taste for literature himself and in later years occasionally spiced the fabric of his descriptive prose with a verse that, if not particularly good in itself, was at least in the best Elizabethan manner. The highly conventionalized poetry (the tribal chants and death songs, for example) of the Indians made no impression then or later upon what we have come to think of as Southern poetry. To John Smith, Virginia was only the lengthened shadow of England.

For more than a century the South remained in spirit and in fact a continuation of England. Richard Rich wrote in 1610 that "wee hope to plant a nation where none before hath stood" but the context shows clearly that he meant an English colony. A man like George Sandys found it a temporary haven, a place where as treasurer he must spend some years of his life. But his desires centered about the London from which he felt himself in temporary exile, and it was for men in London that he polished so carefully his classical translation of Ovid's *Metamorphoses*. Most men of position felt themselves temporary residents in the new land. Yet, inevitably, a dual allegiance came into being. A Virginia planter like William Byrd, educated at the Middle Temple and with a wide acquaintance in London, might consider himself an English gentleman, might complain of English friends that "distance they reckon the same as death"— but he found that distance too great to traverse, and he found also that it led to constant governmental misunderstandings which fretted him and his friends mightily.

On the seaboard a colonial aristocracy developed rapidly. Indentured servants, after they had secured freedom by work, and free men with little money, tended to move west and take up land, leaving a settled landed gentry which in turn imported more servants or more slaves. In a land where social lines had not become strait and well-defined, this gradual transformation was not unusual, although it was, naturally, limited to the shrewdest and most capable men. The number of *bona fide* members of the English aristocracy was numerically small, as U. B. Phillips notes: "A thin sprinkling of the genteel class came from England until Cromwell's time, when fairly numerous opponents of the Roundheads sought asylum in the colonies." More important was the idea of aristocracy, which from the beginning was firmly planted in the Southern colonies. To men at that time this ideal way of life was most nearly approximated by William Byrd with his thousands of acres, his slaves, his fine house, and his library of four thousand choice volumes. If few men could do that well, they were at least headed in the same direction.

The settled country and the frontier had divergent interests and were often in opposition. Only a few times did these differences lead to open and dramatic conflict, as in 1676 when Nathaniel Bacon rebelled against Governor

Berkeley and organized the frontiersmen to fight against the Indians, or as in 1785 when John Sevier and his fellows west of the mountains revolted against North Carolina and organized the short-lived State of Franklin.   Such outbreaks are rare and incidental; a truer picture can be gained by a comparison of the sections in quieter times.

The seaboard South had an established religion; such a religion did little to encourage thought or writing.   The Episcopal church was in authority and ministers saw little need to defend it.   They were not, as were the Puritans, "leading a great body of men out of this castellated state of mind"; they were rather set upon holding to traditional ways and beliefs.   The racial and religious homogeneity of this powerful aristocracy was not fully broken up until after the Civil War.   But it received before that time many a rude jolt.   The waves of population brought Huguenots to South Carolina after the Edict of Nantes (1685); the founding of Georgia as an asylum for dissenters and outcasts in 1732 brought Lutherans, Moravians, and Salzburgers, and brought, along with the English, the propagation of Methodism; but, most important of all, the years brought a steady stream of Scotch-Irish to the frontier.   The seaboard welcomed these immigrants, partially for the mercenary reason that landowners could sell farms to them, but more because of the reason advanced by Governor Gooch of Virginia in 1738: that the Presbyterians would serve as a buffer between the seaboard and the Indians.

Since it influenced the leaders primarily, and through them permeated in diluted form the thought of most men, the influence of deism and rationalism in the latter part of the eighteenth century was important, although not so important as it was in the Middle Colonies; it contributed, along with the views of the Presbyterians, Baptists, and

Methodists, to American independence and to the separation of church and state in the new republic. Not until Revolutionary days did these sects and these philosophies displace the established church, but they did succeed in helping to make it conservative and lifeless. While Cotton Mather wrote his four hundred books, and Puritan divines produced before 1750 a body of work tremendous in volume and not unimpressive in quality, the Episcopalians wrote almost nothing; it is perhaps not without significance that today men blame many of our evils upon the Puritans, but neither blame nor praise is given to the Episcopalians.

The Puritan also had turned to education as one form of betterment and had founded schools. The Southern gentleman preferred to educate his children at home under supervision of a tutor, and then to send his sons to England for college or legal education. There was considerable opposition to free schools. Governor Berkeley in 1670 had expressed the dictatorial spirit regarding education, when he declared: "I thank God there are no free schools nor printing [in Virginia], and I hope we shall have none these hundred years, for learning has brought disobedience and heresy and sects into the world, and printing has divulged them and libels against the best of governments." Apparently the first newspaper established in Virginia was *The Virginia Gazette*, published by William Parks at Williamsburg in 1736; the first college, William and Mary, was founded in 1693. Schools and newspapers soon became common enough throughout the region, but the true Southerner continued to look to England for his education, when the family's resources would permit.

Education in newly settled regions was of necessity fragmentary. Thus John Marshall received almost no formal schooling until in 1780 he temporarily left the army to study law for six weeks under George Wythe, the greatest lawyer in Virginia, at William and Mary. And Wythe, although called by Thomas Jefferson the best Greek and Latin scholar in Virginia, was entirely self-educated. Fairly typical of the education given to sons of well-to-do planters was that given to Jefferson. His father was almost entirely self-taught, but Peter Jefferson was a capable mathematician who enjoyed the works of Addison, Swift, Pope, and Shakspere, and desired that his son have a classical education. Thomas was educated in private English and Latin schools conducted by clergymen until in 1760 he entered William and Mary. Then he studied law under Chancellor Wythe. His nephew, Peter Carr, went to Edinburgh; Thomas Randolph to France. Over and over these stories could be repeated in the lives of other men. In the years that followed came the gradual founding and development of state and sectarian universities. Schools like the universities of Virginia and of North Carolina gained a favor which did not extend to elementary public schools, however, until the nineteenth century, and in most Southern states not until after the Civil War.

The Southerner largely copied the educational system of England. Equally he looked to England for his literature. The seventeenth-century Southerner read the Elizabethan dramatists and the Restoration wits; in the eighteenth century his descendants turned to Dryden, Pope, Fielding, Swift, Johnson, and Goldsmith. More and more, however, the planters and lawyers studied the works of the philosophers, of Hume and Hooker and Harrington and, particularly, Locke. As men became more interested in governmental theory they tended to abandon *belles-lettres* and to concentrate upon political philosophy. The lawyer and the plantation-owner were alike respected; men returned from London or Princeton to sit under Chancellor George Wythe of Virginia, and receive a training at once broad and intensive. Such training took for granted a thorough knowledge of Latin literature: a man was expected to quote his Horace or Cicero as readily and correctly as his Locke or Pope. This development was natural enough in regions controlled by the aristocracy. The frontier regions at once emulated it and revolted against it; the struggles of Patrick Henry against privileged classes in Virginia is best known, but his attitude and his contentions could be matched in every other colony.

The aristocratic yet acquisitive planter of the seventeenth century had largely been replaced by the lawyer. If William Byrd can be cited as the ideal of early Virginia and of the early South, equally can Chancellor Wythe be considered the ideal of the eighteenth century.

The Revolution almost seemed to remove definite barriers. Before that time only three small areas were settled; immediately after the war, wave after wave of men crossed the mountains. Along the eastern coast the farmer was pushed out or absorbed by the plantation-owner; he "found it of no advantage to live within hail of ocean-going ships; and most of those who owned tidewater farms sold them to neighboring planters and moved inland." The Virginia planter depended upon tobacco, and would traffic with no middleman, but shipped directly to England; around Charleston and Savannah, in the rich indigo and rice—and later cotton—districts, there developed a system of marketing through towns. Geography caused the relative poverty of North Carolina, with its poorer soil and broken topography. From these sections largely, after the Revolution, men moved into the west, and they sought, primarily, land. Harriet Martineau wrote (1837): "The possession of land is the aim of all action, generally speaking, and the cure of all social evils among men in the United States." By 1836 the South was formed, in so far as its human geography was concerned. But the process of its settlement has less importance, as background for literature, than some of the conditions which arose in that process.

These new states, contrary to modern belief, were not unified either sectionally or nationally. Certain definable influences can be traced, certain beliefs and trends and ways of life. But this tracing results in over-simplification, when, as here, only the broad outlines can be drawn. Holland Thompson has neatly contrasted the diverse elements in the ante-bellum South: "There was a South of the plantation, and of the upland farm; of the Coastal Plains and of the mountains; the South with lands almost incredibly fertile and the barren South where living was hard; the civilized South, and nearby the South ignorant and rude; the austere Calvinist South, and the South of romance; the haughty aristocratic South and the democratic South."

The most important unit was the state. It took precedence over the nation, and men resigned from the United States Senate to serve as governors of their state. Even the state, in early days, was insufficient: John Sevier and his fellows west of the mountains, in 1785, calmly seceded from North Carolina and established the state of Franklin; just as calmly, after Tennessee was admitted to the Union, its citizens proceeded to negotiate with Spanish governors of Louisiana in a manner little short of treasonable. "These United States" was the term used, in its literal sense; Alexander Stephens employed a significant phrase when he wrote that Calhoun "would like to see this Confederacy abolished." Yet this independence of states and localities can easily be overdrawn: it was a Tennessean who wrecked Nullification, and some of the bitterest foes of Nullification were South Carolinians. Vernon L. Parrington's analysis remains pointedly true: "It is the North that has changed, and not the South, and the nationality that sits so easily upon us would have seemed ominous to the simpler world that determined the ideals of the Old Dominion. The southern mind has grown old-fashioned, but it is native and of long and honorable descent. It derived its singularity from the eighteenth century in which it took shape; and it retained the clear impress of its origins long after the eighteenth century had become an anachronism in America ... this political agrarianism, parochial in its outlook rather than national, suffices to explain the singularity of the southern mind in the eyes of a later industrialized America."

Before the South did become a unified section (chiefly through the welding force of outside attacks made upon it, and even then less completely than is generally realized), it was influenced chiefly by three philosophies: of physiocratic agrarianism, developing through Jefferson; of imperialism which, under Calhoun, took the ideal of a Greek democracy; and of the frontier. These divergent philosophies finally took shape to form the Southern mind, a political and economic mind which liberals like William P. Trent partially misunderstood and called feudal. He considered only the planters.

The superficial aspects of the life of the plantation owner are well-known. His tradition became in the hands of romancers the Southern tradition: a stately house surrounded by broad fields, with a dignified, goateed master and good-looking, capable mistress, with daughters at once beautiful, pure, and flirtatious, with sons wild yet noble, and with slaves contentedly working in house or fields. Here hospitality reigned supreme and good living was ennobled until it became an art. Such is the novelist's conception of the South—a conception not without elements of truth.[1] But this picture omits from consideration the yeoman farmer; as John Spencer Bassett discerningly notes: "This class of men has received but little attention from those who have written of Southern society, and yet it was the backbone of that society. There was little that was ideal about such men. They were humdrum, but they were honest, pious, and substantial, and they were numerous." Some owned a few slaves; more of them worked their fifty or one hundred acres entirely by themselves; they shaded, as a class, from small plantation owners to poverty-stricken farmers. With the exception of the mountaineers, however, all of these men were distinctly Southern in sympathy, when war came. The reason for that attitude must be traced to the heritage of Jeffersonian agrarianism—a heritage which did much to form the mind of the South.

The political idea of democracy had evolved in American minds primarily from John Locke; the economic and later political doctrine of the South came largely from Quesnay and the French Physiocrats. Although Franklin introduced physiocratic agrarianism to this country, Jefferson first gave the philosophy a wide currency among a receptive audience—and in John Taylor of Caroline he found an agrarian economist who could elaborate and expound this doctrine. Briefly, the Physiocrats believed that "agriculture is the single productive form of labor, that from it alone

---

[1] V. L. Parrington writes, in *Main Currents in American Thought*, II, 29: "It is not so much that the worst did not get into the romantic tradition—shortcomings in Virginia life which even Wirt hints at—as that the best did not get in. The plantation master of the romantics falls grossly short of the reality that Virginia provided. The simple dignity of John Taylor, the ingrained Puritanism of Lee and Jackson, the Catholic culture and fine integrity of George Wythe, have been left out of the tradition. The Virginian created by the romantics is absurdly inferior to such men. . . ."

comes the *produit net* or ultimate net labor increment," and that all manufacturers and middlemen are parasites. But Jefferson and his followers rejected the benevolent despotism advocated by the French philosophers, and replaced it with the more congenial idea of democracy. To this he added "the doctrine of the terminable nature of contract," a doctrine which he amplified to include the view that "no society can make a perpetual constitution, or even a perpetual law." In this was the origin of the theory of states' rights; in this can be found one of the germinal ideas which later governed Southern thought. Long before slavery became an issue, John Taylor in 1814 pointed out that there was created "a fundamental conflict between the capitalistic and agrarian interests which was the origin of parties in the United States."

This agrarianism was never abandoned; it remained a determining factor in Southern thought. But it was elaborated and subtly transformed until the ideal of a Greek democracy replaced the humanitarian Virginia concept of Jeffersonian democracy, and the definite belief in the right of a state veto replaced the looser idea of a terminable contract. This was largely the work of two political philosophers—John C. Calhoun and Alexander H. Stephens—who rationalized the position of the South, and gave to that section a clear-cut philosophy. When slavery, after 1820, became too profitable to be voluntarily exterminated, and added this economic factor to equally vital philosophic considerations, Calhoun shifted the argument to democratic imperialism, which denied the natural rights theory of the Declaration of Independence, and held that democracy is possible only in a society which recognizes inequality as a law of nature. Liberty was "a reward to be earned, not a blessing to be gratuitously lavished on all alike." Calhoun also distrusted the merchant class, and he argued with sustained logic that slavery was preferable to wage servitude. To the "checks and balances" in the Constitution he added also the checking power of each state, and it was on this principle that South Carolina attempted Nullification. Logically, also, he turned to a strict construction of the letter of the Constitution, for he argued that "Two powers are necessary to the existence and preservation of free States: a power on the part of the ruled to prevent rulers from abusing their authority, by compelling them to be faithful to their constituents, and which is effected through the right of suffrage; and a power to compel the parts of society to be just to one another, by compelling them to consult the interest of each other—which can only be effected . . . by requiring the concurring assent of all the great and distinct interests of the community to the measures of the Government."

This ideal of Greek democracy, with its center in the plantation system, ran counter to frontier influence. For the constantly moving frontier was in a state of flux, which led men into contradictory positions. Thus, Andrew Jackson was instantly willing to disregard the orders of the federal government, when he attacked Florida; he probably said of John Marshall's decision on the Georgia Indians that "he has made his decision, now let him enforce it," but he also delivered the famous toast that the union must be preserved. Lawless and law-abiding, according to the particular question at issue—such was the frontiersman. And Jackson, who is confusedly regarded as a democrat, illustrates another point: there were several kinds of democracy on the frontier. Jackson represented the acquisitive land-owning class, the gentry; he was never one of the "wool-hat boys." The democratic frontiersman is better personified in David Crockett, the opponent of Jackson on the Public Lands question. Although Jackson might seem, and be, nationally the defender of the plain man, his real philosophy was that of the land speculator and frontiersman grafted on to the agrarian beliefs of Thomas Jefferson. His attack upon the National Bank was a direct attack upon consolidation of government, upon the growing power of capitalism. In that respect he agreed (though he probably would never have admitted such agreement) with Calhoun and South Carolina, but Jackson and the frontier generally never recognized the true basis of contention. And by 1836 the frontier had progressed westward beyond the boundaries of the South. A new question came then to plague Southern leaders: what would happen, in a government run by a numerical majority, when the South had become a hopeless minority?

Slavery, right or wrong, was ever-present, and it offered a convenient moral weapon with which to attack the South. But the basic conflict was between diverse systems—and the Civil War, eventually, was not fought over slavery. That was only a superficial cause, but its tangibility, in the propaganda of abolitionists, made it appear to overshadow all other issues. The conflict developed out of two entirely different philosophies of government which in turn had evolved from different economic systems: narrowly and immediately, a conflict between local and national sovereignty; basically, a conflict between agrarianism and industrialism. The Southern mind was a conservative, agrarian mind; the small farmer and the large planter, the yeoman and the slaveholder, were eventually forced into the same position because their philosophies possessed definite elements of kinship, and were at complete variance with the philosophy of industrialism. Always the Southerner remained loyal to the Union as he interpreted the Union, and Alexander Stephens late in life could truly declare that "no stronger or more ardent Union man ever lived than I was"—but the majority of Southerners, like Stephens, thought of the country as a confederacy, and the majority also, like Robert E. Lee, felt that first allegiance went not to the nation but to the state.

A religious transformation came over the South after 1800—a change which can be traced partially to the Calvinistic beliefs of the Scotch-Irish. Men like Calhoun and Jackson were hard, upright, honest, unbending; they lacked pliability; they might break but never bend. Deism had ceased to be largely influential. Methodism had spread throughout the Old Southwest. Perhaps the Biblical defense of slavery (which led Alexander Stephens to write: "To maintain that Slavery is *in itself sinful*, in the face of all that is said and written in the Bible upon the subject, with so many sanctions of the relation by the Deity himself, does seem to me to be little short of blasphemous!") completed this transformation of a cavalier religion into a puritanical religion. In Charleston, particularly, this attitude assumed a moral rather than a theological cast.

It made generally true the Southern contention that actual slavery was more civilized and decent than wage slavery. U. B. Phillips, in his *American Negro Slavery*, gives a temperate, informed judgment: "There was clearly no general prevalence of severity and strain in that regime . . . little of the curse of impersonality and indifference which too commonly prevails in the factories of the present-day world where power-driven machinery sets the pace, where the employers have no relations with the employed outside of work hours." The plantation was a community and that community was part of a stabilized order, a conservative way of life: if a man owned land and slaves, he accepted the personal obligation which such ownership imposed upon him and did not take refuge in an abstract relationship known as freedom. Not always, certainly; an imposing array of cases can be cited to show cruelty, mismanagement, illicit sexual relationships, and general lack of consideration for the Negroes. But an even more imposing list of exceptionally merciful masters can be drawn up, and there seems little reason to disagree with the verdict of F. P. Gaines, historian of the Southern plantation, that "In the large, the Negro who did his share of the work received a modest sufficiency of life's necessities and was not often subjected to any form of physical torture, either of punishment or of over-work."

Most Southerners had, in truth, grown blind to the evils of slavery; gone were the days before 1810 when Southern leaders fondly hoped and expected that slaves could be emancipated. As a result of Abolitionist attacks and of Nat Turner's Rebellion, they had been forced to defend their "peculiar institution," and they had developed a theory of government upon it. But that imperialistic theory was only superimposed upon the Jeffersonian theory of physiocratic agrarianism and of local sovereignty—and it is well to remember that the great majority of Southerners fought rather for agrarianism than for slavery, and that three states did not secede until Lincoln called for volunteers to invade the South.

The "irrepressible conflict" had been years in the making. In 1850 secession had seemed inevitable, and only a specious compromise held the Union together for a decade. The lines had become tautly drawn until Southern fire-eater and Northern abolitionist alike were ready for war. From the Southern point of view the ominous specter of the Republican party, with its strictly sectional policies, overshadowed all other matters and seemed to end a voluntary compact. The immediate issue was clearly defined, the basic issue thoroughly beclouded, when in 1858 Abraham Lincoln delivered his famous "house divided" speech. The following year the fanatical John Brown threw the South into a panic with his raid on Harper's Ferry. After Lincoln's election in 1860 seven states seceded and formed the Confederate States of America. Even then war might have been prevented or postponed, but the efforts of Douglas and Crittenden came to nothing while the president-elect and his party attended to their political fences. In April, 1861, Fort Sumter was fired on. War had come.

The story of that war is too well-known to need retelling here. The South began with high hopes of quick and complete victory, and the first year of conflict seemed to bear out these hopes. But it was the weaker section, and it was fighting a defensive war. Victories in Virginia were nullified by unspectacular but effective Federal campaigns in the west. Gradually the South was hemmed in, with one part— Texas, Louisiana, and Arkansas—cut off from the main body. The club of "King Cotton Diplomacy," confidently expected to force European intervention on the South's behalf, failed when England found our war a most profitable enterprise for her citizens. Even the states' rights theory operated against the successful prosecution of the war. After four years of dogged, gallant fighting General Lee surrendered at Appomattox, and the Confederacy collapsed.

The war had taken a horrible toll. While the North prospered and grew rich, the South served as battleground. Men who had gone into war jubilantly lived to see houses and property destroyed, relatives and friends killed, and their section ruined. In part this destruction was the natural result of the war being fought on Southern soil; in part it was due to a deliberate policy of destruction on the part of men like General Sherman, in his far-flung campaign, and like General Butler in New Orleans. Whether caused by military policy, as in Sherman's case, or simply by unintelligent brutality, as in Butler's, this deliberate destruction has left far more bitterness in its wake than all the horrors of legitimate war.

More horrible even than Sherman's march was reconstruction. Truly it deserves the titles of *The Tragic Era* and *The Age of Hate*. The Confederate soldiers had returned to raise crops on lands sown with bullets, and to patch up twisted and broken lives. The Negroes were free, but no provision had been made for them. All was confusion. Then to sectional despair was suddenly added a national confusion when John Wilkes Booth assassinated Abraham Lincoln. Death removed the one man who might have controlled the Republican politicians. To his place succeeded an honest and capable Unionist Democrat, Andrew Johnson of Tennessee—but Johnson had no power over Congress, and narrowly escaped impeachment at its hands. Government became strictly a party affair, the Southern states (the fact of whose secession the North had refused to admit) merely conquered territories to be governed by military rule until Congress decided that they could safely be re-admitted to the Union. Dominating that Congress were fanatical Thaddeus Stevens and vindictive Charles Sumner— party politicians bent primarily on keeping the Republican party safely in office.

The South was divided into military districts, and ruled by army generals. The local governments were taken over by white carpetbaggers, by Southern unionists who generally deserved their title of "scalawags," and by the freed Negroes.

These men sat in legislative halls, represented their states in Congress, and made a travesty of government. Corruption was everywhere, until state and city debts became unbearable. Only the hooded terror of the Ku Klux Klan, under the leadership of General Nathan Bedford Forrest, held the carpetbaggers and Negroes partially in check. James Truslow Adams, a temperate historian, not overkind to the South generally, has written: "There is no parallel for the situation in the history of modern civilized nations, and it is almost incredible that it occurred within our own country. No civilized victor was ever more ungenerous. The war had left the South prostrate; Reconstruction left it maddened."

Hardly less irritating was the attitude of Northerners who meant to be kind. The spirit of the South, as Frank Owsley notes in "The Irrespressible Conflict," must be changed; President Wayland of Brown University "regarded the South as 'the new missionary ground for the national schoolteacher,' and President Hill of Harvard looked forward to the task for the North 'of spreading knowledge and culture over the regions that sat in darkness.' " So Northern historians wrote *error* across the ideals of the lost cause, and Northern missionaries prepared to re-make one of the authentic cultures which this nation had possessed.

Thus was born the "Solid South." Except for occasional periods when local emotions or economic conditions have caused it to split, the section has remained closely unified. The free Negro was as much of a problem as the slave: one experience of his political control was more than enough. And the South, generally, has remained agrarian; it has suffered, as it suffered before the Civil War, but in greater degree, from high tariffs and protectionist policies. But its life and society have grown increasingly complex. For ten years, after the war, little could be done by native men. Schools were founded by the new "missionaries," and businesses established by them. In that decade the one significant change in the section was the growth of cities.

The ante-bellum South had little need for cities. Farm and plantation were really small communities, almost entirely self-sustaining. But the dangers of Reconstruction forced men to band closely together, and towns grew mightily almost overnight. Since few men possessed money, a system of tenant-farming or share-cropping developed, with the farms taken over by Negroes or poor whites; in many cases the owner superintended the farm work by day and returned to town at nightfall. The sons of these men knew little of farming, and that little was unpromising. They tended to move from the towns to the rapidly developing cities.

By 1880 the period of stagnation was over. If money could not be made from raising cotton or tobacco, it could from the manufacture of products from these crops. The South must be revived, men said, "not with cotton in the fields, but cotton in the mills."

Cities sought eagerly for these new industries. New towns like Birmingham were founded, with the development of coal and iron ore as their main objective. At first these industries were financed by local men, and their progress seemed heart-breakingly slow. But, significantly, they were founded to utilize local products, chiefly tobacco and cotton and iron ore, and they might have grown integrally out of the structure of society. These industries succeeded so well that Northern capitalists, like Northern missionaries of twenty years earlier, became interested. Andrew Carnegie and his competitors bought into the Alabama iron industries, and capitalists invested in new industries in many places.

By 1900 the period of self-development had largely passed

and the era of exploitation had begun. But long before that time two schools of thought contested for supremacy in the South: the old school conservative and agrarian, the new school progressive and industrialistic. The composite mind of the South since the Civil War has been torn between these two philosophies, but it has turned more and more to the group which advocates the development of industrialism.

A term was coined by the progressive leaders: "The New South." There had been an old South of slavery and secession, but that, said Henry Grady, was dead. A new order had come, a new and better way of life. If only his section could be awakened from its lethargy, if only it would become progressive and industrialized, then all would be well and prosperity would come again. Grady's early death soon silenced his prophetic voice, but able men were not lacking to carry his message. Publicists like Walter Hines Page excoriated the "Southern mummies" who were stubbornly agrarian—which in his eyes meant backward—in thought. In 1881 he published an article called "An Old Southern Borough." He portrayed a sleepy North Carolina town inhabited by Southern gentlemen, living in the past, unconscious of the present. They read Horace, Vergil, Addison; above all, they read Sir Walter Scott, and continued, as their fathers had done, to pattern their conduct on his bookish notions of chivalry. In contrast to these idlers, Page pictured the new order which had arisen; young men who advocated a burial of dead issues, a united country. These young men envisioned a South cured of all its troubles by three agencies: education, industrialism, and science. That message Page hammered home relentlessly, in articles and editorials. Even in a novel which is no more than propaganda, he presented the hero and ostensible author Nicholas Worth as confronted by three ghosts which dominated

Southern life: the ghost of the Confederacy, the ghost of religious orthodoxy, the ghost of negro domination. In the end the protagonist abandoned teaching and politics to manage a cotton mill, convinced that the salvation of the South depended on economic progress—which in life, as well as in Page's mind, was most often synonymous with mere activity.

Grady and Page are here used as representative of a powerful school of thought in the South. They did much to call attention to what Page called the "Forgotten Man," to interest philanthropic and educational agencies in Southern problems, and most valuable of all, to stimulate local activity in many fields. This stimulus led—as was inevitable in a world of men—to fully as much harm as good. The public school system, established in most states immediately after the Civil War, developed rapidly, but it came, as public school systems seem always to come, to spread factual knowledge more and more thinly as it touched a greater number of people, while it inexorably crowded out such excellent private academies as were established about the same time by men like W. Gordon McCabe in Virginia and Sawney Webb in Tennessee. The classics were slightly taught, or not taught at all, in the schools; the reading of an educated and curious person in Nashville would not differ greatly from that of a person elsewhere.

There was a certain lag in this as in other respects; men turned more slowly from Vergil and Shakspere to Darwin (or to popularizers of Darwinian theory) and Dreiser—but they were, after all, human, and even the influence of a cultural tradition, combined with inertia, could not long hold them from the way of a world which came ever nearer to each man's doorstep. The benefits of science brought also the philosophic doubts which accompany that learning

when it forsakes facts and becomes speculative.   The impact
of science upon religious thought led, contradictorily enough,
to laws which denied the truth of evolution and at the same
time to a loosening of the religious structure.   In short, the
South as it lost its autonomy became more like New York
and Nebraska—as Atlanta tended to become more like
New York City, Birmingham like Pittsburgh.   Civilization
and thought followed, though more slowly than in other
sections, the American current toward urbanization, mechanization, and standardization.

   The progressives, while always speaking reverently of the
past, repudiated that past as rapidly as possible.   But
there were other men who saw that more than a war had
been lost—that, in truth, a philosophy of life had been
destroyed.   The geographic South was defeated, said Richard L. Dabney after Appomattox, but the spiritual South
could yet be saved by a wholesale migration to Brazil.   Not
many men cared to go to that extreme, but men were not
lacking who recognized that picturesque values (more easily
discernible than philosophical values) were rapidly vanish-
ing.   Local colorists set about the task of preserving on
paper the customs and idiosyncrasies of unstandardized
localities.   A Henry Grady could attempt to make the
sections love each other, a Sidney Lanier could sing the
paeans of a new and mighty nationalism in his "Psalm of
the West,"—but a Thomas Nelson Page could see that this
world around him was a grossly materialistic world, and he
went back to one where abstract principles counted for less
than personal relationships.   Joel Chandler Harris, who
with Grady had attempted to advance progress and reconciliation, came in his later years to doubt the value of that
progress, came to doubt the application if not the inherent
truth of the New South doctrine, "put business above
politics"—and he turned to writing directly of neighbor-

knowledge and of personal kindness and of all the intangible values which he had indirectly put into his stories of Uncle Remus.

Not all men were blind to philosophical values. In one mighty, old-fashioned sentence, C. C. Jones of Augusta struck to the root of the question: "Under the absurd guise of a New South, flaunting the banners of utilitarianism, lifting the standards of speculation and expediency, elevating the colours whereon are emblazoned consolidation of wealth and centralization of government, lowering the flag of intellectual, moral and refined supremacy in the presence of the petty guidons of ignorance, personal ambition and diabolism ... not a few there are who, ignoring the elevating influence of heroic impulses, manly endeavour, and virtuous sentiments, would fain convert this region into a money-worshipping domain; and, careless of the landmarks of the fathers, impatient of the restraints of a calm, enlightened, conservative civilization ... would counsel no oblation save at the shrine of Mammon." These leaders were mainly old, bewhiskered, and indubitably archaic; they were of an age rapidly passing, Jeffersonian democrats in a nationalistic country fast abandoning both Jeffersonianism and democracy. Such men could readily be discredited with opprobrious titles like "professional Southerner." For allies they had, primarily, the patriotic organizations, and, queerly, the Populists; they had on their side, also, inertia. Inertia could be overcome; the patriotic organizations seemed also buried in the past; the Populists, after several active campaigns which brought the poorer whites into power in several states and which, briefly, seemed on the point of re-establishing agrarian control, lapsed back into desuetude as the cities and industries increased in size and wealth and influence.

Today, the South remains a battlefield of two surviving

philosophies of life. The exponents of industrialism, here as elsewhere, range from ultra-conservative individualists to communists; the advocates of agrarianism from those who favor localized industrialism to men who disbelieve completely in industrialism. Only through the efforts of agrarianism does the South retain a flavor of individuality, an intangible but real unity which yet differentiates it from other sections of the country.

III

Southern Poetic Theory

IN THE period which preceded the Revolutionary War, few men in the South concerned themselves with literary theories or criticism. In that, as in the verse which they wrote, there was a satisfactory tradition at hand: the tradition of English classical verse. Men with profound and philosophical minds studied political theory; they expressed their reflections through the medium of prose. Poetry was a graceful accomplishment. At times a critic like the anonymous Gentleman who wrote *Poems on Several Occasions* might attack in rhyme the corruption of the Virginia drama, and buttress with his support the position held by his contemporary in England, Alexander Pope. The drama, thought the Gentleman, should be in the tradition of Shakspere; he deprecated the clowns and harlequins who infested the stage, and he concluded vigorously:

> From foreign Trifling and unmanly Tone
> We turn to downright nonsense of our own.

In the main, such ideas were accepted so implicitly that men felt no need for stating them. Only one observation, long a commonplace, need be made: the manner was more important than the matter of poetry.

This concentration upon form was in time to lead to extended consideration of theories and philosophies of poetry; in the early days this conventional acceptance was in striking contrast with the bold analysis of government made by leaders throughout the colonies. The first serious study of prosody was not by a practicing poet, but by that intensely curious and many-sided thinker, Thomas Jefferson.

Jefferson's taste in classical poetry was catholic yet impeccable; his taste in English poetry—save for his temporarily overpowering passion for the works of Ossian and his fondness for republican sentiments expressed in verse—sound. But the reader of his historically important and intrinsically interesting "Thoughts on English Prosody" quickly realizes that Jefferson's analysis is the work of a gifted, untrained enthusiast who has reversed the customary attitude: instead of approaching Greek and Latin prosody from a background of English study, he considers native poetry from the point of view of a classicist. This essay, addressed to Monsieur F. J. de Chastellaux, was probably written while Jefferson was Secretary of State; in a preliminary letter the author explains his earlier adherence to the classical system of scansion by long and short syllables arranged into regular feet, which he had taken for granted as constituting the harmony of English verse. Although this system was employed by Samuel Johnson as the basis for his views on prosody, it is incorrect. English prosody, he has come to think, depends rather upon emphasis and accent.

If this discovery was new to Jefferson, it was by no means unknown to earlier English writers. On this foundation he erects certain rules which are somewhat startling in their rigidity:

That the accent shall never be displaced from the syllable whereon usage hath established it is the fundamental law of English verse.

There are but three arrangements into which these accents can be thrown in the English language which entitles the composition to be distinguished by the name of verse. That is, 1. Where the accent falls on all the odd syllables; 2. Where it falls on all the even syllables; 3. When it falls on every third syllable. If the reason of this be asked, no other can be assigned but that it results from the nature of the sounds which compose the English language and from the construction of the human ear.

The author provides for no exceptions. Since he was no poet himself, this omission is not surprising. His scansion of lines was at times decidedly erratic; his statements sometimes acute if farfetched, as when he writes that "the language of Homer enabled him to compose in verse of six feet, the English language cannot bear this." But his observations were made at first-hand, they represented his independent thoughts on the subject. For that reason there is distinctive value in his conclusions that the accentual basis of English verse leads to the same threefold distribution to which the hypothesis of *quantity* had led Dr. Johnson: trochaic, iambic, and anapestic. His metrical analyses of these measures have little intrinsic value.

Jefferson was primarily interested in technique from the reader's standpoint. The writers of poetry were equally interested in a philosophical quality, which they felt vitiated much of their work. Richard Henry Wilde slowly evolved a theory as to his country's literary sterility: America was too young for poetry. With its great forests, mountains, rivers, and towns, it had "matter that the eye and mind, heart, fancy, memory could dwell upon," but for the poetic mind "without human passion, action, thought, Nature however beautiful is void." In his dedication to *Hesperia*, Wilde expressed his idea directly: "Few write well, except from personal experience—from what they have seen and felt—and modern life, in America especially, is utterly commonplace. It wants the objects and events which are essential to poetry." A realistic romantic, he believed that no American could write successfully a story about a foreign country; he recognized his own limitation in "want of inven-

tion"; but, since he was above all a romanticist, he could
not rid himself of longing:

> Could we our country's scenery invest
> With history or legendary lore,
> Give to each valley an immortal guest
> Repeople with the past the desert shore,
> Pass out where Hampdens bled or Shakespeares rest,
> Exult o'er Memory's exhaustless store,
> As our descendants centuries hence may do—
> We should—and then shall have—our poets too!

This strikes deeper than the frequent complaints of lack
of intellectual stimulation and companionship, of lack of
encouragement from an appreciative audience. These things
Wilde attributed to his country's immaturity. Rather, his
statements antedate the romantic criticisms of such men as
Van Wyck Brooks and Randolph Bourne. For that type
of mind which draws sustenance from tradition and even
more from books, these criticisms have definite validity,
but they have only partial truth.

Southern magazines, rapidly increasing in number, were
constantly publishing poetry and criticisms of poetry.
These magazines were mainly English in spirit, in content,
and in format. The distinctively American magazine
evolved under the guidance of Edgar Allan Poe, but before
and after his period of editorship there were able and solid
journals. A fine example of this type was the *Southern
Review*, under the editorship of Hugh Swinton Legaré, but
the *Review* had several distinguished rivals. Legaré was
an erudite critic, and in particular his review of William Cul-
len Bryant's poems has elements of importance. For Legaré
was the Samuel Johnson of Charleston, and his words
carried authority with the Carolinian poets. In this work
he praised simple, natural, precise language—"the language

of people of this world such as they use when they utter
home-bred feelings in conversation with one another around
the fireside or the festive board, not the fastidious, diluted,
inexpressive jargon used nowhere but in second-rate books,
and called elegant only by critics of the Della Cruscan
school. . . . As to that more various elevated, powerful, and
imaginative diction—itself a *creation*, and the most dazzling
of poetic creations—such as we read in Pindar and the Greek
tragedians, especially Aeschylus—such as we see in many
parts of Shakespeare, and in almost every line of Milton—
there is none of it here." To these sane words on diction,
Legaré adds a brief analysis of the sonnet; Bryant's sonnets
he thought good, but far from masterpieces. He concludes
with a significant statement of the value of poetry: "Decided
poetic merit is a great desideratum, in the social character
of our country. A most exalted merit it is—precious in
itself, still more precious as an index of what is felt and
thought by a people, and as tending to foster and to warm
into enthusiasm, all the sentiments that do most honour to
human nature."

Poetry itself Legaré thought "but an abridged name for
the sublime and beautiful, and for highly wrought pathos."
In the middle of an essay which defended classical literature
against the claims presented by an advocate of science,
Legaré defines poetry in the terms of romanticism:

. . . It is spread over the whole face of nature—it is in the glories
of the heavens and in the wonders of the great deep, in the voice
of the cataract and of the coming storm, in Alpine precipices
and solitudes, in the balmy gales and sweet bloom and freshness
of spring. It is in every heroic achievement, in every lofty sentiment, in every deep passion, in every bright vision of fancy, in
every vehement affection of gladness or of grief, of pleasure or
of pain. It is, in short, the feeling—the deep, the strictly *moral*

feeling, which, when it is affected by chance or change in human life, as at a tragedy, we call sympathy—but as it appears in the still more mysterious connection between the heart of man and the forms and beauties of inanimate nature, as if they were instinct with a soul and a sensibility like our own, has no appropriate appellation in our language, but is not the less real or the less familiar to our experience on that account. It is these feelings, whether utterance be given to them, or they be only nursed in the smitten bosom—whether they be couched in metre, or poured out with wild disorder and irrepressible rapture, that constitute the true spirit and essence of poetry, which is, therefore, necessarily connected with the grandest conceptions and the most touching and intense emotions, with the fondest aspirations and the most awful concerns of mankind.

These words were not without effect on able young poets in Charleston.

William Gilmore Simms succeeded to the literary dictatorship which Legaré had held. His influence extended throughout the section, as editor of several successive magazines, as well as author of highly popular novels, biographies, and poems. A small number of his critical articles were collected in *Views and Reviews*; an even larger number are yet scattered in the files of magazines no longer easily procurable. The sweeping range of his interests led him to edit *A Supplement to the Plays of William Shakespeare*, to consider for other writers "The Epochs and Events of American History, as suited to the Purposes of Art in Fiction," and, at one time or another, to express his views on critics, poets, literature, economics, and other subjects. At least one distinguished critical essay came from his pen; "The Writings of James Fenimore Cooper" deserved Bryant's praise: "A critical essay of great depth and discrimination, to which I am not sure that anything hitherto written [on Cooper] is fully equal." In his remarks on poetry scattered through his essays and letters, Simms was on the side of common sense: although he admired Poe's genius, he judged Poe as "bizarre, rather than great or healthful." His advice to Thomas Holley Chivers is a good summary of his theory: "Rhyme is the mere decoration of thought . . . mannerism is a fatal weakness . . . seek for simplicity and wholeness—avoid yourself in your topics—write no more elegies, and discard all pet words, all phrases—discard all attempts at mysticism. Be manly, direct, simple, natural, —full, unaffected, and elaborate." This was sensible advice to a man who infrequently transcended common sense, but whose brief flights into the sublime made any reasonable counsel seem out of place and superfluous.

Simms's poetic theories are not intrinsically important, although in later life he would state his views with a Johnsonian arrogance which at least once offended the discriminating Timrod. More important than his dogmatic ideas, however, was his warm and friendly encouragement to such young poets as Timrod, Hayne, and James Mathewes Legaré. If his ideas were often rather simple and occasionally mistaken, his influence in its totality was quickening and remarkably fine.

His theory of the novel is highly important; as he saw it, "the modern Romance is the substitute which the people of the present day offer for the ancient epic." For his definitions he went back of Sir Walter Scott to that neglected but important chronicler of chivalry, Froissart. Although Simms applied his theory primarily to the romance, it helps to explain some of his longer poems. This theory was shared—independently, it seems—by the Virginian Philip Pendleton Cooke, who applied it both to tales and poetry. Cooke entitled his one volume, significantly, *Froissart Ballads*; in the preface he states that he has been "as faithful

to the text of Froissart as the necessities of verse permitted."
Highest praise from Cooke goes to the old minstrels and
bards, the makers of lays, whose high art leads back to the
ancient days, and who vivify the legends of Arthur, Robin
Hood, and other nobly picturesque figures of chivalry. Unfortunately, neither Cooke nor Simms wrote a good poem
in this *genre:* the theory was better fitted for the prose
romance.

This summary glance at the most significant critical
thought reveals a keen interest in the way of writing, as
regards both philosophy and technique. All of it is pertinent and interesting: here, in embryo, are major questions
which remain as open to discussion as they were in the days
of Wilde and Legaré. In politics the Southerner of the old
school tended to be a theorist and philosopher; in literature
he was similarly occupied, although his achievements were
not comparable. In this form, however, can best be discerned the duality of Southern intellect, the intermingling
(if not the perfect union) of classical and romantic tendencies
and thought. The literary influence of nineteenth-century
England was direct and immediate and powerful, as the
poetry of the writers clearly shows; but almost equally
powerful were the living books of long-dead Greek and
Latin poets.

For all this preoccupation with theory, no critic developed
a system or a philosophy which radically changed the
thought of his own and succeeding ages, until Edgar Allan
Poe helped to evolve for a changing culture a philosophy
which was suited for it. It is well to remember that these
men, after Jefferson, were all contemporaries, and most of
them friends and correspondents; the work of one man might
well influence another. Only Legaré can justly be termed
a learned man, by the standards of that day; by our looser

requirements, which rate education in terms of degrees without differentiation as to subject matter, all were erudite. They wrote in a style no longer popular; perhaps their thinking, like their phraseology, is out of date. In the final analysis this may reflect not on their age but on our own.

The views—or perhaps the rationalizations—of Wilde and Simms and Cooke have a sensible quality which make them easily understandable. Their limitations are apparent. If their universe differed from our own, it was well-ordered and coherent. Their contemporaries—Chivers and Poe—can not so readily be tagged and placed in tight compartments: although masters of rationalization, these two poets elude the comprehension of rational men. One has received but slight attention; the other has been the subject of countless articles and biographies which have generated far more heat than light. The critical ideas of Chivers are curious and fascinating, but they help to explain, mainly, the poetry of Chivers; the ideas of Poe help to adumbrate his age.

Chivers's critical theories are remarkable, in language as well as in ideas. He envisioned poetry as "that crystal river of the soul which runs through all the avenues of life, and after purifying the affections of the heart, empties itself into the Sea of God. . . . Poetry is the power given by God to man of manifesting these relations. . . . Poetry is the soul of his nature, whereby, from communing with the beauties of this earth, he is capable of giving birth to other beings brighter than himself; and of lifting up his spirit to the presence of those things which he shall enjoy in another state; and which he manifests to *this* through the instrumentality of certain words and sentences melodiously concatenated; and such as correspond with the definite and wise configurations of the mouth in the communication of thought through language." He goes beyond Sir Philip Sidney, who wrote that a poet was by the Romans "called *Vates*, which is as much as a Diviner, Fore-seer, or Prophet"; to Chivers the poets are the "Revelators of the Divine Idea through the Beautiful." But Chivers could not be content with simple expression of these transcendental ideas. He clothed them in metaphorical words; he quoted from many languages the various definitions of a poet, and of poetry, and he considered how these definitions supported his own belief in the divine nature of art and artist. He agreed with Poe in the statement that Milton's *Paradise Lost* is too long a poem to be entirely pleasing, and is poetic only in passages, "the others being only the relatively connecting links of the whole. It is, therefore, obvious that the idiosyncratic merits of any poet depend entirely upon the manner in which he has realized his dreams of the *crystalline revelation of the divine idea*." But Chivers did not believe, with Poe, that a poem must necessarily be brief; indeed, this preface is to a poem which is intended to be at once epical, lyrical and symbolic, and "an experiment upon the minds of the Chosen Few."

This poem, *Atlanta*, is an elaborate glorification of poetry. S. Foster Damon writes in his biography of Chivers, "Its symbolism hardly needs explanation. Man's finer self is stolen from him by his baser passions; but eventually he tricks them into serving him. All night they cross the inner sea; and with the dawn appears the Island of Poetry, where his ideal lives, still unblemished. In the glorious cave (the ageless symbol of the body, made famous by Plato) he perfects himself in union with his higher self, through the medium of complete love." Mentally Chivers had, long before this was written, taken refuge in that island of poetry, as compensation for the defeats which he felt in the practical world; he prefaced several volumes with his lyrical theories, and he wrote Simms in 1852 that he would soon publish a volume which would give "an analysis of Poetry from its Gothic up to its Greek manifestations."

This analysis was to be "a new thing under the sun"— as original as his poems, which were "all original." In truth, Chivers was in all that he did an original, in the old sense of that word, with its kindred meaning of eccentric. His critical ideas, however, if we can judge from his prefaces to *Nacoochee*, *Memoralia*, *Atlanta*, and *Virginalia*, are not precisely new; they can be traced in varying form in the works of older and more normal critics. Essentially they are romantic, but they are not the nonsense which a careless reading of Chivers's luxuriant phrases might lead one to suspect. He believed that the *existere* of a poem must be coeternal with its *esse*, that in every poem there are two beauties—the outward beauty of art, the inward beauty of nature or passion—that a poem which unites perfectly this body and soul is a pure poem. Few critics would dispute this, any more than they would dispute Pope's dictum that the sound should be an echo of the sense. More debatable is Chivers's theory of the refrain: he saw it not as an ornament, or a vital part, but as "an essence—a life—a vitality— an immortal soul." As a general theory, in the way in which Chivers meant it, this statement is nonsense; only when applied to the specialized type of poetry which Chivers wrote does it have any validity. Poe's words in "The Philosophy of Composition" probably express all that the over-exuberant Chivers meant: "In carefully thinking over all the usual artistic effects—or more properly *points*, in the theatrical sense—I did not fail to perceive immediately that no one had been so universally employed as that of the *refrain*. The universality of its employment sufficed to assure me of its intrinsic value, and spared me the necessity of submitting it to analysis. ... As commonly used, the *refrain*, or burden, not only is limited to lyric verse, but depends for its impression upon the force of monotone—both in sound and thought. The pleasure is deduced solely from the sense of identity—of repetition. I resolved to diversify, and so heighten, the effect, by adhering in general to the monotone of sound, while I continually varied that of thought: that is to say, I determined to produce continuously novel effects, by the variation *of the application* of the *refrain*—the *refrain* itself remaining, for the most part, unvaried."

When compared with those of Chivers, Poe's critical theories seem a model of rationality. They are also, in part, rationalizations of their author's own creative limitations. Even more, they are an attempt to develop a theory which would be applicable to the magazine age.

His belief that a poem must be "the rhythmical creation of beauty," without didacticism and largely without passion, was adapted precisely to his type of writing. Yet it is difficult to agree wholeheartedly with Joseph Wood Krutch that Poe's psychological limitations are basic causes for his theories. With at least equal justice this thesis can be reversed, since as early as 1831 Poe (following his chief master in criticism, Coleridge, and barely paraphrasing one of Coleridge's most famous definitions) declared that "a poem, in my opinion, is opposed to a work of science by having, for its *immediate* object, pleasure, not truth; to romance, by having for its object an *indefinite* instead of a *definite* pleasure, being a poem only so far as this object is attained." In this essay the young poet stated in embryonic form his philosophy of literature: only the poet could be a critic of literature; only the indefinite poem, not concerned with direct moral issues, could be truly beautiful. (Yet critics, on the basis largely of his poetry and tales, continue to speak of Poe as un-American.) Even his theory of the necessity for a poem's brevity was implied, in the preface to *Poems* (1831), in his remarks upon Milton and the epic.

Norman Foerster in his *American Criticism* has given an excellent summary of Poe's artistic creed:

The end of art is pleasure, not truth. In order that pleasure may be intense, the work of art must have unity and brevity. In poetry, the proper means of arousing pleasure is the creation of beauty; not the beauty of concrete things alone, but also a higher beauty—supernal beauty. Music is an indispensable element in poetry, and is especially valuable in the poet's straining toward the supernal, since music comes nearer this goal than any other art. In the prose tale, on the other hand, the artist may seek to produce effects other than those of poetry,—effects of horror, terror, passion,—limiting himself in each case to a single effect.

This summary, founded mainly upon "The Poetic Principle," gives Poe's rounded and integrated theory; he has developed consistently the rather scrappy suggestions in his early preface—which, naturally, is inferior to "The Poetic Principle"—but, since so much nonsense has been written about Poe, it has an unusual value. There was nothing wishy-washy about the man's thought: he formed a tenable if definitely limited theory early in life; he developed and expanded that theory (although always within the same limits) until it became a consistent aesthetic.

Thus he did not deny truth as part of a poem, but held that truth as such—that is, truth with a moral—could better be dealt with in prose. Humor he thought "antagonistical to that which is the soul of the muse proper"; sadness combined with beauty "invariably excites the sen-

sitive soul to tears.   Melancholy is thus the most legitimate
of all the poetical tones."   Poe's failure to recognize in
metaphysical poetry any element of what he considered
the essence of poetry, his denial even that it was poetry, is
not surprising, although, undeniably, it is narrow: poet-
critics have, in the main, consistently believed that only the
verse which they have written is *poetry*.[1] This does not
mean that the author of "The Raven," then, can be utterly
trusted when in "The Philosophy of Composition" he rationalizes for himself and for the world the method by which
that poem came into being; what it does mean is that the
student who is not overly obsessed with Freudianism can
gain from poem and criticism a valuable knowledge of
Poe's ratiocination.

From Poe's theories, also, he can gain a knowledge of the
aesthetic which was beginning to rule in that time, and which
largely dominates in our own.   Poe's distrust and dislike
of epics was not accidental; he may have taken suggestions
from Schlegel or Kames or Blair that a poem should, to be
effective, be reasonably short, but such suggestions were
valuable only because as seeds they lodged in fallow ground.
Poe was integrally a part of his environment; he was by
profession a magazine editor.   Assuredly he was expressing
his sincerest beliefs when he wrote:

The increase, within a few years, of the magazine literature,
is by no means to be regarded as indicating what some critics
would suppose it to indicate—a downward tendency in American taste or in American letters.   It is but a sign of the times—

---

[1] I have seen no wiser statement on this than Henry Timrod's observation
("A Theory of Poetry," *Atlantic Monthly*, XCVI, 325): "A very little examination
will generally prove that they [poetic theories] have grown out of the idiosyncrasies
of the poets themselves, and so, necessarily, seldom attain a greater breadth than
suffices to shelter the theorist and the models from which he has drawn his arguments and his inspirations."

an indication of an era in which men are forced upon the curt, the condensed, the well-digested—in place of the voluminous —in a word, upon journalism in lieu of dissertation. We need now the light artillery rather than the Peace-makers of the intellect. I will not be sure that men at present think more profoundly than half a century ago, but beyond question they think with more rapidity, with more skill, with more tact, with more of method, and less of excrescence in the thought. Besides all this, they have a vast increase in the thinking material. They have more facts, more to think about. For this reason, they are disposed to put the greatest amount of thought in the smallest compass and disperse it with the utmost attainable rapidity. Hence the journalism of the age, hence, in especial, magazines. Too many we cannot have, as a general proposition; but we demand that they have sufficient merit to render them noticeable in the beginning, and that they continue in existence sufficiently long to permit us a fair estimation of their value.

In addition, he belonged to the romantic, the lyric, period. Expression of mood, of heart, of subjectivity in general do not make for sustained expression: at base these moods are thin and tenuous. When portrayed at length this tenuous thinness becomes definitely apparent. In this general connection Ludwig Lewisohn wrote that "the literary sterility of the South ceases, like that of many other problems, to have any problematic character so soon as we attain to the true conception of literature as, on its lowest terms, the expression of an experience that is differentiated from the experience of the social or tribal group." As a definition of romanticism—that type of romanticism, in particular, of which Lewisohn is a modern master—this definition can hardly be excelled. The germ of it can be traced back to the Renaissance, and to the rise of protestantism. But as a conception of literature it is exceedingly narrow, with its basic untruth immediately obvious. Insert the word *mod-*

ern, however, before either *conception* or *literature*. Then all is clear: the lyric, the subjective, the romantic—that which gave rise to the cult of the genius—come into being. The aesthetic of romanticism can be found only dimly in Edward Young and in Wordsworth; the exegesis of that aesthetic was the work of Coleridge and, after him, of Poe. In addition, it was Poe's function to restate this aesthetic in the terms which were to be almost universally employed by men who wrote for what may be denominated a magazine-literature.

Poe's theories on prosody are relatively unimportant, when compared with his theories on poetry. Even so, they are not to be dismissed lightly. His method of using the refrain has been quoted above; his insistence upon melody, as well as harmony, in a poem naturally led to employment of such devices as repetition and alliteration. Although he never carried his experiments in sound to the extreme which Chivers did, he was so fascinated with the "tintinnabulation" of word-sounds that in "The Bells"—with its reiterative rhymes, its assonance and alliteration, its parallelisms and refrains—he deserved Emerson's judgment of "the jingle man," for this experiment in onomatopoeia (in spite of the symbolism which suggests youthful pleasure, marriage, disaster, and death) descends to mere echolalia. Yet it is consistent with his theories that harsh consonants should never disturb the music of a line, and that poetry, generally, is "an inferior or less capable music." He was less consistent in his practice with regard to certain exceedingly strict rules he laid down: that in diction the poet should avoid archaisms, contractions, inversions; that rhymes should not be inexact, identical, or light; and that contractions or elisions are not permissible. Undoubtedly Poe's liking for mathematical certainty, combined with a desire to avoid the metaphysical aspects which he deprecated in Wordsworth and Coleridge, caused him to make exact statements without appending the badly needed qualifications. This can easily be understood, and pardoned. But in the background of Poe's "Rationale of Verse"—a defect more obvious with Lanier, since he made it the foundation of his theory—there is a fundamental misconception: he was attempting to make a science of that which is, at most, a technique. When compared with this, his errors with regard to linguistic facts and to metrics and rhythm are decidedly minor. True, his tendency to apply scientific principles to all things was as thoroughly in accord with the thought of his age as his philosophic theories were; factual misconceptions, however, can be lightly swept away in this case, at least, but the heritage of thought which the age of Poe bequeathed to us has become a part of that which we know.

The critical work of Henry Timrod—brief in quantity but excellent in quality—represented an attempt to controvert the statements (although not, basically, the romantic philosophy) of Poe. As a preliminary to this main task, he answered the essay of his older friend, William J. Grayson. A distinguished lawyer with intellectual tastes which led him to prefer Dryden and Pope to the overwhelmingly popular romantic poets, Grayson argued for a type of poetry which seemed to Timrod only a metrical prose. "The poetry of the day is, for the most part, subtile and transcendental," Grayson wrote, yet "the school of Dryden and Pope is not entirely forgotten." Since even "the most fastidious appetite may tolerate an occasional change of diet, and exchange dainties now and then for plainer fare," he thought the heroic couplet offered, at least, "some variety to the poetic forms that are almost universally prevalent." With excessive modesty Grayson advances these ideas, which are not without strong elements of truth but which were quite alien to nineteenth-century thought—even in the South, where the influence of the eighteenth century remained strongest. Perhaps wisely, Timrod dismissed Grayson's remarks as totally inadequate, to be easily refuted through the establishment "of a theory altogether opposed to it."

Timrod's main intent was to refute Poe. He based his first attack—on the transiency of excitement which makes brevity essential to a poem—firmly upon the high seriousness of poetry and upon the "thoughtful sublimity and the matured and almost inexhaustible strength of a healthy intellect." Neither the writing nor the reading of poetry was a light matter, to be undertaken in a few moments of leisure; the enjoyment of a sustained poem requires not so much uninterrupted reading as sustained thought. The reader of *Paradise Lost*, "instead of sitting down to the study of the third book as to a new poem, brings with him all the impressions of his former reading to heighten the color and deepen the effect of that which is before him." This is far from saying, Timrod adds, that length makes a poem more valuable, or even that *Paradise Lost* is uniformly excellent: "However noble the theme, there will be parts and aspects which do not admit of the presence of genuine poetry. Herein, however, I differ from Poe; inasmuch as I maintain that these parts may be raised so far above the ordinary level of prose by skillful verse as to preserve the general harmony of the poem and materially to insure its beauty as a work of art. And in the distinction between poetry and the poem, between the spirit and its body, which Poe recognizes when he comes to develop his theory, but which he blinks or ignores altogether in his remarks upon *Paradise Lost*, I shall look for the justification of my position. I hold that the confusion of these terms, of the subjective essence with the objective form, is the source of most of the errors and contradictions of opinion prevalent upon this theme."

In some respects Timrod agreed with Poe. The author must regard each poem "strictly as a work of art." As such, it has "one purpose . . . the materials of which it is composed should be so selected as to enforce it." In another essay, where he defended the sonnet form, Timrod elaborated on this singleness of purpose: "The sonnet is designed, as it is peculiarly fitted, for the development of a single thought, emotion, or picture. It is governed by another law not less imperative than that which determines its length . . . the law of unity." Considerations both of art and of technique precluded a true poet from being an improvisator, from writing under the spur of inspiration: "A distinction must be made between the moment when the great thought strikes for the first time along the brain . . . and the hour of patient, elaborate execution." The hours of insight must be separated from the hours of labor.

Poetry is not limited in subject matter, as Poe insists, for appropriate subjects can be found not only in the mysterious and the beautiful, but equally in the sublime and terrible, the commonplace and homely—in whatever subject the individual poet can transmute into poetry. These varied sources cannot be reduced until "the simple element of beauty" suffices for all: "Two other elements at least must be added; and these are power, when it is developed in some noble shape, and truth, whether abstract or not, when it affects the common heart of mankind."

The indefinite must not be pushed too far; generalized imagery can not with advantage replace concrete imagery: "Poetry does not deal in abstractions. However abstract be his thought, the poet is compelled, by his passion-fused

imagination, to give it life, form or color.   Hence the necessity of employing the *sensuous* or concrete words of the
language, and hence the exclusion of long words which in
English are nearly all purely and austerely abstract, from
the poetic vocabulary."   To this Timrod adds: "The poetry
of words has never so strange a fascination as when it seems
to suggest more than it utters."   To Timrod, and to his
friends, these specific statements and general ideas seemed
a complete refutation of Poe's principles, but when the
critical essays of both men are examined from the vantage
point which historical perspective gives, it is clear that,
like Wordsworth and Coleridge before them, they complement rather than contradict each other, that they were
describing the same shield from different points of view.

Lanier's critical theories, like Poe's, divide naturally in
two categories: the philosophical and the prosodical.   Unlike Poe's, his technical observations are not an integral
part of his larger conceptions; although the two run along
together harmoniously enough, they never fuse.   While
Lanier's ideas also help to explain his age and his section,
they are, in the final analysis, a part of a submerging current,
not a fountainhead.   For that reason, Lanier's work can
be more nearly valid, yet far less important.

His belief in the sacredness of art and of the religious
rapport of the poet is akin to that of Chivers.   At times his
words take on something of the earlier poet's wild, mystical
zeal, as when he admonished the young artist: "Unless you
are suffused—soul and body, one might say—with that
moral purpose which finds its largest expression in love—
that is, the love of all things in their proper relation—unless
you are suffused with this love do not dare to meddle with
beauty, unless you are suffused with beauty, do not dare to
meddle with love, unless you are suffused with truth, do not

dare to meddle with goodness,—in a word, unless you are suffused with beauty, truth, wisdom, goodness *and* love, abandon the hope that the ages will accept you as an artist." That was his own creed, and he employed it, to the detriment of his reputation as a critic, unsparingly. Whatever justification can be made for some of the strangest judgments by a good writer on record can be found in Lanier's excessive enthusiasms and his burningly intense belief in a narrow morality.

In this study even a consideration of these flights from reason would be unnecessary if Lanier's ideas could be justly considered or explained without an attempt to understand Lanier himself. Not only was he an abnormally spiritual man; he was ill. When D. C. Gilman described Lanier, he wrote that "one said, 'He looks like Moses'; another, 'He looks like Christ.' A German physiologist simply said 'Tuberculosis'. " The optimism which this disease is known to foster may well be the basis for Lanier's desire to undertake everything, but to be content with a haphazard mastery of each subject. Surely, the specter of lack of time, the threatening nearness of death, must have driven his acquisitive curiosity onward, while it left him no time for working out the subjects which he touched. In justice to Lanier, one must remember this constantly, and must remember, also, that too many of his books are not finished products, but publications edited and printed by others after his death. This final item palliates the frequent errors in quotations and citations, and the superficial and dogmatic judgments which Lanier might well have revised.

An opportunity to reflect upon and to correct the manuscripts of these posthumous works would, beyond doubt, have greatly improved them. Time might have brought him a richer insight, health a broader and finer outlook.

These were denied him. Remembrance of all this brings with it an overwhelming pity for the man, a poignant wish that all his prose except his letters could have been swept unknown into limbo, and only his poetry left. For there is no blinking the fact that Lanier's philosophies of life and of poetry are weak, and that occasional flashes of insight do not compensate for his fevered rhapsodies.

The precarious state of his health caused him to live "so exclusively in a world of artistic speculation and scientific questioning that things spiritual came to be more familiar to him than things material, and moral facts to be taken as much for granted as physical facts are." Although his religious convictions prevented his really accepting Darwin's theories, his romantic faith in science caused him to admire Newton and Darwin intensely. By intuitive reasoning he convinced himself that no compromise, even, was needed, for science did not endanger—science, indeed, might strenghten—both religion and poetry. He worked faithfully, if confusedly, to integrate the contradictory gods of religion and of science.

The artist was free to do as he willed with those tools which God had given him. Fine and true work could be accomplished only by those who lived in accordance with God and nature. If he believed, as we are told, that great music is but the rhythm of a great personality, he also paraphrases, in *The Science of English Verse*, with entire approval Herbert Spencer's proposition that "where opposing forces act, rhythm appears, and [Spencer] has traced the rhythmic motions of nature to the antagonistic forces there found, such as the two motions which carry the earth towards and away from the sun and so result in the periodicity of the earth's progress, and others.

"Perhaps this view may be made, without strain, to bind

together even facts so remote from each other as the physical and the moral. When we compare what one may call the literal rhythm which rules throughout physical nature with that metaphorical rhythm or proportion which governs good behavior as well as good art; when we find that opposition in the physical world results in rhythm, and that no opposition in the moral world—the fret, the sting, the thwart, the irreconcilable me as against all other me's, the awful struggle for existence, the desperate friction of individualities, the no of death to all requests—may also result in rhythm; when we perceive that through all those immeasurable agitations which constitute both moral and physical nature this beautiful and orderly principle of rhythm thus swings to and fro like the shuttle of a loom and weaves a definite and comprehensible pattern into the otherwise chaotic fabric of things: we may be able to see dimly into that old Orphic saying of the seer, 'The father of metre is rhythm, and the father of rhythm is God.' " Here, truly, all is confusion. Religion and science and art were three powerful magnets, drawing his mind hither and yon. Lanier was powerless to separate them, and he lacked the power to fuse them into a complete philosophy, either for the world or for himself.

This lack of philosophical integration carried over into his more direct theories of poetry. Lanier's demand for a heavy moral content seems as dated as Poe's demand for pure beauty. At least a partial reason for this is Lanier's phraseology: although he states his argument in chaotic and old-fashioned terms, he seems nearer the heart of creative expression than Poe. The most kindly critic can not say as much for his most elaborate treatise on versification, *The Science of English Verse*. The title alone reveals one fundamental misconception: there is an art of poetry, a technique of versification—but a *science of verse* is a contradiction of terms. The second fundamental error is Lanier's confusion of art-forms, his belief in the identity of music and poetry: "The art of sound must always be regarded the genus, and music and verse its two species. Prose, scientifically considered, is a wild variety of verse. . . . When we hear verse, we *hear* a set of relations between sounds; when we silently read verse, we *see* that which brings to us a set of relations between sounds; when we imagine verse, we *imagine* a set of relations between sounds." From this definition Lanier develops the thesis that the laws which govern versification and musical composition are identical, for "there is absolutely no difference between the sound-relations used in music and those used in verse."

With these and similar statements Lanier dismisses the vital element of intellectual content. That, one may say, he took for granted, although this supposition will, of itself, damage his theory considerably. His poems treat social and political topics, and he was greatly interested in contemporary ideas; but in his theories he did not include these elements, and indeed leaves little room for them. Less obvious but equally important is another factor which weakens his theory: although words and music may, as Richard Wagner observed, complement each other, one can never replace the other. In attempting that replacement, which necessarily required an identity between the two forms, Lanier failed—as many another critic before him had failed in the attempt to make poetry and painting kindred forms.

In science, this misconception in the premise would at once establish the falseness of other observations. In a loose technique, like versification, the corollary does not inevitably follow. Men who employed the classical method of scansion have written very excellent verse in English; Sidney Lanier, who disdained the accentual method, wrote poems which can in most instances be scanned quite satisfactorily in that manner. It may be true that most poetry is normally read in $\frac{3}{8}$ time, but that is no reason to say it was written in that time, or that it can not be read effectively with due regard to accent. In brief, Lanier worked in a field where precise scientific statement is ineffective for the simple reason that one method may be as good, where the result is the basis of judgment, as another. For that reason Lanier's observations are of some value: if they rarely touch the whole of poetry, they do give a stimulating discussion of one important portion—sound. To other critics has gone the duty of fitting that part into the whole.

Lanier divides sound into four particulars: duration, intensity, pitch, and tone-color. Each of these he defines carefully; each sound "for the purpose of verse, is represented by one syllable." This comes eventually to mean that each foot, which may be composed of a varying number of syllables, is equal in temporal quality to every foot in the line; Lanier frequently substituted *bar* for foot, and he wrote that "In a strain of music any bar is exactly equal to any other bar in the time it occupies." Therefore, every poetic foot must be equal in time. And "rhythm of any sort is impossible, except through the coordination of time. Time is the essential basis of rhythm. 'Accent' can effect nothing except in arranging materials already rhythmical through some temporal recurrence."

G. W. Allen, in *American Prosody*, has given a remarkably accurate summary of Lanier's conception of rhythm: "Briefly, the rhythms in Lanier's system are as follows: (1) The *temporal relation* is 'primary' rhythm, that is, the time covered by each separate sound ('verse-sound,' or syllable) and the pauses and silences. (2) *Accent*, which indicates the beginning of a new bar, forms a 'secondary' rhythm. (3) But English speech is not pronounced in syllable or sound groups but in 'phrases,' necessitated by the dependence of human speech upon respiration. Thus the *phrase* forms a 'tertiary' rhythm. Subheads of tertiary rhythm are alliteration, rhetorical emphasis (which includes both intensity and pitch accent), and logical accent. (4) The 'fourth order of rhythmic groups' is the *line*—meter is the number of verse-sounds in a line. Rime also has a rhythmic function because it marks the end of the line. (5) The 'fifth order of rhythmic groups' is the stanza. This rhythm, of course, is ordinarily marked by rime-schemes, but may be indicated by phrases and full stops."

After extended analyses of many poems in the light of his theories, Lanier concluded his volume with a one-page chapter which says that his science consists only of hints, not laws; that "For the artist in verse there is no law: the perception and love of beauty constitute the whole outfit; and what is herein set forth is to be taken merely as enlarging that perception and exalting that love. In all cases, the appeal is to the ear. . . ." Of what value, ultimately, is this platitude? Is the body of the study as valueless as its hypothesis and its conclusion? When all the false and worthless elements are stripped away, certain other elements of value do remain, but they are suggestive hints on the relation of melody and harmony to words, on the complementary nature of music and words. This value itself is not what Lanier intended, for he considered the laws of these arts as identical.

That Sidney Lanier was consciously aware of pictorial as well as harmonic qualities in his verse is apparent from reading the "Hymns of the Marshes," the "Song of the

Chattahoochee," or half a dozen other of his poems. That he was in part a local colorist can be discerned in his novel, *Tiger Lilies*, in *Florida*, with its gorgeous word pictures, and in his dialect poems. In a manner almost underground, since the author's name is rarely attached to it, one poem has circulated so extensively that it has taken on the quality of a folk product. "Thar's More in the Man Than Thar is in the Land" is not distinguished poetry, but it warrants the title of Lanier's most popular poem, and it is a good example of local color poetry. Essentially, however, Lanier wanted to get away from a section where old values were rapidly disintegrating: "You are all so alive, up there, and we are all so dead, down here" he wrote in June, 1866, to a Northern friend. This is not the mood of the local colorist, but of one who desires to be in the vanguard of change. It is not surprising that Sidney Lanier—who preferred burial in Baltimore to burial in Macon—never developed a theory of local color, never developed his beginnings in that field of writing.

The gifted Irwin Russell died young: he knew what he was about, but he never stated his ideas. Certain aspects of a life he cherished were disappearing from the world; something was happening to the Negroes in their freedom which recalled the vivid impressions of youth, when world and Negro alike had seemed more happily exuberant. Because it was a part of him, native to mind and almost a part of blood, he put on paper (with an artless artistry, equalled only by Joel Chandler Harris in his stories of Uncle Remus) his recollections of a Christmas night in the quarters.

When his theory was defined, poetically, it was the product of two young and sophisticated men, who had found a "tropically rich store of material, an unurbanized beauty, the possibility of legend, folk-song, romance, historical narrative, glorious landscape, and an untired mood." Southern poetry should be regional, of and about places and persons; it should be distinctively sectional.   Du Bose Heyward and Hervey Allen, like many another poetaster, discovered that the surface qualities—picturesqueness of locale and speech, in particular—were easy.   That easiness was deceptive, although the same elements which made it false in spirit also made many persons accept it as authentic. It is not easy to attain, but easy to handle.   What few men seemed to realize was that local color when employed with discretion made an excellent background to give added reality, but a thin and quick-fading foreground.

The one tenable theory of this nature has been stated, and its difficulties analyzed, by a distinguished poet and critic, Donald Davidson, in *The Attack on Leviathan:* the craft of a poet must come "as part of a generally diffused tradition which has local roots and which he naturally appropriates as his own. . . . There ought to be something virile and positive in its art, as an art linked by devotion to a concrete place rather than animated by a loose enthusiasm for a 'national' culture which has no organic unity behind it." Whether the poet is concerned with local or with universal subjects, this influence of a stable and vital tradition should have a deepening influence.   Too often it does not have, since the tradition has either been discredited and discarded, by men like Grady and Page, or it has been falsified, by men like Heyward and Allen.

Allen Tate and John Crowe Ransom, equally, have joined in the contentions of Davidson, but they have gone beyond him in poetic theory and constructed a tight, logical philosophy which excellently explains what they are doing so well, but which leaves much to be desired in its failure to recognize other *kinds* of verse as poetry.[2] The three general attitudes possible in the modern world, in the order in which they have respectively dominated the minds of men, are the creative spirit, romantic irony, and the spirit of the practical will. Unquestionably, today, the scientific spirit, with its substitution of the will for the imagination, its "confidence in the limitless power of man to impose practical abstractions upon the world," is in the ascendant. Appropriately, W. B. Yeats has called the rhetoric of romantic poets "the will trying to do the work of the imagination." But the true function of the creative spirit is "the quality of experience and not its control by the will." It is not concerned with propaganda or didacticism or melody or pure beauty, but only with totality of vision and of experience. To convey this there is no substitute for sense, for what T. S. Eliot has called "tough reasonableness"; in the effort to make the impact of this greater, the modern poet is capable of

---

[2] A distinction needs to be made between *kinds* of poetry and *degrees of excellence* in poetry. It would be foolish to attempt to evaluate the degrees of excellence in, say, Shakspere and Jonson until one analyzed the difference in *kind*, and recognized that the two men were doing quite different things. Only then do degrees of excellence have much meaning. Only by this method, also, does the old statement of judging an author according to his intentions have much meaning; we can judge the excellence of his work within its kind (which is radically different). For brief but valuable discussions of this point, see Foerster, *American Criticism*, 50-1, and T. S. Eliot, *Selected Essays*, 136-9. The failure of Ransom and Tate to admit this distinction weakens, rather than strengthens, their dialectic: as when Tate writes (in *Reactionary Essays in Poetry and Ideas*) that "We must understand clearly that such lines as

> 'Life, like a dome of many-colored glass,
> Stains the white radiance of Eternity'

are not poetry, but are the frustrated individual will trying to compete with science." That it is a weak kind of poetry, because of the defects which Tate brilliantly analyzes—the lack of wholeness of vision and of a sure grasp of the totality of experience—many persons, including the present writer, would agree; but to state as absolute and final that it is not poetry seems unnecessarily to narrow the meaning of *poetry*.

going over his smooth metres and laboriously roughening them. This point is relatively unimportant; the essential point is that the poet must work in the severe and subtle tradition of English verse, with a thorough comprehension of technique—a tradition and a techinque to which Spenser, Shakspere, and Milton *belonged*, as well as developed. Viewed in this light, the conventions of subject matter and of style which poets have adopted prevent only a weak "personal expression"; these conventions deepen its content, rather, by giving a formal, postponed, and reflective pleasure instead of an immediate and approximate pleasure. This aesthetic of poetry—developed in Ransom's *The World's Body*, Tate's *Reactionary Essays*, and the uncollected essays of Cleanth Brooks, Robert Penn Warren, and other Southern critics—gives meaning to traditionalism, dignity and content to poetry.

Such theories do not make for great popularity, since the poetry which comes out of them has almost a classic quality with a certain necessary involvement which is alien to the romantic and scientific spirit. If these theories do not embrace all of poetry, they give a valid, tenable foundation on which one type of poetry—in at least some respects the best type of poetry—can be written. This quality John Peale Bishop emphasizes when he writes that "poetry must be traditional."

Only because it diverges from the modern attitude does the theory of the Fugitive group of poets seem revolutionary. In general the conservative South has had little interest in radical experimentation. To speak of imagism, for example, as ever becoming a part of Southern poetic thought would be absurd; it deserves a brief notice here only because it was in part the product of a brilliant Southern poet, John Gould Fletcher. Poetry, to his mind, was to render mood alone. Each mood could best be represented not only by sound but by color patterns conjoined. He aimed at "a presentation of daily life in terms of highly-orchestrated and coloured words." The poetic form in which he developed this presentation most individually he called Symphonies; Fletcher himself describes them as "examples of the use, or the abuse, of the *allusive* method . . . . My aim in them was to describe certain predominant moods in the terms of things happening. Thus one gets expectancy described as a traveller looking at blue mountains in the distance, and despair described in terms of a stoker on board a ship. Each mood was to be presented not as abstract sorrow or joy or rage, but as something seen, heard, felt, and actually happening. By these means, I approached close to that 'methodical confusion of all the senses' which was described as the visionary state by no less a poet than Arthur Rimbaud."

In form these poems "seemed to be entirely shapeless," but Fletcher's defense is not easily overthrown: "I have always felt it more important for a poet to create his form according to the state of his feelings and the condition of his material, than to borrow one ready-made and to attempt to squeeze his feelings in it. Only a few metrical forms are really of universal applicability, perhaps the sonnet and blank verse are the only forms in English that can be used indiscriminately by all poets without loss of quality. I may have pushed metrical variation too far towards anarchy; for having employed it in preference to uniformity, I still feel I owe neither explanation nor apology." These definite theories were influential on other poets, but it is perhaps well to note that the influence was on English and Northern rather than on Southern poets. They came early in his life, and his later poetry reveals that his statement, "since then I have tended increasingly to hold that poetry is also thought, and that thought and emotion play the part in poetry of counterpoint and melody in the works of musical composers," is the key to much of his finest work. The early poems were written by an expatriate, the later poems by a man reintegrated to his section. Although a knowledge of his ideas gives a richer quality to the reading of Fletcher's poems, it is important here only in that connection.

For theory and practice alike, in the South, tend among the better poets to be traditional. Of bad writing, of confused thinking, of radical experimentation, of local color writing and sentimental sweetmeats, no section and no country or age have a monopoly. What the intentions, implied or stated, back of this work may be does not greatly matter. Partisan defense would be foolish, as it would be useless. But it is never without value to consider carefully the theories of articulate poets of any time or place, for out of that consideration comes a better understanding of poetry. Since the Southern poets generally have been inclined to ponder and to discuss the *how* as well as the *why*, they have worked out a rich body of poetic theory, which, though uneven in quality and validity, sets an intelligible background for their work.

IV

Southern Poetry

IF RICHARD Rich in 1610 carried his versified story of
Virginia to London, it is equally true that the English
colonists carried with them to Virginia their own songs,
ballads, and poems. The early poetry was English poetry
transplanted; the early ballads were English ballads twisted
gradually to the pattern of a new environment. Captain
John Smith was, from a literary as well as general point of
view, only a lesser Sir Walter Raleigh; George Sandys a
temporary American counterpart of Michael Drayton or
George Chapman. To men like Smith or William Byrd or
George Washington or St. George Tucker writing was the
accomplishment, not the career, of a gentleman. The
ability to write an appropriate poem, make a good speech
or turn a neat phrase, and relate effectively a dramatic or
useful anecdote were, one or all, likely to be a part of his
equipment. But they were not necessarily important: no
man was in likelihood of losing a lady for want of a sonnet.
Only Sandys, however, of these men had any professional
pride in his poetry; the others were gentlemanly dabblers
in the art of letters. Subjects for poetry were strictly occasional: the death of a great man, the winning of a victory,
the song to a loved one. In his youth George Washington
partially completed an acrostic to Frances Alexander, but
when inspiration failed him he abandoned the attempt as
unimportant. This attitude was typical.

To attempt a complete description of the early poems
produced in the South would be fruitless. But several
works deserve mention because they illustrate trends, and
one poem deserves more attention because of its intrinsic
merits than it generally receives.

That poem is "Bacon's Epitaph." It is one of the very few poems written in America which merits the adjective *great*. Yet it is completely in the Southern tradition: it came out of conflict between frontier and seaboard; its author was so little a man of letters that today he is unknown; it was strictly an occasional poem, in the best seventeenth-century manner, for a dead leader. The poem is richly allusive, classical in tone, sincere and dignified in emotion. Moses Coit Tyler wrote of it with justice as "this noble dirge, which has a stateliness, a compressed energy, and a mournful eloquence, reminding one of the commemorative verse of Ben Jonson"; even more, these nobly rhetorical couplets remind one of John Webster at his best. "Bacon's Epitaph" was the first and perhaps the greatest of the mono-poems which make up so much of Southern poetry.

Of slighter caliber was the first volume of poems published in the South: *Poems on Several Occasions by a Gentleman of Virginia* (1736). It is more impressive than such miscellaneous performances as appeared in the poet's corner of the *Virginia Gazette* solely because one man had written a quantity of verse which he thought good enough to collect into a volume. In his preface the Gentleman warns the reader that "the following pieces are the casual productions of youth," but he desires only honest judgment, for "I am well assured that giving an undeserved Applause to bad Poems, is a much greater and more dangerous Piece of Injustice to the Author, than even discouraging those, which are good." The poems deserved only moderate applause. Technically they reveal a limited command of blank verse, heroic couplets, and the simpler verse structures. The lyrics are pleasing, but slight in content: here are epistles after the manner of Horace, with a tendency toward moralizing; pastorals to Sylvia, with the faint licentiousness fashionable in that form; four imitations of Anacreon; and a satire, "On the Corruption of the Stage," which has interest only because the final line ("We turn to downright nonsense of our own") indicates that Virginia before 1736 had attempted sufficient dramatic efforts to earn the disapproval of the Gentleman's classical taste.

Although unimportant as literature, this easily available exhibit perfectly illustrates certain important features of Southern poetry. To attempt to compare it, favorably or unfavorably, with the works of Michael Wigglesworth or Anne Bradstreet would indeed be an attempt to measure the veriest of pigmies. But this difference is important: the Virginian's poetry is less indigenous and more graceful. If he never reached the goal of authentic poetry (as Anne Bradstreet did once in the poignant "Before the Birth of One of My Children"), he never stooped to the philosophical banalities of her "Contemplations," or to the pathological horrors of Wigglesworth's *Day of Doom*. The manner and attitude of the Virginian are highly civilized; he is more interested in a girdle than in a prayer, for poetical purposes; but he has back of him no content of thought shaped either from a personal philosophy or from a fund of common ideas which needed expression. Wigglesworth wrote directly out of a Puritan's conscience: he was a *choragus* for one section of Puritan thought; he had something in hand which he felt needed to be said, and he said it in wretched verse. The Gentleman had only a graceful attitude.

This attitude can be traced to the Southern view of poetry as a genteel accomplishment. There was no lack of serious thought in the South, but when Byrd or Wythe or Jefferson or Washington had something of importance to communicate, he put it into prose. Poetry was limited almost to *vers de société*. When Eben Cook in 1708 wrote his vigorous Hudibrastic satire on Maryland, he used verse to vent his spleen—but he was exceptional in this. Satire was usually light and pleasant, more nearly related to the polite thrusts of Matthew Prior than to the stiletto shafts of Alexander Pope. Occasionally it was robust and Rabelaisian, as in the jingle about the establishment in Williamsburg of a paper mill:

> Nice Delia's smock, which, neat and whole,
> No man durst finger for his soul;
> Turned to *Gazette*, now all the town
> May take it up, or smooth it down.

Mainly, poetry was polite and decorous. Only with the coming of the Revolution did it acquire a sharp edge, and even then the poets produced nothing memorable. There was no dearth of writing, but mostly these poems were modeled after older works, and rarely is an authentic note struck. The pretty picture of "Virginia Banishing Tea" had counterparts equally good, or bad, in other sections; the elegies, martial calls, and ballads were all feeble and derivative. The South, and the nation, had no poetic Jefferson—only a Freneau. Out of the frontier came one or two homely songs whose apt images are yet memorable: no line expresses better the ideas of combatants than "'Twas on a pleasant mountain / The Tory heathens lay." But such sharp aptness of phrase is rare.

During the days of war there appeared in the *Virginia Gazette* a rhymed catalogue which celebrated "The Belles of Williamsburg," and it was popular enough to bring forth a sequel. The authors were Dr. James McClurg, author of a medical treatise upon the human bile, and St. George Tucker, the annotator of Blackstone. This was the stuff of which poetry was made, by gentlemen-versifiers who had more important work to do in the world, but who would, occasionally, turn to verse for the expression of social ideas or of personal emotions. The lawyer wrote, shortly before his death, the best of the early Southern lyrics, "Resignation," with its plaintively haunting note of melancholy, but even his reflections on the transiency of life and the approach of death lack finality.

After the Revolution several volumes of versified trivialities appeared, which might on occasion (as in the case of John Shaw's dainty lyric, "Who Has Robb'd the Ocean Cave?") gain wide approval because of sentimentality and singing rhyme rather than intrinsic value. For a few months or years Baltimore, Richmond, and Charleston had each its magazine, before 1800, but nothing memorable came out of them. Poems and magazines were pale imitations of English models, and it seemed in no way strange that Washington Allston, poet and sculptor, should go from Charleston to live in England.

Allston did what most men wanted to do. Among those who remained in Charleston the foremost poet of early days was William Crafts, a Harvard-educated wit who modeled his conversation after Robert Treat Paine, and his poetry after Alexander Pope. His *Sullivan's Island* follows slavishly Pope's *Windsor Forest*; his longer, more important work, *The Raciad*, recounts in couplets not often sprightly the great social and sporting event of the Southern city. Crafts gathered round himself a group of kindred spirits, who met together and talked and on rare occasions read poems: if they were not greatly interested in producing literature, they were at least interested in all things literary. An abler poet and a better man was Samuel Henry Dickson, but with him, in typically Southern fashion, poetry was only a hobby. His profession was the practice and teaching of medicine, and he left as monument not deathless verses but a flourishing medical school.

Neither Crafts nor Dickson was intensely interested in the writing of poetry.   On the basis of surface appearances the same statement can be made of Richard Henry Wilde, lawyer and congressman, but the statement would be utterly false.   Wilde in his own opinion failed in life when he failed to write poetry which would endure.   This was in part due to the vitiating nature of his belief that a great literary work could be written only in a land rich with legend and tradition and culture; in part to external circumstance, for his finest poem, "My Life Is Like the Summer Rose," brought not fame but charges of plagiarism, from men who should have known better.   Consciousness of literary sterility combined with a driving ardor for poetry caused him to take up scholarly research, but this substitute for creative expression never fully satisfied him.

For all his misgivings, Wilde had a spark of genuine poetry within him.   That he could have been a great poet in any time or place seems doubtful; in addition to theories and circumstances, he would have had to overcome a defect within himself.   His poems do not develop in idea, theme, or story.   Although he imitated Byron, he failed where the Englishman best succeeded: in communicable movement. Ironically, even in Wilde's sonnet, "To Lord Byron," this defect appears, for the lines seem to stop on a single idea, the words pile up without developing the thought.   In his long unfinished poem, *Hesperia*, this static diffuseness nullifies the total value of a work which, in short sequences, is often powerful and arresting.   The man reveals himself in the poem, although unintentionally, and the man revealed is worth knowing: a reflective philosopher, a satirist who attacks abstractions like gold rather than persons, a traveler with an eye for scenery, which he describes without quite fusing the objects into a word-portrait; above all, a man who could speak with justice of "my inexpressible weariness of life and spirit."

As a poet he depended too much on eye and soul, upon that thin romantic atmosphere which, he felt, was thin because of lack of richness in his environment, and too little upon intellectual content. He had a knack mainly for writing melodious and impressive single lines (his best line, perhaps, was "On that lone shore loud moans the sea," with its graphic imagery accented by monotonous alliteration and rich vowel-color). On a few occasions, however, his inclination toward rhetorical oratory seems a natural part of the poem, as in the poignantly memorable "Farewell to America," or in the depth of feeling which strikes sharply through the deceptively light surface of "To the Mocking-Bird." The scanty records of Wilde's life do not show a man of infinite sadness, but the poems do; a congenial and successful person, to the world, but to himself a fit companion for the Lord Byron whom he admired so greatly. From this troubled and frustrated poet who judged himself and his work so stringently came one almost perfect lyric and a body of work which has been unjustly neglected.

If Wilde has with justice been relegated to the position of author of one poem, Edward Coote Pinkney has for no reason at all been accorded the same fate. In five years of writing, before his death at twenty-six, he produced half a dozen excellent lyrics and at least one stirring ode.[1] In

---

[1] T. O. Mabbott and F. L. Pleadwell (*The Life and Works of Edward Coote Pinkney*, v–vi) have written a paragraph of such excellence as a summary that it well deserves inclusion here: "The importance historically of the first of the Southern lyrists, Poe's most immediate forerunner, and of the most noted poet of the United States Navy is evident enough. But Pinkney's verses have more claim to attention than their historical interest alone would entitle them to hold; they

personal character Pinkney represented a wide and influential strain in the Southern group: he was a moral cavalier, who was touchy as to his honor and quick to challenge any man who impinged on it, who wrote gallant love songs to one fair lady at a time, and who was affected by classical, neoclassical, and romantic thought and poetry. If his lyrics can be best compared with those of Thomas Carew, his indebtedness to Wordsworth's songs to Lucy cannot be overlooked; if in his longer work he took as models chiefly Lord Byron and Thomas Moore, he drew also upon Milton and Donne and the Elizabethan dramatists, upon Catullus and other Roman poets. For Pinkney was studious and learned, gay and moral, a young man who was gradually shaping and refining his thought and his poetry.

---

are in themselves poetry 'of the first water,' at their best 'perfect chrysolites,' as Willis has called them, at their worst never what any poet need blush to own. True, like every young poet, Pinkney had masters, though unlike many a young man he was of catholic taste, and numbered among his models poets ancient and modern, not only Tom Moore, but also the Cavalier lyrists; not only Byron, but Wordsworth as well. If some poems are imitative, others are strikingly original, and all have more or less a markedly individual flavor, unlike that of any other verse, distinctive, and in itself the sign of the true poetic gift. One of the fragments, *Cornelius Agrippa*, a palpable imitation of *Don Juan*, will illustrate this point. Compare it, in subject and treatment, with *Don Juan* and any other imitation of Byron, and the poet's innate originality is at once revealed. Then read one of the finest of the lyrics, 'Look out upon the stars, my love,' or the tremendous closing quatrain of *The Voyager's Song*, or the gallant *Health*, and the poet's power rings out clear. Distinguished particularly for enthusiasm, warm and vivid imagery, and what Hubner terms 'classic elegance of diction' Pinkney may be considered a worthy predecessor of the three other great Southern poets, Poe, Timrod, and Lanier; while his absolute preëminence in his own special field of English literature is perhaps as notable as that of Poe himself in his. Yet, except for the selections in the Anthologies, few have read Pinkney's poems; the slight bulk of his work, published before his early death, militated against his reputation; and of late years copies of the early editions of his *Poems* have become so scarce that many a student who desired to read other poems by the author of *A Health* has found it impossible to procure them outside of the very largest libraries."

There is clear evidence in his poetry that he was working out a personal philosophy which would have deepened and enriched his individual lyric gift; out of his experimentation with more ambitious poems might have come a poem that was derivative only in the good sense of the word, that was distinctly his own while it remained securely in the tradition of English poetry.

This consideration gives to his career, inevitably, a sense of brilliant promise rather than a complete fulfillment. Yet his incompleteness is far from failure: Pinkney, like his section, was cut off at the period of greatest achievement, and, again like his section, his real values have been strangely neglected. In his thin sheaf of poems can be found some trash and much immature and incomplete work, but in at least a dozen poems, also, can be found the singing note of the true lyric poet.

The year that Pinkney died in Baltimore (1828), William Gilmore Simms of Charleston was editing his first magazine. Three years before he had published his first volume of verse: a monody in heroic couplets on the death in 1825 of General Charles Cotesworth Pinckney. At the time Simms was a young law student who watched from outside the group of wits presided over by William Crafts; in the years that followed he knocked almost vainly at the door of the literary group which, under the leadership of Hugh Swinton Legaré, founded *The Southern Review* and made Charleston a center of literary effort. Not only was Simms a poor man of an undistinguished family, but he was also arrogantly free with his opinions. His vigorous opposition to Nullification, for one example, prejudiced many people against him. Also, the leaders of the community thought better of the learned essays of Legaré than of any poems and stories; as for creative literature, in particular, they had a marked preference for English over American books.

Simms continued to write and to publish poetry, but he soon abandoned the heroic couplet for the looser Byronic forms. Only by accident did he turn romancer, and he never abandoned poetry—he valued his poems, in fact, more highly than his novels. His enormous energy, mental and physical, needed many outlets. The range of his poetry was astonishingly wide. He wrote long romantic narratives in verse after the manner of Byron and Scott, sonnets after the manner of Wordsworth, and occasional poems of many types. In this final respect, Simms as poet was typically Southern. He preferred the occasional subject, preferred to write at white heat while men were stirred mightily by some immediate event.

In that was his fatal flaw, poetically. Brief and subjective lyric poems can be dashed off, in spite of all that critics may say, and some of them are surprisingly good; long poems even of the romantic type require a sustained thought—an effort which the Southerner grounded in the tenets of inspirational romanticism was unwilling to give to fiction or verse, but which he gave unsparingly to political theory. Simms shared this attitude, with the result that his long poems contain vivid and stirring passages, but mainly they contain a facile correctness which rarely attains distinction. Although his poetic masters were Byron and Wordsworth, his mind was more like Dryden's. But he lacked Dryden's severe genius; he could expand an idea much more easily than he could prune back the luxuriant growth of his fancy.

By 1860 Simms had published eighteen volumes of poetry. If Pinkney wrote too little, quantitatively, to gain him the critical consideration he deserved, Simms managed to smother some really excellent work under the weight of too much mediocrity. This bulky inequality is enough to explain why casual readers have passed him by, but it does not explain why the anthologists or, even more, his biographer, have paid so little attention to separating the good from the bad. For Simms could write powerfully, if not perfectly: in the rank undergrowth of words in "The Edge of the Swamp" there is caught a miasmic atmosphere redolent with local color; in many short poems the man's mental vitality more than compensates for his lack of artistry. That he lacked utterly the faculty of self-criticism was best revealed when he expanded and sadly vitiated his finest poem, until it lost the grandeur and finality of the first version: "The Lost Pleiad" is an orchestrated expression of the transiency of the most stable objects, a poem which cuts through the conventionalities of that overused subject and gives to it a lasting freshness and significance.

Simms was a man of positive defects and flaws. These are obvious enough, but their obviousness has for too long obscured his equally positive merits and achievements. From his entire poetic work only a small volume of excellent poems could be selected, but that volume would entitle Simms to rank with the better American poets.

Equally drastic principles of selectivity must be exercised on the work of Thomas Holley Chivers, of Georgia. S. Foster Damon has appropriately written that Chivers "straddled the famous fence between the sublime and the ridiculous, and quite as often fell on the one side as on the other. . . . He knew nothing about correctness. He made up words; his grammar was shaky; his rhymes were often common; he repeated his metaphors over and over; he padded his stanzas; he borrowed the best lines of other poets; he mixed his mythologies; he said silly, inconsequential things; he lacked restraint of every kind. He was morbid—worse yet, fashionably morbid; he believed in angels and was always writing about them; he was appallingly sincere; he printed far too much, under the impression that everything versified at the proper heat of enthusiasm was sacred. Nevertheless, through all his work, good and bad, runs the curious undercurrent of power which is the peculiar manifestation of genius."

All this is true. It can be discerned by a careful reading of any typical Chivers poem, such as "Lily Adair." He was an eccentric, an *original*. On the surface his poetry is more easily identified with persons and places, with his background and his immediate life, than Poe's. To a large degree all that Chivers wrote was autobiographical. Poetry was a cathartic by which he partially purged his system. When marriage failed, he pitied in verse his broken life; when he beheld the Mississippi, he demanded with "mystical ardor" that it speak to him; when one of his children died, he wrote agonized yet liquid elegies. He gave to autobiographical facts a tinge of metaphysical idea, which transmuted the best of these poems into a borderland between this world and the next. It was not, exactly, a matter of all being grist that came to his mill; it was rather the absolute faith which Chivers had in the poet being the revelator of the divine will. While he dramatized himself and his sufferings, at first in Byronic fashion and later in his own original manner, even his most absurd dramatizations seem an integral part of his morbid subjectivity.

He was much possessed by death. Over one-third of his poems deal with that subject. But he tended to escape quickly from the here to the hereafter, and his faith in immortality was unshakable. Moreover, he trusted implicitly the power of his musical words to sweep the reader into transcendental ecstasy at any moment. For Chivers had seen visions, which colored most of everything he wrote; he was a Swedenborgian, an associationist, a mystic without a sense of balance.

Let it be said here, also, that he was a poet. When all the qualifications—and they are numerous—have been listed which must be made, there remains an intrinsic value to his best poems which cannot be denied. "Inspiration and technique are the twin wings on which every poet soars; and both of Chivers' lacked many feathers. But occasionally in his eccentric flight, he shot high," wrote Damon, putting his finger upon the fundamental weakness of Thomas Holley Chivers. These things the Georgia poet had, although unevenly; what he lacked was the intellectual power to discipline them to his purpose. Inspiration and technique are not enough: at best, they result in the straitly limited poetry of a Coleridge or a Shelley. Chivers was not, in his kind, comparable in ability to the two Englishmen, who in their turn are not comparable to Webster and Jonson and Donne, much less to Shakspere or Dante or Homer. But the field of poetry is wide, and capable of including diverse types and wide ranges of excellence. Only a prejudiced person would claim for Chivers a high place: all of his poetry is extraordinary, a great part of it is incredibly bad, but a residue of lyrical poetry (comparable, Damon suggests, to Beddoes' work rather than to Blake's) is purely melodious and thinly authentic.

To this writer, at least, it seems impossible that we should ever again attempt an evaluation of the life and work of Edgar Allan Poe without a consideration also of Chivers. This distinction may be tentatively suggested: that Poe had a wild genius disciplined by artistry, Chivers a wayward talent which occasionally became genius. The two were literary brothers. Each man in his youth followed Byron, each in his early maturity Coleridge; each evolved strikingly individual theories and types of poetry which have obvious similarities. Each borrowed freely from the other and from any other poet whose work seemed attractive. Each was an unusual product of his time and of his peculiar environment (Poe by adoption the son of a Virginia gentleman, Chivers by birth a wealthy Georgian), yet each escaped from that environment into a cloudy, haunted other-world.

This is important because later critics have evolved strange theories to explain the "mystery" of Poe. That he was at times a drunkard, and possibly an opium addict, is true enough, but these explain strange vagaries in his conduct without explaining his creative achievement in the least; that he was sexually impotent may have been true, but there seem few reasons to believe it, and many reasons not to believe it; that he was a literary "man without a country," unique and unlocalized, is unadulterated nonsense. Much misinterpretation might have been avoided if only slight attention had been paid to Chivers. For he took no drugs, he preached abstinence from tobacco and alcohol, he fathered seven children, and he was, quite plainly, a citizen of Georgia. Yet his critical theories parallel Poe's; his metaphysical speculations go far beyond Poe's; his poems have the same ghost-haunted atmosphere, and his visions are just as far removed from everyday reality.

To understand these men requires an understanding also of their age—a subject far too involved for analysis here, and one rarely treated. They were part of the romantic movement which had so many facets, but which, in the main, can be said to have completed the work of protestantism in making the individual all-important. It was a heady doctrine, which in the form of transcendentalism almost swept the cool Emerson from his moorings; in the form of

German philosophy, it unseated Coleridge. Men were affected in different ways: Poe detested transcendentalism as such, while every philosophical thought he uttered revealed a similar source; Chivers was attracted by it, and went beyond it into spiritualism. Both men, in that period of rootless intellects, explored the mental frontier: Poe pseudo-rationally, in *Eureka;* Chivers mystically, in *Search after Truth.* These wild books have numerous parallels by American writers of that day; they are in no sense unique; they are American variants of a widely scattered development of thought.

Poe's mind had more of balance than did the mind of Chivers or, for another example, of Bronson Alcott; his mind, indeed, seems that of an inferior, and American, Coleridge. That is, Poe could rationalize rather than philosophize about his beliefs; but in each case, if the reader will allow the first premises, the dialectic and the logic hold together with surprising tightness. Poe's theories of poetry require certain elements, previously discussed; his practice may have caused the theories, or the process may have been reversed. In all probability theory and practice developed together, the one as a normal part of the other.

At its best his poetry represents mood exalted at the expense of intellect. His aim was a dark beauty, secured in part by indefinite imagery and melodic, almost hypnotic, rhythm. That Poe could recognize and state poetically an intellectual truth he demonstrated in the "Sonnet—To Science": the destruction of age-old myth by science is his theme, and it is a worthy one. (The fascination which science held for Poe is more readily seen in his stories). If he could realize such facts, he could not as poet remain greatly interested in them; he infinitely preferred his "ghoul-haunted woodland of Weir." Only a few poems deal with a specific locale. They catch instead an atmosphere, a somber mood, a haunted spirit. His range was exceedingly narrow, his productivity small. His theme is slightly varied, yet basically constant: the death of a beautiful woman, the realm of the spirit, the psychological state of the poet when his mind is partially in another world. Combinations or variations of these themes are at the heart of nearly all of his finest lyrics.

The plot that Poe tilled was strait and infertile. From it, however, he wrung a few exquisite plants. With infinite pains he reworked his poems, elaborating here and pruning there, republishing his revised poem, and then subjecting it to additional revision. Perhaps it would be more appropriate to compare Poe with a lapidary, for he was constantly polishing his small and finely-cut gems. Even the best are likely to have one flaw: Poe's phraseology was lush as well as liquid. His greater defect can be summarized in Poe's own judgment of Bryant, whom he denied a place with "the spiritual Shelleys"[2] because "the objects in the moral or physical universe coming within the periphery of his vision" are exceedingly limited; "The relative extent of these peripheries of poetical vision must ever be a primary consideration in our classification of poets." Where Poe's periphery ended it is most important that a great poet's shall begin: in completeness of vision. He saw only one phase of those realities which are of the human spirit. His "shuddering harmonies of the murky subconscious, and roseate harmonies of sensuous longing posing as spirituality"

---

[2] As Norman Foerster notes, this is a sound canon if properly understood: "it explains why Chaucer, for example, great as he is, is not among the greatest— his periphery is short. But Poe forgets that what makes Chaucer great despite his restricted periphery, is his extraordinary truth and completeness of vision within his limits, and that the spiritual Shelleys ... are inferior to him because, with all their reach of vision, they are wanting in this truth and completeness."

are complete in themselves—but they are not extensive in scope or sympathy. Within his narrowed range Poe's achievement is remarkably high. It is this quality which gives him a certain pre-eminence over Emerson or Whitman, whose vast peripheries of vision are rarely clarified or expressed in words of finality. What Poe had to say is communicated poetically and with finality. But there is more to be said—and failure in this regard makes Edgar Allan Poe a limited poet.

Deliberate experiments in prosody began with Poe and Chivers. Each desired to write in original forms. Poe stated his ideas clearly in "The Philosophy of Composition," in "The Rationale of Verse," and in other essays; all his efforts were directed toward "the creation of novel moods of beauty, in form, in color, in sound, in sentiment." As G. W. Allen has observed, "All of Poe's experimentation with rime, alliteration, 'indefinite' imagery, and even meter, progresses toward the attainment of this one ideal, and is realized most successfully in such poems as *Ulalume*, *Lenore*, and *The Raven*. Here we have the 'essential' Poe (at any rate in versification); here his theory and practice most unmistakably converge."

Only in "The Bells" did Poe carry this experimentation with onomatopoeia to an extreme, with his attempts to represent four moods through jolly sleigh bells, mellow wedding bells, loud alarum bells, and solemn tolling bells. Generally he attempted to fit meter and stanza form to the precise mood of the poem, to make every poetic device accentuate the sense by fusing sound and sense (or atmosphere) into a whole.

Chivers was bolder and less successful in his experimentation. In his first volume he calmly invented a stanza of nine lines, rhyming *ababcdcdd*, in an attempt to round out with an extra rhyme the tonal qualities of a common form; in a late and revised version of "Georgia Waters" he returned to this stanza form with a slight variation in the rhyme— *ababcbcbb*. Usually his experiments were directed toward the cult of sound. Melody, musical overtones, hypnotic sound, meant more to him than idea or thought. This was responsible for his belief that the refrain was not an ornament, but an essence, of a poem. For the sake of euphony he did not hesitate to invent new words, or to twist the meaning of strange and archaic words until he secured the liquid melody that he thought vital. Certain words and refrains do yeoman service many times. He was attempting, as Damon notes, to build songs "out of pure sound and a rich stream of apparently unrelated images." The richness of open vowels, of luxuriant alliteration and repetitive devices were not enough to satisfy him: "He was interested in the songs of birds, the metallic diapason of bells, the weird thin music of the Chinese, the puffing of a railroad." In one poem he imitated with great success the rhythm of the negro songs, using negro dialect. In several poems he wrote in the cadence that Whitman used most often. Only one of these experimental poems need be quoted here, his "Railroad Song":

> Clitta, clatta, clatta, clatter,
> Like the devil beating batter
> Down below in iron platter—
> Which subsides into a clanky,
> And a clinky, and a clanky,
> And a clinky, clanky, clanky,
> And a clanky, clinky, clanky;
> And the song that I now offer
> For Apollo's Golden Coffer—
> With the friendship that I proffer—
> Is for Riding on a Rail.

Like his other experiments with sound it was intended to be recitative, and it antedated the similar experiments of Vachel Lindsay. However, these poems were buried in almost forgotten magazines; although interesting in themselves, they had little effect upon Southern poets.

Poe and Chivers belong to that class loosely denominated by the word *genius*. Simms did not. But he valued their friendship, and they in turn valued his; they kept in touch through correspondence. Simms submitted his work to Poe, who gladly published it; and he preached to both men from afar the unwelcome doctrine of his prejudiced common sense.

More nearly akin to Simms in mind and work was Philip Pendleton Cooke, who attempted with little success to recapture the old bardic ardor in his ballads on historical subjects. Cooke also wrote with great rapidity. Only once did he attain a marked popular esteem, with the delicately pleasing "Florence Vane." A better poem, possibly because it expressed spontaneously Cooke's ideal of the way of living, was his "Life in the Autumn Woods." Cooke did not have Simms's vitality, however; his character, his work, and even his promise all are pleasant, but all seem definitely slight. By 1850 Poe and Cooke were dead; after 1853 (when he published three volumes of poetry) Chivers practically passed from the literary scene.

Simms continued. And the group which gathered around him in Charleston was no mean one. To its leadership he came late, after the death of Hugh Swinton Legaré—but to leadership he had come, until in the 1850's he was the "Nestor" of Southern letters, the master of "Woodlands" and the friend of literary aspirants. This group had a convenient meeting place in Russell's Bookstore, for "Lord John" Russell was more interested in good conversation than in sales. In the afternoon, when work was done, certain men would drop in to browse and talk: Simms, William J. Grayson, James L. Petigru, Samuel Henry Dickson and his namesake and son-in-law J. Dickson Bruns, James Mathewes Legaré, and other distinguished persons. Younger men were coming to the shop to take the place of those who died, like Legaré, or of those who moved away, like Dickson. To this coterie belonged Basil Gildersleeve, Henry Timrod, and Paul Hamilton Hayne. Here books were discussed, poems read, and theories debated. A smaller club of nine men met frequently at Simms's town house—the "Wigwam"—and facetious neighbors who lived blocks away would comment next morning on the poet's thunderous declamations.

Even the names of some of these Charleston intellectuals have been forgotten; in a few instances, justly. One gifted poet has dropped from sight, with a resultant loss to our poetry: James Mathewes Legaré's one small book, with the unpromising title *Orta-Undis*, contains five poems which have, beneath the gentle moralizing and simple verse structure, a graceful and individual statement of old truths in pleasingly new combinations. His book is uneven, his poetry often derivative but sometimes authentic. Legaré remained strictly within the Southern tradition: a classicist, his title poem is in Latin; an occasional poet, he wrote an excellent and memorable tribute to his kinsman, Hugh Swinton Legaré; a lover of nature, he wrote well on that popular and difficult subject. In these poems his romanticism, his indebtedness to Wordsworth, Schiller, and Tennyson, can be found, but playing over this romanticism is the precision of mind natural to a classicist. Ironically enough, his most widely reprinted poem was an oriental legend, "Ahab-Mohammed," in the manner of Leigh Hunt's "Abou Ben Adhem." For Legaré wrote better poems—slight enough, it is true, yet poems which reveal a fresh, observant eye for nature and for earth, and a rhythm and style which ideally fitted his gentle muse.

Legaré was a minor figure. By some odd trick of fate, Timrod has been relegated to a rôle which Legaré deserved. In his early days Timrod was the conventional poet, following closely in the footsteps of Wordsworth. That he understood the meaning and purpose of poetry he clearly revealed in his critical articles; in the youthful *Vision of Poesy* he wrote:

> My task hath been, beneath a mightier power,
> To keep the world forever fresh and young . . .
>
> I turn life's tasteless waters into wine,
> And flash them through and through with purple tints.

But the vision, though high and noble, is the work of youth, and as poetry it is weak and uneven. One feels beneath the lines desire, not conviction; dreams, not philosophy or reflection. In the assertion that "the poet to the whole wide world belongs" there is a wealth of meaning: all the rootlessness of one who had learned the technique, had mastered the art of poetic reference and communication, but had never really had anything to say. He wrote pleasing tributes to ladies and graceful poems about nature, but he suffered much from his inability to loose the feelings that stirred within him.

The war awakened all his dormant emotions. The whole wide world was forgotten in his absorption with something which lay nearer his hand and his heart. His technique and intellectual turn of mind now served him well: although sincerity and throbbing emotion beat through his words in passionate undertones, the passion never carries the verse into formlessness of thought or reference. Instead an almost classic coolness and restraint appears, from first to last, in his war poems. This quality more than any other marks Timrod's undoubted surperiority over his comrade Hayne—over, for that matter, every Southern poet except Edgar Allan Poe. The friendly Northern critic, Thomas Wentworth Higginson, thought that South Carolina was somewhat to blame for Hayne's poetic shortcomings: it denied him "a nation," and thus made a handicap of his love for the state. But the geographical sweep of a man's affections has nothing to do with his poetic intensity; in Timrod's case the state was enough and nation or world would not have made Hayne a greater poet: the diffuseness of his writing thinned out the content. Not that Hayne felt less deeply than Timrod—it was not that; Hayne failed in the attempt to communicate that feeling. He had certain natural advantages: "the passion for the poet's calling, the thirst for natural beauty, the spirit of brooding peace, the reminiscent note, the mystic strain." But the thirst for natural beauty was a sensuous and surface thirst; although he lived for twenty years at Copse Hill, Hayne never seems to have acquired a feeling of the richness and fertility of earth, or of man's dependence upon it.

Possibly Hayne had felt too deeply the tragedy of war and defeat, of poverty and reconstruction. In his poetry there is a certain negative quality, a turning away from what was immediately about him, which shows more glaringly in his complete works than it possibly can in a selection. A kindly man, he had no desire to cherish animus, and his letters and poems to various Northern poets ring plaintively with a desire for fellowship and friendly feeling. But the ugly, stubborn facts were all about him, obtruding even into the quietude of Copse Hill—and he could neither bear nor deny them. True, he never, as Lanier did, spoke directly the messages which a progressive nation desired to hear; he retired within himself, although his correspondence with American and European poets was surprisingly large. But his retirement was real enough, in the sense that he preferred not to think of what had happened, or what, under an industrialistic regime, was happening to the South. Literature meant escape; poetry meant beauty. And he could find beauty in the pines, in the clouds, in the birds, in the lush vegetation that grew so plentifully around him. Beauty was not much in men, and when he thought of nobility it brought him back too swiftly to older days which wrung a man's heart to think upon.

The escape was involuntary, perhaps, and surely from the standpoint of one individual's happiness it was far better than any amount of, most likely, unavailing thought. Hayne never shirked a direct task. He edited the poems of Timrod before his own poems were collected, and he wrote for that volume a preface which is just and generous, which deserves, indeed, more adjectives of praise than captious men in our day would ever permit to be given it without a cynical sneer. For back of it, and hovering close to the surface, are the unshed tears of men who could not weep, and who rarely, very rarely, yielded to the hysteria which every man at that time must, in part, have felt. Hayne told the pathetic story of Timrod's life with tenderness, with ungrudging admiration, yet with a certain calmness of phrase which tears the heart. The man was infinitely gentle, and great.

Yet it is as poets that we must, finally, be concerned with Hayne and Timrod. That Hayne was a minor poet is certain: his reputation must rest upon a few competent and noble sonnets, and upon a few truly fine lyrics. He wrote narrative poems which can be read as easily as the similar works of Tennyson or William Morris can be read. Although the average level of craftsmanship which he attained in all his work is amazingly high, his finest achievements are never far above that standard. Lanier noted his obvious faults: "First, we observe a frequently recurring *lapsus* of thought, in which Mr. Hayne falls into trite similes, worn collocations of words, and common-place sentiments. . . . The second fault. . . is diffuseness, principally originating in a lavishness and looseness of adjectives." These faults suggest a diffuseness of thought as well as of words, a lack of that predestinate iron which is the heritage of great poets. He could write poignant monodies for his friends after their deaths, kindly tributes to fellow poets and to his son—but he was at his best when he sang of the pines or when he considered the fleeting transiency of his own days.

Timrod's frail body lacked strength, but his mind possessed the clarity of thought and the iron which Hayne's mind somehow lacked. He saw a poem as a whole, yet as composed of lines, and his best poems combine a clear distinction of line with a sense of rounded completeness. His early nature poems are Wordsworthian in tone and character; even his excellent sonnets owe something to that earlier poet. In the best of this work—particularly in "I Know Not Why" and "Most Men Know Love"—he began to speak in his own tongue. When war came he spoke boldly: in long odes like "Ethnogenesis" and "The Cotton Boll," in spirited lyrics like "Carolina" and "Charleston"— all first-rate poems. "The Cotton Boll" belongs definitely to the land, rather than to nature as such; "it is the voice of the agricultural, commercial, and militant South." Timrod could express this quality, but he could express even better the sadness and horror of war. In "Spring" he achieved a perfect balance with his idyllic yet half-sad picture of a world breaking into bloom thrown abruptly in contrast with "the call of death":

> Yet not more surely shall the Spring awake
> The voice of wood and brake,
> Than she shall rouse, for all her tranquil charms,
> A million men to arms.

Not only was it Timrod who sang of war; it was Timrod who wrote for the dead a memorial poem "that approximates perfection." His "Ode" has the supreme artistic merit of throbbing with vibrant emotion in its effect upon a reader, yet of possessing a classic coolness of phrase which might have been carved from stone. The poet indulges in no histrionic exhibitionism, but this controlled and inevitable verse leaves nothing to be said:

> In seeds of laurel in the earth
> The blossom of your fame is blown,
> And somewhere, waiting for its birth,
> The shaft is in the stone!

Before 1860 the stimulus of war produced few notable lyrics in the South; from the War of 1812, perhaps the greatest occasional song ever produced in America, "The Star-Spangled Banner"; from the Mexican War, Theodore O'Hara's "The Bivouac of the Dead." Key wrote nothing else of importance; O'Hara, at most, wrote only two other poems. One of these has close kinship with "The Bivouac": it honors Daniel Boone, it follows the same form, and it too is elegiac. Each man succeeded in expressing with finality the emotions of a people. These poems have almost an anonymous value, seeming to stem out of the general consciousness rather than from one man's mind; it is that happy quality which gives to them enduring worth.

No single poem written during the Civil War quite attains this height; two works, however, almost achieved it. The nearest approach is Randall's "Maryland, My Maryland." Written at white heat one night, read to his students next day, and published in the New Orleans *Delta* within a week, it spread over the entire South when it was set to the music of the German college tune "Lauriger Horatius" (itself founded on "Tannenbaum, O Tannenbaum"). Something of universality and of anonymity "My Maryland" does possess; it has been spoken of as "the Marseillaise of the Confederacy," but this statement is over-strong. The concentrated lines suggest the passion of a people proclaiming liberty, but the song falls a little short of finality— a lack easily explained in the fact that men were too widespread, no longer homogeneous enough to feel great passion as a tribal possession. Loyalty too was divided and uncertain, for North and South were still one nation; the foe was not quite foreign.

The song which permeated even more widely through the South, which indeed as to music answered every requirement, was "Dixie," written by Dan D. Emmett for Bryant's Minstrels in 1859. The older version has the homely picturesqueness of a folk ballad: it was stirring, not dignified. After the manner of folk ballads the text underwent many sea changes—in some instances improvements, in others, detriments. But as a song it quickly became the possession of a people, gaining in time the unofficial rank of a national (after the Confederacy was defeated, a sectional) anthem. This came about almost in spite of the words, for the text was altered and changed many times, while men and women sought vainly to write words for the music which would be both dignified and popular. The effort was vain. Most attempts were silly or sentimental or bombastic; the best version is Albert Pike's somewhat pompous "Southrons, hear your country call you!" Pike's version is literary, made for the printed page instead of the camp or singing group. "Dixie" as usually sung at present may well be described as the finest ballad which America has produced.

Other songs attained a tremendous popularity with the soldiers: "The Bonnie Blue Flag," "Lorena," and "Listen to the Mocking-Bird" are probably the best examples. Even more interesting are the verses improvised for the occasion by the soldiers themselves. A writer in the *Southern Bivouac* (July, 1885) has described this making of homemade epics:

As the long contest dragged on, and war, losing much of its earlier illusions, became a stern, bitter, and exceedingly monotonous reality, these "high-toned" lyrics were tacitly voted rather too romantic and poetical for the actual field, and were remitted to the parlor and the piano stool. The soldiers chanted in quite other fashion on the march or seated at the campfire. In these crude rhymes, some of them improvised for the moment, there was less of flourish but more of meaning, not so much bravado but a good deal more point. They were sappy with the homely satire of the camps, which stings friend and foe alike. Innumerable verses were composed and sung to popular refrains. The Army of Virginia and the Army of Tennessee had each its history rudely chronicled as fast as made in this rough minstrelsy. Every corps and command contributed some commemorative stanza. The current events of campaigns were told in improvised verse as rapidly as they occurred and were thereafter skillfully recited by the rhapsodist who professed to know the whole fragmentary epic.

These improvisations have chiefly folk values. The poets were not idle. Every person who could write patriotic

verse, it seems, did so, North and South: the result on
both sides is an amazing mélange of excellent, fair, bad,
and terrible poetry.   The course of the war can be traced
in the poetry, can be traced, indeed, in the work of the
best Southern poet, Timrod.   He anticipated the war with
his hopefully prophetic "The Cotton Boll"; hailed the birth
of the Confederacy with a stately ode, "Ethnogenesis";
rallied the South in general with the passionate "A Cry to
Arms," and South Carolina in particular, somewhat later,
with the ringing lyric, "Carolina;" wrote nobly an elegy to
"The Unknown Dead"; cried pathetically for the end of
bloodshed and the return of peace in a bitter pastoral,
"Spring;" mourned the destruction of his native city with
"Charleston;" and at last, when war's fever was over, Timrod wrote the noblest of his poems (the finest that came out
of the war), the "Ode" to the Confederate dead.

Yet Timrod's war poetry was but a part—although the
finest part—of his poetic achievement.   If the same continuity cannot be found in the work of another individual,
it can be found in the sweep of poetry which tended to
submerge individual personalities under stress of emotion,
and to give most of the poems a distinct kinship with
related poems by other men.   However sharply defined each
elegy may be, for instance, it relates to other elegies in
attitude and often in phraseology, until the conclusion seems
inescapable that these grew out of a folk consciousness as
much as they did out of an individual's brain.

If the war brought forth no poem which assumed universality, defeat did.   (This question is not one of literary values
alone, by any means; none of these poems considered from
this angle—"The Star-Spangled Banner," "The Bivouac of
the Dead," "Dixie," or "The Conquered Banner"—compare
with the best work of Poe or Timrod, to stick to Southern

poets; it has to do with the acceptance almost as a heritage of a poem by a people). Abram Joseph Ryan had served as soldier and chaplain through the war, and to the Confederacy he had given his whole allegiance. Expressing his own emotions, he dashed off "The Conquered Banner," and it was accepted immediately as the poem of defeat. Father Ryan had many of the qualities of the scōp, the bard of the people; he almost improvised his poems, he felt a little more deeply what all were feeling, and gave adequate expression to that common emotion. Ryan left no memorable poem of the war, but immediately afterward he wrote three of the finest poems that we have: the other two, "The Sword of Robert Lee" and "A Land without Ruins," are of the same general type, but they failed to strike quite the same note.

The tragic histories of Edgar Allan Poe and of Thomas Holley Chivers might well have been the subjects for Greek dramatists: each man possessed a fatal flaw within himself, although that flaw is partially indefinable. Neither man had balance; neither acted, in literature or in life, with moderation. Timrod's was a modern tragedy: he was crushed and beaten by outside forces—grinding poverty which led to sickness and to death—over which he could have no possible control. Timrod in early days had too much balance; he could not turn himself loose and write. The result is that he left no bad poems in the sense that certain poems of Poe and particularly of Chivers are bad; but in that early work no magnificent passages sweep the reader away. The war released him, and the war in turn ruined him.

To a lesser degree the war also ruined many another Southern poet. In Hayne's case health was spared; he lived on in a poverty which was not quite a matter of starvation, but which forced him away from the social life he had known and loved. How plaintively he cherished the autographs of Simms and Timrod, written on the bare walls of his hut; how faithfully he corresponded with men whom he could not visit—these tokens show a mental starvation which is only a little less pathetic than the bodily starvation of Timrod. And Hayne needed the stimulus of conversation, the wit of verbal battle, more than most poets. Left alone, he mellowed rather than ripened.

The war which set abstraction free did more than cut off men in their prime. It changed an entire way of life, it uprooted an old, sound culture and substituted for it a new civilization. The result of that uprooting can best be traced in the life and poetry of Sidney Lanier. In Lanier's failure there are elements both of modern and of Greek tragedy; after the war he struggled manfully if unavailingly against the relentless forces of poverty and of disease. But his relative failure as a major poet must also be sought within himself; he attempted to substitute a vague emotional sensibility for philosophy and thought.

This is easily illustrated. A contemporary critic wrote that "Mr. Lanier's poetic sensibility and poetic purpose cannot make up for a lack of clear expression in his writing. This lack is the evidence not so much of want of practice in composition as of discipline of thought." Set against this criticism the poet's reply, in a letter to this brother: ". . . It has naturally caused me to make a merciless arraignment and trial of my artistic purposes; and an unspeakable content arises out of the revelation that they come from the ordeal confirmed in innocence and clearly defined in their relations with all things. I do not hate the people who have so cruelly maltreated me; they knew not what they did. . . . "

This characteristic evasion of the real problem is at the heart of one's difficulty in judging the work of Lanier. To evaluate the work of Poe it is necessary only to understand the strict limitations which he, or nature, imposed, then to place Poe's performance within that limit and to set that narrow but precise art in the tradition. Artistic evaluations are never exact, but a reasonably just approximation is not difficult. Timrod likewise thought and wrote with precision. But the voice of Lanier is a large voice with a sweep and breadth which has caused Edwin Mims to write that "there are moods when the imperfection of Lanier pleases more than the perfection of Poe—even from the artistic standpoint." This dimensional power requires examination in the light of Lanier's confident intention to be a great poet: "I *know*, through the fiercest tests of life, that I am in soul, and shall be in life and utterance, a great poet."

As always, qualifications must be made. Many poems are sadly in need of revision; those poems which Lanier did revise are greatly improved over the earlier versions. He had little time for revision. On that score many imperfections can be forgiven him. Also, his theories that music and poetry were governed by identical laws may have hampered his work. This point is doubtful: what Lanier succeeded in doing was in presenting musical effects (which is far different from using musical methods).[3] These are

---

[3] T. S. Eliot (*Selected Essays*, 282) in writing on Swinburne makes a point which is equally applicable to Lanier: "The beauty or effect of sound is neither that of music nor that of poetry which can be set to music. There is no reason why verse intended to be sung should not present a sharp visual image or convey an important intellectual meaning, for it supplements the music by another means of affecting the feelings. What we get in Swinburne is an expression by sound, which could not possibly associate itself with music. For what he gives is not images and ideas and music, it is one thing with a curious mixture of suggestions of all three."

incidental; they can be allowed to one who speaks out of a large and wise philosophy.

But this largeness is in part confusion founded upon abstraction. This appears in the first lines of "The Symphony":

> "O Trade! O Trade! would thou wert dead!
> The time needs heart—'tis tired of head:
> We're all for love," the violins said.

The trade which he attacks in rhapsodic fashion is embodied in the nationalism which he praised so highly in "Psalm of the West"—a problem which Lanier never considered. He would solve the evils which trade had brought with a single phrase, *Love they neighbor*, and he added, explicitly, the corollary that *All men are neighbors*, thus reducing love to a humanitarian abstraction which, in the attempt to embrace equally those who live in New York and Shanghai with those who live next door, inevitably makes personal affection approximate close to zero. This is perhaps best illustrated in the chaotic "Psalm of the West":

> And Science be known as the sense making love to the All,
> And Art be known as the soul making love to the All,
> And Love be known as the marriage of man with the All—
> Till Science to knowing the Highest shall lovingly turn,
> Till Art to loving the Highest shall consciously burn,
> Till Science to Art as a man to a woman shall yearn,
> —Then morn!

Even the capitals are indicative. It is, as Robert Penn Warren has observed, "probably, a defect of taste to prefer 'darling Tennyson' to Milton; it is a defect of another order to confound science with art, the abstract with the concrete, the practical with the contemplative." This defect is plain: to Lanier, the world was governed by Platonic abstractions. His mind was soft and sentimental, capable even, in that same poem, of depicting the Civil War as a joust between Head (the North) and Heart (the South), with a remarkable power for reversing what little imagery he put into this queer poem. Once again he had evaded the central problem while he talked in honeyed abstractions.

To my mind this goes beyond a statement that Lanier did not understand the function of ideas in art. It explains the man—a man confused, muddled in his philosophy, and with no love for thought. "Metaphors come of love rather than of thought," he wrote, and if by love is understood a vague emotional sensitivity, what he called an "etherialization," then Lanier's failure as a philosophical poet is explained.

When as poet he attempted only to feel and to see, Lanier approached greatness. He beheld more than conventional landscapes: he saw details of nature in sharp objectivity. "In 'Corn' for once an American poet strode into our splendid native golden fields and sang what his eyes saw, and deeper, what the harvest of the fields can be for man." The poem only partially deserves this high praise, for in it are more than traces of the vague, cloudy rhetoric and tortured fancy which Edmund Gosse detected as substitutes for passion and imagination:

> Old hill! Old hill! thou gashed and hairy Lear
> Whom the divine Cordelia of the year,
> E'en pitying spring, will vainly try to cheer—

This straining for effect at any cost mars a fine poem; it was a fault which Lanier could never eradicate. At least, however, he recognized it: "I have frequently noticed in myself a tendency to a diffuse style; a disposition to push my metaphors too far, employing a multitude of words to

heighten the patness of the image and so making of it a
conceit." What he failed to recognize is perhaps even more
important, that too often his metaphors and conceits—as
above, and in the poem "Clover"—do not represent anything. They have only a blurred relation to the subject.

His fondness for secondhand metaphors drawn from books
gives a faint, unconvincing literary odor to many of his
poems. When he sees nature through a Shaksperean play,
as in "Marsh Song—At Sunset," he invariably keeps the
idea abstract; it never achieves the status of experience.
Fortunately he sometimes forgets his unassimilated reading,
forgets his belief that the artist must be "afire with moral
beauty just as with physical beauty," forgets his philosophy,
and writes. Then he becomes the poet. Then he writes
such valid and impressive poems as the artless and spontaneously spiritual "Ballad of Trees and the Master" and
the quick-moving, brutal, uncharacteristic "Revenge of
Hamish."

When one forgets the message intended for the brain and
concentrates on the pictorial harmonies intended for eye and
ear, one can find a definite beauty in "Sunrise" and "Song
of the Chattahoochee." In this he excelled. With good
reason have critics acclaimed "The Marshes of Glynn" his
finest poem; the philosophical moral is bedded so deeply
that the reader is hardly conscious of it, while the gorgeous
sweep of scene is carried by an uneven melodious effect
which weaves and twists through forest patterns, through the
live-oaks and the marsh-grass, the marsh and the sea. The
effect is hypnotic:

> How still the plains of the waters be!
> The tide is in his ecstasy.
> The tide is at his highest height:
> > And it is night.

Entire sections of it are magnificently sensuous, and those sections have much value and poetic validity.

In his spontaneous lyrics and his sensuous descriptive verse Lanier achieves striking and original effects. I do not refer to his virtuosity in such a poem as "The Symphony," with its simulation of each instrument in an orchestra. That is only a clever experiment in technique by a dexterous artificer, which concentrates attention on the superficial form. In better and less obvious poems he skillfully used alliteration, tone color, vowel sounds, and mixed rhythms to give musical effects and pictorial values: the ultimate effect is that of a richly embroidered sensuosity, which, unlike Swinburne's, never shades into sensuality. When he neglects his philosophy he writes authentic poetry. It is impossible to agree with John Macy that only "three volumes of unimpeachable poetry have been written in America, 'Leaves of Grass,' the thin volume of Poe, and the poetry of Sidney Lanier"—(there are, also, Emerson and Timrod and Emily Dickinson). In Lanier's case the elimination of bad poems must be too drastic. Yet, in the six or eight which remain, there is the distinctive mark of a poet who wrote far better than he knew, who achieved a limited but fine body of work which in the main is unlike that which greater poets have done.

Father Ryan and Father Tabb, the two Catholic poets of the South, indicate two divergent attitudes. Each had served in the war, but to Ryan, for all his piety, the war and the South were consuming and passionate subjects of tragedy. He was not a great poet, but he was handling with dignity a great theme. Tabb was a younger man; after the war he studied and taught in Baltimore; in his poetry the influence of the war can hardly be traced. The one was a mystic who could never rid himself of reality; the younger a realist who could not quite achieve mysticism. Possibly that is why Ryan's poetry, for all its limitations, remains so attractive, while Tabb's polished epigrams are quickly read and rarely remembered.

Lanier hymned a new nation; Ryan eulogized a dead nation; Tabb withdrew into a cloistered school. An able poet different from any of these men devoted his brief and troubled life to the effort of recapturing tranquillity in a period of emotional stress. He caught the difficult spirit which gives an inner reality to the superficial aspects of local color; with reason Joel Chandler Harris wrote that "Irwin Russell was among the very first of Southern writers to appreciate the literary possibilities of the negro character." His dialect poems are slightly sentimentalized, and his work is incomplete: before his death Russell was planning a series of poems and novels which might have placed him with Harris and his stories of Uncle Remus. As it is, only one poem raises him above the rank of an erratic, wandering, yet richly gifted minstrel. That poem is "Christmas-Night in the Quarters"—a masterpiece which has been inexplicably neglected, but which is not surpassed by a more famous poem in the same *genre*: Whittier's "Snow-Bound." For his ideas of poetry Russell owed much to Robert Burns, but any direct indebtedness is hardly discernible. Yet, like Burns, he attempted to portray—never to exploit or to degrade in making out a case—characters whom he knew and loved. He never portrayed a single character who captivated the imagination of a people, but in "Christmas-Night" he wrote an operetta of the Negro in convincing dialect, and with a skillful fusion of the religious, humorous, pathetic, and noble elements of life which his friends in the quarters possessed.

In the South, as in the country generally, the years from

1880 to 1910 were relatively barren. A few people yet living spanned these years, but they wrote no intrinsically great poetry. William Hamilton Hayne continued to write in the tradition of his father; if as poet he was of smaller caliber, he yet produced a volume of respectable worth. In Tennessee John Trotwood Moore painted glowing landscapes in prose and verse, and wrote at least one ballad of a Confederate soldier, "Sam Davis," which transcends verse and becomes poetry. Similarly, Walter Malone concentrated primarily on the surface aspects of nature, won fame with a poem, "Opportunity," which said well what many persons wanted to hear, and wrote an epic poem, *De Soto*, which almost attains greatness but which few people have cared to read.

Only Madison Cawein received much critical attention or acclaim. His poems of nature had more deftness, evoked more distinctly an atmosphere of a person who writes of a land that he knows. This impression is largely due to Cawein's greater skill and craftsmanship; in lesser degree, possibly, to a greater body of sustained work over a score of years. Edmund Gosse thought that his early work suffered from a lack of criticism in the South, but a more reasonable estimate is that Cawein lacked the faculty of self-criticism. Even Gosse preferred Cawein's pantheistic poems and gentle lyrics. A few of these have distinctive beauty, but mostly they are rather commonplace restatements of old and well-worn subjects. Cawein's work, however, has at times a drive and bite for which he is not given credit; he mixed these poems, together with his best poems of nature, with such a profuse welter of mediocre verses of the same general type that great selectivity is required before one realizes that he is, at intervals, an able poet.

These writers belong definitely to the past. Such poets

as Olive Tilford Dargan and Cale Young Rice have elements
of kinship with them, but they have significant differences.
They continue to write and to publish volumes—a fact
which makes consideration of their work tentative and incomplete. Miss Lizette Woodworth Reese has, unfortunately, become known as the author of one poignant
sonnet, "Tears," while the remainder of her work is neglected. Yet she has an individual way of observing small
things in life and in nature, and of transmuting her observation into gentle, precise poetry. Rice has written with
facility of the surface aspects of many nations; his range of
subject matter has been astonishingly varied. It is picturesque, and at times bitter, but there is no fusion of artist
and subject, of matter and manner—a fusion which Miss
Reese, in her slight lyrics of the countryside she knows, has
achieved.

When they have noticed his work at all, critics have
placed William Alexander Percy with the other poets who
apparently antedated the "poetic renascence." Although
his first verses were not published until 1911, this classification has some reason: Percy has written in traditional
forms of ancient and medieval subjects; he was brusque and
outspoken only in statements against metropolitan life and
people:

> Too much is said too loudly; I am dazed.
> The silken sound of whirled infinity
> Is lost in voices shouting to be heard.
> I once knew men as earnest and less shrill.

This quality of withdrawal was not likely to attract the
shrill voices; neither was the deceptively quiet poetry which
he wrote. Possibly the underlying philosophy, also, will not
again be popular: that man, although foredoomed to failure

and conscious that in this world faith is ever likely to be defeated by fact, wins a victorious acceptance over defeat since the entire human person is greater than his physical self or the inevitable accident of circumstance. This conquest of athos over pathos has been the source of high tragedy in such diverse writers as Shakspere and Schiller; in Percy's hands the theme never becomes quite overpowering, but it is given adequate and moving statement.

What has been called the "renascence" of American poetry, about 1912, had little immediate effect upon the South. It was not without effect upon gifted persons—such as Conrad Aiken and John Gould Fletcher—but it permeated through the consciousness of the section slowly. Both Aiken and Fletcher became cosmopolitans and experimentalists: only by the accident of birth could Aiken be considered a Southern poet. Fletcher has, since 1930, returned definitely to his region, and has advocated regionalism, which he has interpreted through the medium of imagist poetry. He has expressed with exactness his intent: "To describe an incident or a scene along with its connotation of emotion, the connotation being *implicit in some part of the scene itself.*" Through impressionism and imagism he developed a highly allusive method, which brings out overtones and connotations primarily from things *seen*; at the same time he developed his own forms: pictorial in detail, symphonic in movement—an orchestration of highly colored words. His poetry, wrote Conrad Aiken in 1919, "contains little of the emotion which relates to the daily life of men and women. . . . It is a sort of absolute poetry, a poetry of detached waver and brilliance, a beautiful flowering of language alone." This was extreme criticism, then; since that time Fletcher's poetry has caught the impact of past upon present, of fallowness upon barrenness (as in

"Earth"), but this content has often gone unnoticed because he wrote in untraditional forms.   Although the value of his experiments need not be discounted, the attention given to his technique has obscured somewhat the conservative religious and philosophical voice which speaks through his later poems.

It is significant that in 1912 Fletcher thought it necessary to leave the United States, like Ezra Pound and T. S. Eliot; their influence was felt from abroad, but it was tenuous and indirect.   More immediate was the recognition about the same time of Edwin Arlington Robinson, the emergence of Edna St. Vincent Millay, Robert Frost, Carl Sandburg, Edgar Lee Masters, and other poets who revivified an art which had seemed almost dead.   Not until 1920 was the Southern poet stirred to action.   Diverse groups began to write poetry and to publish little magazines.

With a single exception these groups may be divided in two categories.   One was up-to-date, smart, and sophisticated; the other interested in the realistic-romantic possibilities of local color.   Two examples of each type may be cited: in New Orleans Julius Friend and John McClure edited *The Double Dealer*; in Richmond Emily Clark (with some assistance from James Branch Cabell, Ellen Glasgow, and other established writers) edited *The Reviewer*.   These magazines were smart and sophisticated, but rootless.   In a letter written, significantly, to the editor of *The Reviewer*, H. L. Mencken summarized their inadequacy: "Friend is failing in New Orleans because he is trying to print an imitation of *The Dial* and *The Smart Set*."   The attempt to write and to publish works of literary merit was an exciting game, but none of the editors had a clear idea of what literature was.   When the first enthusiasm had faded, neither the magazines nor their chief contributors seemed very important. They gained more attention than several groups which concentrated on local subjects, like the Virginia group which published *The Lyric* at Norfolk. Most promising of the local colorist schools was that at Charleston, which published a yearbook instead of a magazine, and which, under Hervey Allen, DuBose Heyward, and Josephine Pinckney, evolved definite theories of how such poetry should be written. This promise never materialized; Allen and Heyward sought picturesque values only, and soon abandoned poetry for fiction. Of all their verses, only Heyward's "The Prodigal" has the stamp of durability. Miss Pinckney's verse has a more authentic quality: to observation she added sympathetic insight—and she has continued to write poetry.

For some reason these groups have dissolved and the poets who composed them have failed to develop. The "Fugitives" of Nashville began modestly in 1922 to publish a small magazine of verse, *The Fugitive*, which was voluntarily abandoned four years later; the authors cloaked their identities under absurd pseudonyms, sponsored no cause, and issued no manifesto. At first glance they represented only another symptom of the intellectual ferment which promised so much, in widely scattered sections of the South— and of the nation. But the discontinuance of the magazine and gradual disintegration of the group was not, in this case, a sign of decay. Some of these poets continued to write and to develop, along individual rather than communal lines, but with a basis of intellectual kinship. Three men— John Crowe Ransom, Donald Davidson, Allen Tate—are definitely among the leading poets of our time; two others— Robert Penn Warren and Alec B. Stevenson—have quite as definitely contributed valid poems, and may in no remote tomorrow attain the same recognition. In addition there is Merrill Moore, a gifted *improvisator* who casts his ironic comments on life into an irregular sonnet form, with lines which depend upon stress rather than scansion, and with a break in the unit at any point where the thought requires it; these skillful "American" sonnets cover a wide range, with a unity imposed only by the poet's personal and, seemingly, almost intuitive philosophy.   With good reason John Gould Fletcher has stated that the doctrine of the "Nashville school" and of its affiliates "has become now the central tradition of Southern poetry."   Ransom, Davidson, Tate, and Warren have also been critics of literature, and of life.

Roughly they belong to the modern metaphysical school. Poetry is not simply an expression of an emotion or the evocation of an object; it is closely akin to the ideas which are at base religious, and which make a philosophy. Poetry represents, in the words of Allen Tate, the transmutation of "an intensely felt ordinary experience, an intense moral situation, into an intensely realized art."   Such work is not romantic, or ornamental; it is a part of life, as seen through the completed experience of an individual poet. Normally it would be a personal expression of an integrated person in a defined society.   Under a scientific civilization, however, the artist, writes Donald Davidson, "is *against* or *away from* society, and the disturbed relationship becomes his essential theme, no matter whether he evades or accepts the treatment of the theme itself."   Dislocation of the artist has resulted in that "dissociation of sensibility" which T. S. Eliot has focused as the center of the poet's problem in modern times.

This is the center of Ransom's poetry.   He has written of "intricate psychological cruxes," frequently casting his poem into the minor dramatic fable which Thomas Hardy used, but he has made the protagonists of his poems sufferers "from that complaint of 'dissociation of sensibility.' " The poem itself is a commentary on the situation, its irony deriving, as Warren has noted, from the "fact that these perhaps otherwise admirable people 'cannot fathom nor perform their nature.' " It is a poetry in which wit is employed not as ornament but as part of the texture, in which at times the images are stated precisely but are telescoped in such a way that the intellectualized cross references are difficult to comprehend. Essentially Ransom's poetry is ironical, with an exact precision of thought and imagery; his standard is remarkably high, so that a certain evenness of quality, combined with his preference for short dramatic episodes, prevents generally one poem from standing out: his apparently unconnected poems, in *Chills and Fever* and *Two Gentlemen in Bonds*, fit together naturally and build up to an integrated structure which expresses Ransom's philosophy largely by exposing the insufficiency of people in a world devoid of grace and myth.

Donald Davidson's first volume, *An Outland Piper*, has a strong resemblance to Ransom's work, with an added mystical element which was possibly derived, in manner, from William Blake. Poetically, however, Ransom has worked through negation; in *The Tall Men* and in later poems, Davidson has been affirmative. A major voice speaks: "It surely is clear, to anyone who has read American poetry carefully, that the blank verse here [in *The Tall Men*] is entirely *sui generis*: no other American poet, unless it be Hart Crane in the rare moments when the flame in him broke through his own inflated rhetoric, has so authentically sounded the heroic note." Here is largeness and sweep of vision, but without confusion; only in the attempts at emphasis and minute analysis—too often reminiscent of Eliot—

and in the lack of a defined climax, can defects be pointed out; in the later, more closely integrated "Lee in the Mountains," there is a complete resolution. In his criticism Davidson has made frontal attacks on a scientific and industrial civilization with its abstract literature; in his poetry he has stated his own philosophy in a manner paralleled only, in our time, by Robert Frost.

The poems of Allen Tate, like those of Ransom, can be classified as metaphysical. Where Ransom is most concerned with God, Tate is most possessed by death. This differentiation in subject matter is suggestive rather than final: in many ways the poetry and the philosophy of the two are akin. Tate's poetry is even more exact, with a stringent distillation which telescopes much matter into a few closely packed lines. He revises and refines his work until the fusion of idea and technique achieves a finality of statement which is absolute. Most of his poetry is involved with the question of self-definition, which involves also the metaphysical questions of the bases of life. His approach is oblique, his method consisting of "gradually circling round the subject, threatening it and filling it with suspense, and finally accomplishing its demise without ever quite using the ultimate violence on it." This is a difficult art, perhaps best achieved when the poem is most objectified —as in "Ode to the Confederate Dead"—or when personal intensity is combined with his closely-knit interrelation of thought and emotion—as in "Sonnets of the Blood," "Shadow and Shade," and "Mediterranean." In these works Tate achieves the status of a major poet.

Closely allied in spirit to the work of Ransom and Tate is that of Robert Penn Warren. It has a broader sweep and it is more directly rooted in earth. Also, Warren's language is Saxon, in contrast to the Latinity of phrase employed by Ransom and Tate. But his bold imagery, his compressed, elliptical play of wit are closely related. Inevitably, since his verses in *Thirty-Six Poems* have so much of experimentation in them, he seems a poet of magnificent promise rather than of positive achievement, except in the sequence, "Kentucky Mountain Farm." The same judgment must be applied to Alec B. Stevenson—whose sinuously powerful lines and strict form are well revealed in "Icarus in November." His work is uncollected, but the quality of a few poems raises it beyond the plane of tentative acceptance.

This group includes other poets whose work has not, as yet, become defined; an appraisal of their work would savor more of prophecy than of achievement. It has drawn other poets, as well: John Peale Bishop (whose early work was derivative, if not directly imitative, of Rimbaud, Eliot, and other poets and whose thought was vitiated by an obsession with Freudian psychologies) has emerged in his later poems as a religious poet, with a tonic attitude of skeptical disillusionment as to the nature of the ritual, but with a firm belief that the world must be saved through the Christian myth, and that the ritual must, somehow, be found. Allied to the group on agrarian rather than on metaphysical grounds is Jesse Stuart, prolific and uneven, but with a capacity for writing in brief sequences a direct, highly personal poetry, with no aid from art but with an intense drive and emotion. In the seven hundred and three sonnets which comprise *Man with a Bull-Tongue Plow*, there are many positive defects, but there are also the positive merits of keen, unstudied observation of mountain people and of nature, of the elemental questions of life and love and death.

The type of poetry has changed. There is no lack of

romantic and occasional poetry and poets, but the ablest of the modern writers have voiced through their poetry a philosophy of living. Although it has presented ideas as well as emotions, this poetry has retained a warmth and grace which is traditional—and it has, above all, remained distinctively Southern.

V

A Note on Southern Literature

CRITICS and commentators have long accepted as a truism that literature, and the arts in general, reflects the society from which it comes, even when the art appears in rebellion against the established pattern of living. More recent, and highly debatable, is our acceptance of the obverse point of view: that a culture expresses itself, or is expressed, through a communicable art. Unless they inherit a part of the cultural tradition, later generations necessarily judge it by the enduring tangible and external products; that is, by the success with which some phase of the life has been translated by individuals into books, music, buildings, and other communicable mediums. By this test, a society exists for the sake of expression, not so much for itself as for the benefit of later generations.

In the brief but valuable Introduction to his *Southern Treasury of Life and Literature*, Stark Young attacks this modern dogma: "It is necessary to say that nothing is more false or outside the nature and spirit of art itself than to insist that a society should produce great art. A society exists, as does any human being, first for its own life and wholeness. ... If, in any of the divers artistic mediums, an art arises to express it, so much more fortunate the society, as if one who up to that time had not found this added voice now finds it happily." Although the function of art is "to re-create, emphasize, mold and perpetuate the qualities of a society," the function of a society is not to produce art except in the sense that creating a way of life should also create an art of living. This primary art can be handed down but not communicated save through translation. In the ante-bellum South the pattern existed: what might have happened to that pattern must remain an unanswerable *If*, since it was forcibly broken from without before it was threatened by inner disintegration, but there is no lack of testimony to the richness and the varied harmony of Southern culture.

Valid testimony can be found in Southern literature, but not of the highest order. It is demonstrable that the South produced little great literature. If an adequate literature can be defined as containing all the fullness and richness of a society without quite attaining greatness, Southern writers failed to produce even that. Van Wyck Brooks, in *The Flowering of New England*, makes the point that in New England a valid way of life found full and relatively complete expression, but his volume testifies to the insecurity and inner decay of the culture presented, as the literature itself testifies to a lack of richness and of certainty. Yet New England was fortunate in that the quality of life was translated for later generations into an adequate literature which sometimes touched on greatness.

The South had many voices, as the pages of Mr. Young's volume prove, but there was no large or unifying voice. Before 1750, literature had largely the character of explanation to an English audience, in such work as the rugged prose of John Smith and the supple writing of William Byrd. Essentially it was, as might be expected from the nature of the South's development, a colonial rather than a regional literature, in a sense not found for long in the New England writers. This attitude tended also to emphasize for regional purposes, as contrasted with the more prevalent colonial purpose, the occasional and familiar type of literature. An excellent poem like "Bacon's Epitaph" might appear, but in general the graceful and easy tone was more apparent than the tones of intensity or of greatness.

This separation of the culture and the written word should have been temporary, and quickly remedied. Although the way of life was transplanted and adapted, it became an integral unit of relationship: the man was in, and of, his communal and regional life. Somehow, literature failed to attain a similar integration. Good writers appeared, as the unity of thought and living became a reality, but they failed to close the gap. Thomas Jefferson in his thoughtful prose pointed the way, and John Taylor continued his work on a broader philosophical basis. The political and economic writers were able men, and the validity of much of what they said is scarcely recognized today, for the ideas of Jefferson—to whom lip-service only is mainly paid—as well as of John C. Calhoun and Alexander Stephens were abruptly brushed aside by the Civil War.

In his brief poetic career, Edward Coote Pinkney gave an eloquent expression to one phase of life. Mr. Young writes: "One side of the South was the Cavalier ideas that held among the upper class and, to a considerable extent, filtered down to the humbler. The Cavalier poetry of England connects thus with Pinkney's poems. What is involved here is by no means a mere matter of literary origin and influence. What is also involved is a living thing, a kinship of civilization, ideals, ways of life." But Pinkney died young, and the slight quantity of his poetry has led to consistent under-rating of its quality. Also, he stood alone. Richard Henry Wilde might have carried on the same tradition, but he absented himself in Italy; good poets like Simms, Timrod, and Hayne were part of it, but imbued with a later romanticism, and keyed to a less fortunate idea of writing.

Their work deserves a respect which we have rarely paid to it. They were of their time; if they failed to re-create the time worthily, it was not for lack of high seriousness and hard endeavor. In fact, Timrod succeeded, during the emotional stress of war, in giving more than adequate expression to a city and a cause, with a sustained lyricism that is still enheartening. Poe worked a narrowly personalized vein (in fiction as well as in verse) with a precise and artistic skill; his work perhaps has more of his time than of his region in it, but Hervey Allen has convincingly demonstrated that Poe is not to be removed summarily from among the Southern poets. And the erratic Thomas Holley Chivers left some memorable work, valuable in itself and likewise valuable in adumbrating the romantically religious mind of an interesting person and movement.

Fiction, like poetry, seemed to have no vital connection with the immediate way of life. The oral story possessed this immediacy, and answered a cultural need: not accidental was the gradual translation of "oralure" into the Davy Crockett-Longstreet-Sut Lovingood type of homespun but indigeneous literature. The tall tale and the anecdote belonged, at first to the frontiersman but eventually to planter, lawyer, and merchant as well. Almost surreptitiously they became a part of our literature, but they were thoroughly woven into the texture of our life.

The formal novel was read for its story, or for the solid backbone of history with which authors like Simms and Caruthers strengthened their plots. John Pendleton Kennedy made an excellent beginning toward integration of fiction and life, in *Swallow Barn*, but he did not continue his wisely humorous observations of Virginia. His failure to develop as a writer has frequently been traced to his satisfactory way of life: he was too engrossed with the pleasure of living to expend much time on the business of writing.

Another reason may be adduced. Men like Kennedy,

Simms, and Caruthers were lured from the novel to the historical romance. Good fiction was not enough. Typically, in *Horse-Shoe Robinson*, Kennedy builds an elaborate introduction to convince the reader that he is relating historical incidents about real characters. If the disguise is thin, it nevertheless helps in vitiating the effectiveness of fiction. Caruthers turned from the sane, genial quality of *The Kentuckian in New York* to the watered pseudo-Scott romanticism of *The Cavaliers of Virginia;* Kennedy, though he held to a higher level of achievement, undoubtedly was dropping downward as he went from *Swallow Barn* to the Revolutionary novel and on to the frothy cavalier romance, *Rob of the Bowl.*

There were no Thackerays, to defy romanticism; no Jane Austens, to surmount it; no George Borrows, to ignore it. William Gilmore Simms, rather, justified the romance: it was "to invest individuals with an absorbing interest. . . and it seeks for its adventures among the wild and wonderful." Simms thought the Romance "of loftier origin than the Novel"; he did better work, if judged according to the standards he set for himself, than we commonly allow, but even his solid row of historical romances with their stimulus to local pride offer pleasant avenues of escape into the past, not avenues of illumination or unification. The best of this work is valuable as fragments, but it does not hold in creation for us the pattern, or rounded parts of the varied patterns, which indubitably existed.

After the Civil War, there was no pattern of Southern civilization to re-create. There was a loyalty to the old South, expressed in print by such writers as Thomas Nelson Page and Joel Chandler Harris; there was a heralding of a new South by Henry W. Grady and Walter Hines Page; there was a valiant and not unsuccessful attempt by the

Local Colorists to catch certain values and picturesque qualities before they disappeared under the onslaught of standardization. The region was confused and in struggle, to such an extent that Sidney Lanier and Father Ryan and Irwin Russell might each be regarded as typical of an important phase of Southern thought. The literature of post-war days mirrored more adequately than ante-bellum literature what existed in the South, but conscious effort could not re-create a unified culture when society had been broken and disrupted.

The confusion continues. The impact of national forces —economic, political, and social—has made for quick and uncharacteristic change, partly encouraged and in part resisted. An element of outside exploitation has caused the South to revert somewhat to a colonial, rather than a regional, status. In the field of literature, commercial and editorial pressures have encouraged a similar exploitation, in books that frequently have the tone of exposé and reform worked through the fabric of explanation. T. S. Stribling and Erskine Caldwell have written *about*, not *of*, the South, in a highly popular and inartistic manner, but they are only the advance representatives of a "realistic" group. Prevailing trends and ideologies influence the communistic Olive Tilford Dargan, the sociological Howard W. Odum, the iconoclastic H. L. Mencken, the egocentric Thomas Wolfe. Confusions at home and abroad have led to lumping together as essentially kin the novels of Caldwell and of Faulkner, with no recognition of the purposes or limits of fiction, no recognition of Faulkner's success as contrasted with Stribling's failure in the creation of literature. The same confusions have led critics to deny there could be artistic reality in the dissimilar but valid Mississippi novels of Faulkner and of Stark Young—that there could be varying strata of people worth writing about, as there are varying geological strata worth studying.

In the pages of Mr. Young's representative anthology, John Wade rubs shoulders with Caldwell, though the two men inhabit vastly different Georgias; John Ransom and Donald Davidson are far removed in intellectual purpose from DuBose Heyward and Paul Green; Elizabeth Madox Roberts and Caroline Gordon have only the vaguest geographical relationship with Caroline Miller or Evelyn Scott. Ellen Glasgow and James Branch Cabell have quietly worked their particular Virginia fields, with brilliant results; John Gould Fletcher and Conrad Aiken have spoken in cosmopolitan tones with a Southern accent. Many voices are speaking, for many diverse interests and sections within the region, but the powerful unifying voice and the integrated culture are yet far off. Certain books like *I'll Take My Stand* point a way; a powerful and blended achievement may yet do more than an individual could accomplish. From the agrarian-distributist writers there has come a tenable approach to integration. Donald Davidson, in *The Attack on Leviathan*, has presented the explicit statement for decentralization and regional strength; John Crowe Ransom, in *The World's Body*, and Allen Tate, in *Reactionary Essays in Poetry and Ideas*, have carried this relation on from life to literature. The body of this work, impressive already in quantity, is impressive also in its quality, and in its acceptance of traditional values as something inbred, unquestionable, and vital, not as a surface quality to be explored, described, and exploited.

Yet, at base, the pattern of life is broken, and recreation at present must of necessity be partial, not complete. It would be pleasant to have in our background the translation of life which a Shakspere or even a Fielding could have made; since we lack that translation, we must work with fitting together the broken and incomplete bits of evidence which we have. They should be, as Mr. Young says, a part of the Southern education; they are also, in themselves, a part of the integration which we have lost and must somehow find again.

VI

Six Southern Novels[1]

M<small>R. T. S.</small> <small>ELIOT</small> has written of the drama a sentence which is equally applicable to the novel: "It is essential that a work of art should be self-consistent, that an artist should consciously or unconsciously draw a circle beyond which he does not trespass: on the one hand actual life is always the material, and on the other hand an abstraction from actual life is a necessary condition to the creation of the work of art." There are two frames of reference, interlocking yet distinct, and each frame demands its own consistency. Since the novel is a particularized and specialized, but self-contained, world in miniature, it makes special demands of consistency, of probability, and of artistic reality; since it also presents human though fictionalized life, there is a larger and more remote frame of reference which can never be overlooked or discarded.

Of the six novels considered here, four are decidedly above the average. But only one—*Absalom, Absalom!*—maintains a strict consistency; and Mr. Faulkner achieves this by an intricate artistic method of allowing the story to filter through the minds of various narrators to the reader. By this method, Faulkner can present Thomas Sutpen as possessed demon and as possessed innocent; he can present many possible interpretations with no absolutely

[1] *Absalom, Absalom!* By William Faulkner. New York: Random House. *The Long Night.* By Andrew Lytle. Indianapolis: The Bobbs-Merrill Company. *Courthouse Square.* By Hamilton Basso. New York: Charles Scribner's Sons. *Green Margins.* By E. P. O'Donnell. Boston: Houghton, Mifflin Company. *To My Father.* By Charles Wertenbaker. New York: Farrar & Rinehart. *Lost Morning.* By DuBose Heyward. New York: Farrar & Rinehart. All published in 1936.

final resolution, and do it convincingly. The author keeps himself out of the picture, and he presents a specialized— not a *representative*—world of Yoknapatawpha County, Mississippi, which is as much his own creation as Poictesme is Cabell's.

The material handled sounds melodramatic. Thomas Sutpen comes from nowhere, with a wagon load of wild niggers and a French architect, to buy a hundred square miles of land, build a mansion, and beget a family. *Absalom, Absalom!* is *his* story, although the title fits a son who kills his mulatto half-brother to prevent an incestuous marriage. All the characters are harried and abnormal and violent; they live according to some strange and driving inner design which differentiates them from persons in the everyday world. Only through a masterly artistic restraint does Mr. Faulkner hold this violence and strangeness in check: he employs a long and complicated sentence structure with tricks and devices of writing which slow the reader and require his entire attention; he leads up to a fact, then stops without revealing it, and allows a partial contradiction before the fact is revealed; he presents, ultimately, not facts but hypotheses which may be accepted or rejected. *Absalom, Absalom!* is closely related to Mr. Faulkner's earlier novels: the chief narrator is the protagonist of *The Sound and the Fury;* the setting is similar; and a few minor characters have appeared in earlier books. It may be that Mr. Faulkner has obscured the movement too effectively for his novel to be popular, but he has rivaled and possibly surpassed the powerful and moving *As I Lay Dying*.

At the other extreme in the matter of consistency, in *Courthouse Square* Mr. Hamilton Basso identifies himself with the returned Southerner David Barondess to such an extent that a careful reader has some difficulty in extricating

the editorial comments of the author from the thoughts
of his protagonist. Mr. Basso is much less the artist, and
much more the reformer. It is definitely enheartening for
a contributing editor to the *New Republic* to aim his satiric
shafts at Communism and Fascism alike, and at the pseudo-
sophisticates among the New York literati, but enheartening in a way that has nothing to do with fiction.

David Barondess, a successful novelist, comes home to
a family which had aways been in conflict with their neighbors, first over slavery and then over the rights of the Negro.
By local standards, the Barondesses were "queer," and David Barondess had continued that tradition by marrying a
lady explorer who had gone on an expedition, leaving David
to return alone. The life of Macedon is handled with deftness but with little of sympathetic comprehension; the riot
(which ensues when the mulatto druggist Alcide Fauget
attempts to buy the oldest and once the best house in Macedon for a Negro hospital) is vividly told. Mr. Basso has
drawn a group of people mainly despicable, leavened by
some persons almost too admirable, but he contrives to make
them real and individual. Perhaps he strives too hard to
imply that they are also representative. A larger flaw is
this: that David Barondess is described as more intelligent
than the minor characters, but his conversation consists too
largely of clichés; his cleverness lies in such expressions as
"he hates my guts," addressed to his aunt; and his mental
outlook, a loose liberalism mixed with Freudianism, seems
as unenlightened or at least as unintelligent (since it stirs up
immediate and irreconcilable trouble to the detriment of
all) as the outlook of most of the townspeople.

Mr. Andrew Lytle's *The Long Night* is impressive and
interesting. The first half of the book has a sustained drive
and a continuity that to some degree sustain the second part,

where Mr. Lytle's main character changes from a driven re-
venger to a dispersed and Hamlet-like doubter who in the
end deserts both his vengeance and his army. Although in
one sense this decision comes out of a severe and cathartic
logic, the change of characterization is never adequately
handled within the first frame of reference, possibly because
the author wavers in his point of view to such an extent, in
the later section, that the reader can see as clearly into the
mind of General Albert Sidney Johnston as he can into the
mind of Pleasant McIvor. These shifts mar, although they
can not ruin, a hard tale of an Alabama blood-feud, which
begins when Cameron McIvor is murdered by a gang which
seems loosely patterned on the Murrell gang, and his relatives gather to avenge him. Mr. Lytle knits his episodes
of vengeance into a pattern varied but essentially integrated;
he makes pursuer and pursued alike possessed of good
and evil, of the attractive and the repulsive. He has a
communicable gusto and a flexible, earthy, idiomatic prose
that give to *The Long Night* a definite distinction from the
superb introduction to the abrupt ending.

In recent years the local color novel has been revivified,
although it is usually labeled "regional." If Mr. E. P.
O'Donnell had studied the best work of the local colorists
and added to that the modern element of sex, he would have
had an excellent formula for *Green Margins*. The bayou
country of lower Louisiana is isolated, strange, and exotic,
with great swamps, a mighty and mysterious river, and a
small amount of habitable, almost tropical, land; the people
are little known, inbred, and colorful with all the color of
something near at hand yet basically foreign. In the first
part of the book, Mr. O'Donnell promises something more.
Sister Kalavich in the beginning seems a symbol of Maya,
or of some earth-mother who will enrich the story with an

underlying myth which has never become outworn. Unfortunately, the myth and the potentially significant character are dissipated, until Sister is presented as a woman to whom things happen, as a strong eternal female who waits for a lover. If not a great character, as she seemed at first to be, Sister is adequate; but she and some well-handled minor characters—the gusty Austrian ex-major, Grampaw; the almost-white girl Unga; the Negroes Bonus and Pretty John, and others of the village and swamp dwellers of the Cajun country's mixed races—can only carry in part the typed individuals: the rich woman and the weak artist from "outside," who marvel over country and people; and the lovers of Sister, who seem too remote and, though typical enough, too undefined.

The marks of hasty writing in *Green Margins* are all too plain, in characters that are well-built but never develop, or that are inconsistent (Mocco Kalavich suddenly and temporarily possesses a knowledge of draftsmanship and architecture for which the reader is totally unprepared); in descriptions excellent during such tense moments as the hurricane, but flat and dull in the routine movement of the book. Mr. O'Donnell's faults are plentiful, and obvious, but they result from imperfect execution of a too-ambitious project. He has written a novel that has much to recommend it, in exotic background and strange people and customs; he seems to know the people and the region thoroughly, and he presents them honestly and unpatronizingly. The local color novel possesses a real if limited validity, and *Green Margins* has the virtues, with relatively few of the defects, of the better novels of this class.

Mr. Charles Wertenbaker wrote in *Boojum!* one of the most ingratiating novels of hard-drinking adolescents of the so-called "plastered age." He has matured, and in *To My*

Father he makes a serious attempt to write a mature novel. But the marks of Boojum are still on him, for Charles Chastain and his fellows at Episcopal High School and at the University of Virginia are almost the same adolescents of the earlier books. *To My Father* has an attractive theme: that a man's strength and fulfillment depend on four factors: heritage, home, his own job, and a helpmeet. The theme is better than the performance. Charles Chastain vacillates, drinks, lives unsatisfactorily with a wife and, finally, satisfactorily with a mistress who is to become his wife. He is not consistent, either in the novel or in life, since the author leaves him on the road to happiness and a successful medical career, although he has previously endowed Charles with much charm but little character. Mr. Wertenbaker succeeds better with the troubled doctor-father and the mother, who leave Virginia but who live only to return to it, than he does with the young men and women. The novel abounds in sex of the plain and of the Freudian varieties, from a neurotic impotent Philip Chastain who is summarily disposed of with certain information dragged in only because it is sexy, to a heroine who talks of the necessity for promiscuous amours in order that she may find the perfect mate. *To My Father* has a date set upon it, and that date is a decade past.

The same statement can be applied to DuBose Heyward's *Lost Morning*. It is far removed from the authentic, if heightened and romanticized, local color which saturates and gives dignity and character to *Porgy*, *The Half-Pint Flask*, and the best of Mr. Heyward's poems. Reduced to outline, the plot sounds incredibly trite: an artist has been managed, his art commercialized, by his more practical wife, but he secures release when he loves—in all meanings of the word—his artist-secretary; after the secretary is accidentally killed, he abandons his wife and his etchings for a Bohemian garret and sculpture. Mr. Heyward does not explain how the managed artist is to become a great and independent artist, but he makes the implications of his transformation too obvious for any doubting—and, incidentally, for any belief. The novels and poems of Du Bose Heyward have ranged from excellent to bad; *Lost Morning* must be regretfully but emphatically added to the debit side.

Mr. Heyward puts these words into the mouth of Felix Hollister's wife: ". . . artists are different. Their heads are always in the clouds. They can't take care of themselves like other people." These words seemingly epitomize the belief not only of Mr. Heyward, but of Messrs. O'Donnell, Basso, and Wertenbaker. In their four books are two painters and two writers, and these four characters are weak, neurotic, hard-drinking, and bewilderedly baffled, not by metaphysical problems but by immediate circumstances. And they are crucified by their companions and their surroundings. It is hardly a convincing thesis, since the men presented here have within themselves the seeds of defeat: they might be happier in an artistic Bohemia or a made-to-order environment, but they could hardly, under any circumstances, be valid artists. Messrs. Faulkner and Lytle also present protagonists who are defeated, but they are overcome by moral and not by circumstantial forces. In this difference between the petty and the magnificent, between the semi-emasculated and the masculine, lies the difference between the adequate and the great novel. Neither Mr. Faulkner nor Mr. Lytle achieves greatness in the novels here considered, but at least they are working toward it, and they have handled regional material in a way that is proper to fiction.

VII

Urban Influences on Ante-bellum Writers of the Southeast

WHEN they wrote directly of the city, ante-bellum Southerners were inclined to make an interesting distinction. "Ancient society," writes Hugh Swinton Legaré, "was born in cities; modern, in the country..." With no attempt at originality, he was simply re-phrasing the ideas of Locke, Sismondi, Guizot, and other political philosophers. When he added, a few sentences later, that "cities were, after all, only subordinate parts of still greater communities," he simply stated an axiom which was accepted without question in 1775 and in 1830. Men differed in their opinions of the values to be derived from great cities; there was, in the mind of Francis Lieber, a distinction between the positive good of London, an integral part of the British empire, and the positive evil of Paris, which by its overwhelming concentration ruled supreme over France. Politically, the city was dangerous; commercially, it was desirable, to all save a few men.

To the casual observer, to the colonial legislator, and to the London proprietor of, say, 1730, cities were distressingly non-existent. They were needed as commercial clearing-houses, as centers for government and trade, and for such urban enterprises as printing establishments. In the Southern colonies, too many estates had private ports for centrally located cities to flourish, and in turn to promote the development of the back country; much hard thought was put, as William Byrd expressed it, in building "citys in the air." Byrd wrote in 1733 of his plans for Richmond; in that year, perhaps two Southern towns, Williamsburg and Charleston, could be spoken of as urban.

The first theatre in America was built in Williamsburg, and the second college was founded there. And in 1730 the first permanent press in Virginia was established, which printed books of poetry as well as laws, and a newspaper that encouraged the production of light literature. It is evident to any person who reads the Virginia *Gazette*, or the epistles, pastorals, and anacreontics in the volume written by a Gentleman of Virginia, that here is suavity and urbanity; here is the mark of the city. The Gentleman was concerned in 1736 with the condition of the stage in general, and of the Williamsburg stage in particular. A few years later, a local wag wrote mildly ribald verses about the establishment of a paper mill; some fifty years later, a doctor and a lawyer collaborated on a poem celebrating the belles of the town.

Charleston was only a few years behind Williamsburg: possibly as early as 1703, Antony Aston was giving plays or dramatic monologues there; by 1735, Otway's *The Orphan* was produced by a dramatic company, with a prologue and epilogue written by a local poet. Charleston's theatrical seasons developed before the Revolution into brilliant affairs which attracted well-known English actors, who presented the plays of Shakspere, Dryden, Cibber, Farquhar, and Addison; after the war, the city could boast also of a French theatre and, dubiously, of a few original plays, such as *An Elopement, or a Trip to the Races*, by a Gentleman of this City. Newspaper comments, which may loosely be called dramatic criticism, were made from time to time on these performances; one of them, published in the Charleston *Gazette* in 1737, was apparently the first commentary in this country on a play after it was produced.

Although Richmond had started late, it was given theatrical distinction before the Revolution by the Hallam family. This troupe was to re-appear, with an imaginary Beatrice Hallam as the heroine, in John Esten Cooke's *The Virginia Comedians*. Local plays were rare, though it seems probable, from evidence in the Prologue to *The Candidates* that a play by Colonel Robert Munford of Mecklenburg was produced in Virginia. And for non-dramatic writers, before the turn of the century, Richmond and Charleston had each its short-lived magazine.

These are slight but significant items. Such eighteenth-century cities as Williamsburg, Charleston, and Richmond brought a definite cosmopolitanism to the people. This was one function of the city, to restrain and temper the parochial. Culturally, the city served as social monitor to the country, as politically it was to focus a point of action when action was needed. In literature, the city functions most directly as a clearing-house, by providing printers to publish newspapers, magazines, pamphlets and books; by supporting libraries and literary clubs, theatres and bookstores. It makes easier the securing of books and presenting of plays; it can offer the stimulating play of mind upon mind and tempt men into writing; it can provide an easy outlet for publication.

The city provides, also, occasions for writing and speaking. Certain events required commemorative poems (two excellent examples which center in Magnolia Cemetery are Simm's "City of the Silent" and Timrod's magnificent ode), and, especially in ante-bellum days, commemorative addresses. Oratory was a part of belles lettres, an important art in itself, and the city provided many events and audiences—through clubs, schools, and organizations as well as civic celebrations—which called into play the talents of

Southern orators. Frequently the speeches were re-printed in pamphlet form; they were important factors in the intellectual life of the section.

If this deliberately incomplete summary is accepted temporarily, we can note that the colonial city was not without its influence. A few immediate local influences, tangible and on the surface of the writing, appear in poems and plays on the Williamsburg belles, the Charleston races, and Richmond politics. These early works are important historically, though of doubtful value as literature. More important is the real nature of the urbanity which the colonial cities reflected, the philosophy and influences from which the colonial authors wrote. Essentially, the theatre was a transplanted theatre of London; as such, it disseminated English thought and, in the loose sense of the word, English culture. The same generalization will hold good, though less directly, for poems and essays, and for other cultural agencies. The true urban influence was in the light of London playing across the sea, and, from a distance even greater removed, the lights of Athens and Rome playing continually through Southern minds upon Southern scenes.

It seems probable, also, that foreign cities rather than Virginia towns perturbed Thomas Jefferson. I take it as evident that a great distrust is, in itself, an influence. When Jefferson writes, "Generally speaking, the proportion which the aggregate of the other classes of citizens bears in any state to that of its husbandmen, is the proportion of its unsound to its healthy parts," or that "the mobs of great cities add just so much to the support of pure government, as sores do to the strength of the human body," he reveals a dislike and distrust of the city which becomes a negative factor of tremendous weight in shaping his agrarian philosophy.

Jefferson was not alone. John Taylor's attack on "mo
nopoly and incorporation," on the new capitalism which h
thought more dangerous than any feudal aristocracy, i
basically a variant stating of Jefferson's distrust. Ther
was in these men a positive faith in agrarianism, but adde(
to faith was a profound distrust of that commercialisn
which seemed to them the primary influence of the city
A simpler man was to state their negative position i
succinct terms: Governor Tyler of Virginia told his legis
lature in 1810, "Commerce is certainly beneficial to society
in a secondary degree, but it produces also what is calle(
citizens of the world—the worst citizens in the world.'
This distrust is nowhere more apparent than in the locatio
of colleges and state universities in rural sections—a con
tinuing influence which caused the University of the Soutl
to be placed, in the 1850's, far from any city.

The opposite view, which I have labelled as "urban in
fluence," is most readily seen in the works of John Marshall
if none of his writings can be called literature, his famou:
decisions had a direct influence more powerful than the per
suasive theories of his political opponents. But a clos(
distinction must be made here: Marshall's philosophy an(
his decisions alike worked inevitably toward the increase o
urban power, but it seems doubtful that his thought wa:
shaped by the city. His extensive and scattered invest
ments give him somewhat the nature of an urban capitalist
but to the same extent, only, that they give a simila
character to the farmer, George Washington. In his own
mind, Marshall may well have thought of Richmond as ar
extremely pleasant city to live in, with all the conveniences
including a theatre, that one need desire. This judgmen
would not have been unique.

In Charleston the theatre flourished. But from 1800 to

1820, its cosmopolitanism was tempered by the presentation of plays written by Charlestonians. These writers were numerous enough to form a significant and important group; the best of them—John Blake White and Isaac Harby—scarcely deserve the neglect which they have received. This wholesome tempering of the imported with the local dramatic product furnishes an excellent example of urban influence, since the activity is traceable to the stimulus of a receptive company and an appreciative audience. Although dramatic writing became more scattered and incidental, as other writing developed and became more unified, Charlestonians continued to write plays which were occasionally presented; the most notable, possibly, is Simms's *Michael Bonham* (1855). If no masterpiece appeared, few appeared in the world at that time. A favorable environment can and does stimulate activity, but it does not control the quality of the work done.

Trent suggests, indirectly, a reason why local authors, after 1820, may have grown self-conscious and hesitant: "Crafts and his fellow-connoisseurs sat in state and weighed out their applause with judicial hands." Mr. William Crafts was a wit, an orator, a *bon vivant*; incidentally, it would seem, a lawyer and man of letters. He lived for the theatre, the club, the drawing-room; he possessed the graces of a man-about-town. The surprising item about Crafts is that his poetry lacks the grace and wit which we should expect to find there. It has all the superficial marks of the city on it, and in manner it is definitely imitative of Mr. Pope; his best poem celebrates, for the edification of young belles and beaux, the popular institution of Race Week in Charleston. Here, in short, are the worst phases of city influence—the affectation without the severe criticism and self-examination which sharpen and form the writings of a wit. The

implications are obvious. Charleston in 1825 was far removed from Queen Anne's London: the brilliantly hard
manner of Pope could not be artificially transplanted and
made to clothe sound work in South Carolina, since the
matter was not transplanted and the manner only partially
understood. For, with all the superficial marks of Charleston which decorate his poetry, Crafts at heart was untouched by the city in which he lived: he made use of it as
a director uses a movie prop, to lend a surface reality to
something basically artificial.

No artificiality can be discerned in the work of Hugh
Swinton Legaré, or in the solid articles in *The Southern
Review*, which he helped to edit. Man and magazine belonged to Charleston, and they would add distinction to
any city. Although English in form, the magazine was
broadly cosmopolitan in subject-matter, with its reviews
based on German studies of Athens and Rome as readily as
on English or American fiction and poetry. Its contributors were scholarly men, with a range of knowledge which
seems fairly astounding, and they were mostly Charlestonians. This physical advantage meant that they could see
each other frequently, in stimulating contact. But their
works rarely have the tone of subjects aired in club-like
conversation and subsequently clarified in writing.

Yet they were urban, according to their definition. Most
of them owned land, and farmed it through an overseer:
they were also agrarian, and saw no philosophical contradiction in the terms. Legaré accepts without question the
doctrine that *fixed land property* is "of the essence of civil
society," and he speaks plainly his fear of the great centralized city with its irresponsible mob: "If there were no
other obstacle to the establishment of popular government
in France, the over-ruling influence of Paris would, alone,

be an insuperable one." He feared the city as a political power; he barely touches the fundamental questions raised by Jefferson and Taylor.

To Legaré and his contemporaries, the Southern city was being properly held to its subordinate position. Never once does he note that the economy fostered by Charleston was perilous to state and section, or that the economy fostered by New York was deadly to the South. He did know that something more powerful than the "march of intellect. . . a mightier than Solomon is abroad. It is the STEAM-ENGINE—in its two-fold capacity of a means of production and a means of transport." The face of Europe had been changed by it, mainly for the worse; inequality of wealth and desecration of beauty had resulted; but the good of cheap production and distribution might come of it. Whether for good or evil, "it is in vain to resist it." But such recognition of industrialism appears rarely, and was not connected, in Legaré's mind, with the city. The Southern writer on political problems, trained in the law, tended to think and write from the legalistic view, which could be cultivated, as Alexander Stephens indubitably proves, as well in rural Georgia as in urban Charleston.

In a section largely dominated by rural thought, one in which the philosophy of statesmen like Legaré and Stephens, or creative writers like John R. Thompson and Philip Pendleton Cooke, is so nearly alike though two were urban and two rural, it is evident that the influence of one city in the Southeast will serve as a type for all the cities. I have no desire to minimize the vigorous culture which flourished in the neighborhood of Savannah, or to discount the work of such coteries as the one Richard Henry Wilde gathered round himself in Augusta; but these influences are the same in kind, and it has seemed wiser to concentrate on the typical influences of the largest cities.

Men tended, in fact, to minimize the influence and even the existence of cities. In 1832, John Pendleton Kennedy—immediately after describing a visit to Richmond—wrote that Virginia "may be called a nation without a capital." Kennedy was of Baltimore, and his thinking in the following years was to become more like that of an industrialist than of a planter, as Baltimore was to become more of an Eastern than a Southern city. But this attitude is not apparent in *Swallow Barn;* at most, there are a few marks of an affectionate urban condescension for the peculiarities of rural characters. (This is far removed from the alien and urban attitude so common in our time, perhaps best reflected in the sociological novels of T. S. Stribling, who examines the rural South from the point of view, and for the edification, of New York. Kindred attitudes run through the books of ante-bellum travelers, Northern and European, who describe the South, but are rarely apparent in books by Southerners. Wirt, in his *Letters of a British Spy,* and Kennedy devise an editorial apparatus which permits the alien point of view, but neither man works the device to much advantage.) When he revised *Swallow Barn* in 1850, Kennedy apparently saw no reason to change his estimate: Richmond is still a "beautiful little city," a subordinate part of the state. Some years later the first historian of Richmond, writing in the *Southern Literary Messenger,* seems pleased that his country was not "weighed down by the incubus of a great city."

Virginia, assuredly, was not so weighed down. Yet Richmond, in the twenty-five years between 1835 and 1860, was an intellectual capital. The theatre was brilliantly cosmopolitan, the companies moving from city to city, lingering for a season in Richmond before moving on to New York or Boston or Charleston or Savannah, and re-tracing or varying their steps as their welcome grew thin. In a sense, these companies belonged to the society rather than to the life of the community, a condition which did not encourage the attempts of local playwrights, though it did make available the best plays in the repertoire of drama. Possibly the highest point in the stage history of Richmond came when Joe Jefferson managed a stock company there for a season, with Edwin Booth among the actors.

Richmond had also its library, with 14,000 volumes; its bookstores and newspapers; and its famed local orators. It was a favored place with visiting celebrities: Thackeray's letters, for example, reveal as much enthusiasm for what he called that "pretty little cheery place," as Richmond's newspapers evince an enthusiasm for Mr. Thackeray.

One of Thackeray's most popular poems (the verses on *The Sorrows of Werther*) was reputedly written at the desk of the *Southern Literary Messenger*. This was appropriate, for two of the editors—Edgar Allan Poe and John R. Thompson—had made consistent and reasonably successful efforts to criticize American books according to the standards and quality of world literature. The magazine endured for over thirty years, though constantly hampered by lack of support; in the uneven but sometimes strikingly brilliant issues appeared representative examples of the best thought and writing which the South had to offer. Poe contributed some of his finest work to it; from his experiences as editor, he shaped his ideas of what a magazine should be.

The elusive figure of Poe has been twisted to fit many later conceptions, and I have no desire to do more violence to him by briefly and arbitrarily making him an urban figure. But such a reading of his character seems to me inevitable. He was a child of the city, influenced, as country men are less likely to be, by all the intellectual doctrines current in his day. He drew upon English, Scottish, and German thought freely, shaping that thought to his own purposes; he was essentially romantic, and essentially, also, eclectic. Richmond influenced him profoundly, as Hervey Allen has shown, but it influenced him in its strictly urban sense, not as part of rural Virginia.

A professional man of letters, Poe was dependent on his editorial salary and his scantily-paid contributions to magazines for a livelihood; mainly, on his salary. As editor, he was necessarily attentive to public opinion, and the voice of the city was more immediate and more immediately powerful; it was more to be heeded. But there are more significant indications than salary and opinion. Poe's thought on modern writing, especially magazine writing, forms a scattered but consistent aesthetic for a modern magazine literature. This may be tentatively suggested: his theory of beauty, with its minimizing of moral content, leads naturally to the later Bohemian and urban "art-for-art's-sake" theory; his emphasis on brevity and unity, in poem or tale, and his desire for "the curt, the condensed, the well-digested," put into the smallest compass and dispersed "with the utmost attainable rapidity" all fit precisely into the concept of literature now dominant—and I presume no one will deny that modern literature is dominated by the city.

In brief, Poe is the one creative writer of the old South whose philosophy was fundamentally urban. Here is no matter of influences, incidental or profound; here is an acceptance of a new type of city—of the third great stage in the development of the city—and Poe was, at base, less influenced by intellectual forces in Richmond than by a concept of literature which was to influence subsequent writers in a distinctly urban manner.

Richmond helped to develop Poe's thought; Richmond did not go very rapidly in his direction, as New York did. In this later period, Virginia had lost its supremacy of thought in the South; leadership had passed to Charleston and South Carolina. In the thirty years before the war, the idea of an imperialistic Greek democracy was in the ascendency, and that idea was used to defend a less responsible plantation system whose economy was not self-sufficient, with its absentee landlordism, overseer-management, dependence on a money crop, and, generally speaking, its business rather than its agrarian economy.

In the mind of John C. Calhoun, there was at least no admission of such irresponsibility. To him the Southern states were "an aggregate, in fact, of communities, not of individuals. Every plantation is a little community, with the master at its head. . . . These small communities aggregated make the state. . . ." Since the city existed only as a larger community to serve these smaller ones, it was definitely subordinate and relatively unimportant. Calhoun may have seen plainly what Jefferson feared; he indicates as much in his attacks on the protective tariff of 1828, with its encouraging bounties to the manufacturing interests and cities of the North; but he saw these dangers through the small end of the telescope, and he placed his trust in legal and constitutional checks. The eyes of Jefferson had by far the longer sight: possibly his view was not impeded by legalistic motes and beams.

Francis Lieber, German by birth and South Carolinian only by virtue of a University professorship, expressed well the view directly opposite to Calhoun's, although his ideas are based on the same legalistic premises. He was concerned with liberty; what he wanted was to safeguard freedom with institutional self-government. All his theories

of property and labor, of organic government, and of th
nature of industrialism philosophically justify the industrial
istic and dominant city, but his strongest direct expressio
is an attack as blasting as Legaré's on the stifling politica
supremacy of Paris. Probably no man would have bee
more horrified than Lieber himself with the development o
his theories by John W. Burgess and Theodore Woolsey—
development which transposed a citizen into a subject
Yet, if the city had little influence on Lieber, few me
have had greater philosophical influence on the growth o
cities.

It remained for a business man, who occasionally wrot
pamphlets to justify and advance his business projects, t
recognize the fundamental economic change in the world
and to preach the cause of its adoption by the South. I
Essays on Domestic Industry, William Gregg wrote tha
"a change in our habits and industrial pursuits is a fa
greater desideratum than any change in the laws of ou
government"; in his article, "Charters of Incorporation fo
Manufacturing Purposes in South Carolina," he present
most of the arguments yet current in favor of big business
The letters, pamphlets, and *Essays* represent a developing
and finally a rounded testament of his economic thought
Gregg believed in industrialism; he wanted factories s
large that they could be financed only by corporations, no
by individuals; he considered industry the vital roots o
sectional prosperity; after politic hesitation, he finally came
out flatly for a protective tariff; he paid extremely high
dividends to stockholders and extremely low wages to
workers, then quarreled with a system which did not encourage greater profits; he is awarded by his biographer the
decidedly dubious title of father of the company-owned mil
village. Gregg is typical of the best type of benevolently

despotic, honest, yet essentially irresponsible industrialist; if his essays seemed far removed from literature, the man and writer were alike significant and influential.   His arguments had at least a superficial effect on Governor James H. Hammond; they were echoed and re-iterated in Charleston newspapers and magazines, and most consistently in the pages of *DeBow's Review*.

More typical, and more closely connected with literature, is the attitude of William Gilmore Simms.   In 1858, he expounded vigorously the thesis that weakness in Southern literature could be traced to "the necessary sparseness of a purely agricultural population, and the almost total want of great cities."   Simms continually thinks of the city as a commercial and intellectual clearing-house: "We require first a great city—a mart of our own—with sufficient commerce and population, capital and talent, to make its own independent opinion—to originate its own enterprise—to find the necessary attrition for the sharpening of the general mind—the awakening of a common emulation—the growth of taste—the culture. . . .   It is only thus that we can establish just standards of judgment; only thus that we can secure the adequate audience, for the support and appreciation of art."   This was not to cause a cleavage with the surrounding country; the cities would "irradiate the agricultural world around them," but would remain an integral part of that world.

For years, Simms had called for a Southern literature, in letters and talks, and, most frequently, in the pages of magazines which he sponsored. *The Magnolia*, *The Southern Quarterly Review*, and *Russell's* testify to this driving desire, and he had gathered round him in Charleston a group of men—Dickson, Porcher, Bruns, Hayne, Timrod, and others —who met often and talked freely of many subjects: of politics, history, and slavery; of rum punches, races, and duelling; most frequently, perhaps, of literature. And the magazines to which they contributed were filled with historical essays, with defenses of slavery and even of duelling, and, above all, with continual demands for a Southern literature. Neither Crafts nor Legaré had worried overmuch about the poor quality or scant quantity of Southern writing: there was, after all, an abundant store of international riches on which they could draw. Simms and his friends wanted local books by local authors, though they differed among themselves as to whether these books should necessarily treat local subjects. (As editors, at least, they encouraged translations of foreign works by Southerners, and sometimes adapted or translated such work themselves; one of them, Timrod, bitterly attacked what he called "shallow Southernisms." They were, then, disputing over a philosophical matter: not a precise question, but a general policy.) Careful study of their work will show, I believe, that while their range of knowledge and reading was wide and varied, their intellectual and especially their emotional horizon had narrowed. This is not necessarily a disadvantage; the stream of emotional thought may deepen as it narrows. The poems of Timrod reveal both aspects of this point.

This narrowing can be traced, by steps too complicated for precise detailing here, to the change which came over the South between 1825 and 1850. It can be traced, though but dimly, in Legaré's writing; it is apparent in that of Simms. The South was on the defensive, was slowly but certainly being pushed from her position of pre-eminence. Now, Charleston could admit without qualms the superiority of London, and even more readily that of ancient Athens or Rome; but the superiority of New York was a dangerous supremacy, a condition in the making rather than an accomplished—or, possibly, an admitted—fact, and a condition to be fought.

As best they could, these men fought. They issued clarion calls for Southern books, magazines, and publishers; for Southern support of Southern writers; in short, for the apparatus and the audience which would help in creating a Southern literature. In part, they succeeded. The men who met so frequently in John Russell's bookstore edited, or contributed to, several magazines which published some excellent as well as much mediocre work by Southern writers. Although one complaint that Simms makes most definitely is that "we have not in all the Southern States a single publisher," the imprint of John Russell appears on several books of distinct literary value. Books were published in Richmond, in Charleston, and in other Southern cities, though too often they were books which could be published only at the expense of the author, and had slight merit.

Occasionally, distinguished authors would do the type of work which we euphuemistically call "a labor of love," or they would go to quixotic lengths. Thus, the popular novelist William A. Caruthers allowed *The Knights of the Horse-Shoe* to be published in Alabama—an undertaking which led the *Southern Quarterly Review* to comment: "We are glad to see that this book is issued from a Southern press—a bold step for any author to take nowadays, who wishes to be popular." Always in the lead in these gallant labors was Simms himself, with his editing of magazines and of *The Charleston Book*, with his novels, histories, and biographies about South Carolina subjects, his untiring exhortatory letters, and his constant willingness to give, in almost the literal meaning of that word, a generous share of his prodigal output to Southern publishers and editors.

All these efforts had but a limited success. The South might be, as Stedman surmised, more interested than the North in reading standard literature; it was definitely less interested in reading contemporary books. A book with a New York or Boston imprint was more likely to be accepted in spite of editorial comment on the subject, even in the South than a book with a Charleston or Richmond imprint. Mr. William Gilmore Simms knew this as well as any man and all his quixotry did not prevent his sending most of his manuscripts to New York.

Looking back, we can see that these men wanted only that Charleston should be an urban center, fulfilling the function which men in 1850 thought belonged to the city. It must be obvious that a city can influence literature only by providing conveniences for its production and dissemination and—more fundamentally important—by shaping or changing the philosophy out of which an author writes. It can only shape the thoughts and lives of writers as it may shape the lives of architects, salesmen, or mechanics, but this influence will affect vitally whatever any of them may do. Strictly, the city has no influence in producing literature. This distinction seems to me fundamental. We do not know how literature is produced; we can only go into those elements which can be discerned in the finished product.

External marks of influence can be selected and classified until examples and classifications alone would fill a goodly volume. I have tried to identify the most relevant, only. For the external conveniences and stimuli were, in the ante-bellum South, not sufficient. It is important to note that Timrod's magnificent tributes to Charleston are testimony of his love for a city, but they prove as much, and as little about urban influence as his nature poems prove of country

As much, which is saying a good deal, but is stating only the outer shell of the matter. Charleston as an entity, as an actual place and a spiritual symbol, he knew and loved, just as he knew trees and flowers. But the city as an immediate yet somehow an abstract influence, in the modern sense of what we mean by urban, was foreign to his thoughts.

This point needs illustrating from another angle. In their respective studies of William Gilmore Simms, Messrs. Trent and Parrington attack the city of Charleston as a bad influence upon the author. The South, and Charleston particularly, attempted to keep alive the age of chivalry, says Trent, adding the debatable generalization that the South ignored the fact that modern civilization was a much higher thing. As a feudal city, Charleston had no place for its Simmses, and the author struggled against this neglect through much of his life. In Parrington's opinion, Charleston "can never atone for the undoing of her greatest son"—for making Simms a partisan rather than an artist.

No city makes an artist. It may be added safely, I believe, that no environment can make an artist. The problem is not, as Parrington intimates, one of attitude or of appropriate subject-matter: art has to do with form, with technique, with the handling of subject-matter. Every environmental advantage known to man can help the artist only as he can absorb these advantages and make them a part of himself and his work; the best and most stringent outside criticism is of value only if the artist adapts that criticism and makes it a part of his own equipment. To speculate upon a Simms removed from Charleston may be a pleasant exercise in pseudo-psychology, but when such work is printed as criticism, it serves only to confuse the issues.

Charleston did not exist for the sake of art, or of the artist; the culture of which Charleston was an integral part was a sufficient end in itself. The phrase *an integral part* needs stressing. Charleston was neither an independent nor a dominant entity, in the sense that New York now is in relation to the country, or Atlanta is in relation to Georgia. This urban dependence is at the root of Mr. Trent's more damaging criticism, although he handles the matter frivolously. His charges are applicable to Charleston, to South Carolina, and to the South—and Trent uses these terms interchangeably. I think his usage justified. Basically his complaint is that Charleston was not urban; that it did not give to Simms a philosophy based on modern civilization, but one based on a parochial and provincial culture.

Trent was writing out of an urban philosophy which was largely, if not completely, unknown to the ante-bellum South. For it is essential to note that Legaré and his contemporaries recognized only two stages of urban influence, and that even Francis Lieber did not see—at least during his Southern residence—the beginnings of a third stage which were already manifest in New York and London. The urban dominance which Trent called "modern civilization" scarcely existed in the old South, in the sense that there was an urban philosophy as distinguished from an agrarian philosophy, or that men in Charleston could even conceive of a dislocated and rootless literature of, for one example, the "art-for-art's-sake" type.

The city does not produce such literature, of course; it simply provides a basis for the philosophy which justifies such movements, and influences men to write in that particular manner. This form of urban thought was never powerful in the South, although certain phases of it in another and dilute form can be seen in the works of Poe and Chivers. What the Southern city did, before the Civil War, was to supply imperfectly the external conveniences and influences as best it could; what it failed to do was to govern the philosophy of the Southern writer. Some of us consider this failure an asset. Whatever our opinion, urban influence as we know it today was not wanted and scarcely existed in the ante-bellum South.

VIII

Legaré and Grayson

Types of Classical Influences on Criticism
in the Old South

SINCE there is little need for emphasizing the obvious, I shall only note that pre-revolutionary Southern criticism was, like the literature generally, colonial—dependent on English thought. Our literature was classical in the same way that English literature was, though inferior in quality and quantity. Writing of any type was scanty; as to criticism, there was little need for it, and few mediums through which to present it. It might be possible to compile a lengthy catalogue of critical snippets, but the results would be unimpressive; one would note the occasional comments of William Byrd and his peers, the precise couplets on the corruption of the stage written by a Gentleman of Virginia, and such criticism as might be contained in locally-written prologues, Addisonian essays, and letters. The catalogue would have some value as historical evidence of what we already know, and I would not discount the value of this factual material.

But it does seem important to attempt a definition of the types of classical or neo-classical influences in the South. There is no agreement, even, on the presence or absence of these influences; W. P. Trent writes of the Charlestonians of 1825 that they were "still living, in imagination at least, in the time of Horace. If they had come down the centuries at all, they had certainly stopped at another Augustan age,—that of Pope and Addison." Edwin H. Eby, author of *American Romantic Criticism 1815 to 1860*, contradicts, without qualification, the second part of Trent's generalization: "The spirit of the eighteenth century appeared cold and deadening to the men of the new era. They all criticized Pope and his followers for lack of imagination, lack of feeling, and for mechanical formulae within which literary expression was strait-jacketed." Since Dr. Eby considers Hugh Swinton Legaré a romantic critic, and from the list of Southern critics treats only Legaré and Poe, I shall analyze the work of the Charlestonian at some length.

The question boils down, I presume, to this: in what degree were Southerners men of the new era? That some of them continued to think on literary matters in the terms of Queen Anne's London, even after 1800, is well-known; it is attested in Virginia, for example, by William Wirt, and in South Carolina by William Crafts.

The influence of classicism might come directly from a reading of Greek and Latin authors, or it might come indirectly, through an imitation of English writers. William Crafts had sufficient grounding to be able to deliver commencement addresses in Latin, but not enough interest or knowledge, for the older literature to become a native part of his thought. He remained strictly within the English tradition: we had declared no independence of intellect, he wrote, and "it is not a voyage across the Atlantic that is to disinherit us." It is significant that he claims only "the literary productions... anteriour to the American Revolution," that he includes the English language, Shakspere, Milton, and Pope in our heritage, but is willing freely to give up "the licentiousness of Byron... the milk and water of Wordsworth... the Waverly novels" and other romantic writers and their works. His criticism and poetry alike indicate that his taste was formed by English neo-classicism. When he writes of natural scenery in South Carolina, he follows closely in the steps of Pope; when he writes essays, in the steps of Addison. Even his anacreontics are not modelled upon those of the Greek poet, but on Tom Moore's translations and adaptations.

Although later in time, Crafts seems to belong to an earlier period than Thomas Jefferson. The mind of Crafts was fixed; that of Jefferson was always open to new impressions. His classical knowledge became so thoroughly native to his thought that for years he accepted classical scansion as applicable to English poetry; when he attempted to clarify his ideas, in the treatise, "Thoughts on English Prosody," he shifts to the position that emphasis and accent constitute the harmony of English verse. Both the initial acceptance and the change are worth noting, for in the things they indicate, Jefferson was not unique. In line with the educational emphasis of his day, he approached the native literature from a Greek and Latin background; but he was finally committed to no system. Although he wrote, when he thought his love for poetry was fading, that he could hardly read even Vergil, he could—before and after that—find values in Ossian and Anglo-Saxon, and in some poems which today seem extremely shoddy. If the poet wrote on the grandeurs of nature, of political freedom, or the nobility of man, Jefferson could forgive an amazing amount of wretched versification—and to the degree that he valued subject rather than form, attitude rather than accomplishment, Jefferson for all his classicism was a part of the romantic movement.

What Crafts dismissed so easily, and what Jefferson accepted or rejected on the basis of his personal taste, was to Hugh Swinton Legaré a matter for critical and philosophical examination. From 1828 to 1832, Legaré as an editor of *The Southern Review* was a practising critic, fully aware that the concept of literature and the books produced under the new order had radically changed from the older one. In his first essay he notes that the German critics maintain "there is a fundamental difference between the *beau ideal* of modern poetry and art, and that of the antique; giving to the one the name of the Romantic, to the other, its old title of the Classical Style." To this distinction Legaré returns frequently; in discussing the works of Byron, he quotes Schlegel's passage which finds a key to modern writing in the Christian religion. Legaré assents, "in general, to the justness of these observations. We think that modern literature does differ from that of the Greeks in its *complexion* and *spirit*—that it is more pensive, sombre and melancholy, perhaps, we may add, more abstract and metaphysical—and it has, no doubt, been 'sicklied o'er' with this sad hue, by the influence of a religious faith which connects morality with worship, and teaches men to consider every thought, word and action of their lives as involving, in some degree, the tremendous issues of eternity." In another review, he adds, "What chiefly distinguishes the modern or romantic poetry from the classical is that the former is more concerned with *spiritualities* than *temporalities*, about soul, than body—about the shadowy abstractions of the mind than the objects of the senses."

It is one thing to accept the premises of Schlegel's argument; quite another to accept as a conclusion that modern literature is superior to the ancient. Legaré notes: "The spirit is changed . . . but does this alter, in any essential degree, the *forms* of beauty?" Homer, Vergil, and Milton employ the same method when describing "the sensible phenomena" of twilight; changes come when we describe "certain casual circumstances which may or may not accompany that hour"—the tolling of a bell, the lonely traveler looking back, and other touching but "still extraneous and it may be, transitory circumstances." Obviously these things may change; since that is true, they represent material for poetry, but not for the greatest poetry. "The *spirit* may vary, the *associations*, the colouring or complexion; but, substantially, there can be but one form o beauty, with which human nature, that never changes, wil rest content."

This form the Greeks perfected, not to conceal a lack o feeling, but to restrain and hold in check an overexuberant emotionalism. They permitted none of the irregularities the bombast, or the subjective mysticism cultivated by modern writers; they rigorously exacted unity of design, and "considered a work of art always as a *whole*." Three things were essential: perfect unity of purpose, simplicity of style, and ease of execution. These are the standards by which any literary work must be judged; it is the handling of material, not the material itself, that makes good or bad art

These tests Legaré applies to modern literature. His standards are most fully revealed in his comparison of Byron's *Manfred* (which he considers "as a *whole*" Byron's best work) with the *Eumenides* of Aeschylus. Legaré first notes that parts of Byron's works may surpass *Manfred*, "but such effusions are not, *caeteris partibus*, comparable to works, in which the beauty of design and composition is added to all other beauties." Legaré prefers this work of Byron's because it has less of the characteristics of a lyrical rhapsody, because it has form and is to some degree objectified: "The spirit of Manfred is strictly modern or romantic. The air of abstract reflection, the moral musing, the pensive woe, which pervade it, are a contrast to the sensible imagery and the lively personification of the Greek play. Yet its *frame and structure* are strictly 'classical'."

Manfred, like the *Eumenides*, is "a picture of remorse," but in the Greek tragedy remorse is personified by the Furies, while in the English play the "hero is alone," and the author receives no help from external symbolism or allegory. The very elements which prevent *Manfred* from being a classical play prevent it also from being great as an objectified and completely rounded work of art. Byron succeeds in part, but Aeschylus succeeds wholly.

Since this acceptance of modernity is obviously limited, it is pertinent to ask why Legaré has been termed a romantic critic. Primarily, it seems, Mr. Eby thus classifies him on the basis of his definition of poetry. Legaré paraphrases Sir Philip Sidney: "True poetry—like true eloquence—is the voice of nature appealing to the heart with its utmost sublimity and power"; he interpellates, in an essay defending the classics against science, the statement that poetry "is but an abridged name for the sublime and beautiful, and for high-wrought pathos. . . . It is spread over the whole face of nature. . . . It is in every heroic achievement, in every lofty sentiment, in every deep passion, in every bright vision of fancy, in every vehement affection of gladness or of grief, of pleasure or of pain. . . . It is these feelings, whether utterance be given to them, or they be only nursed in the smitten bosom—whether they be couched in metre, or poured out with wild disorder and irrespressible rapture, that constitute the true spirit and essence of poetry."

The key to this all-inclusive definition is in the final phrases. The subject-matter of poetry is unlimited: in all these things, animate or inanimate, spoken or mute, there is the spirit of poetry; but if we consider his definitions in connection with his other criticism, it seems evident that where realized and not potential poetry is under discussion, Legaré demands of the poet that he give form, design, and wholeness to the matter. The feeling is not the finished product, although it is the initial and vitalizing part of that product. Thus Legaré does not object to the content of Wordsworth's poems, but to the kind of simplicity, which is "often affected, and always visibly elaborate." He dismisses the "mere musings" of James Percival as incoherent, undefined, and shapeless fantasies, product of the brain of "poetical opium eaters." The poetry of Ossian would have been regarded by Athenians "as a mere monstrosity. A people accustomed to ask the reason for everything, would have seen in the vagueness, obscurity, and bombast of this pretended Celtic epic, only the effusions of a melancholy madness."

These defects of romanticism are not traceable, always, to Christianity: Milton and Dante are "the two most sublime poets of modern times, the most Christian in spirit, and the most classical and severe in style." Legaré returns again and again to Milton, and the keynote of his praise can be indicated by this—that *Paradise Lost* is a unified creation, with design in every point of it. Even Shakspere (though "*we* have no tragedies" but Shakspere's) falls into bombast and conceit. Simple and natural work, as in the poetry of Bryant, deserved full praise, and Legaré was delighted to give it, with the qualifying clause that such work could never rank with the greatest.

Legaré's is an independent neo-classicism or humanism, developed from the Greek models, not founded on any English type. He is in sympathy with the English: Byron's "defence of Pope . . . had been worthy of all praise, had he gone a little farther and only gibbeted a few of that great man's detractor's in another Dunciad." His highest praise of Byron is that, like Pope, he formed his taste "upon the models of Attic, not of Asiatic eloquence—of classical, not

of romantic poetry." Byron's taste, notes Legaré discrim-
inatingly, was so formed, but not his poetry—and for that
reason his performance falls short of Dryden's and of Pope's.
But Legaré sees defects in the English neo-classicists: "Pope
is, to some degree, a mannerist, and, so far, falls short of
absolute perfection"; much later, he pronounces Dr. Johnson
"a horribly bad writer ... yet his criticism in everything
that does not soar above a certain height, is usually very
sensible."

Through these quotations I have tried to indicate two
things: that here is a closely reasoned and consistently
applied body of critical standards which Legaré had constantly in mind when he wrote on literary matters; and that
these standards were formed not by the precepts of Horace
and Pope but by independent study of classical and of
modern literature, with the result that Legaré broadens
the base for poetry by widening the scope of its subject-
matter, without loosening the standards of form and unity
and wholeness. His work can not be fitted to Trent's
generalization, or to Eby's; yet, though Legaré's position
can be taken as more typical of Southern thought in 1830
than either of the generalizations I have quoted, his work is
not precisely typical. It is founded on too closely reasoned
a system; there is too much of analysis and too little of
acceptance; there is, in short, more than one can expect
even from cultivated readers.

Legaré, to my mind, represents the classicist tempered by
romanticism. His position is far removed from that of such
romantics as A. B. Meek, who termed the sonnet "poetry
in the pillory," or Thomas Holley Chivers, who believed in
spontaneity and never hesitated to invent his own forms, or
to attempt to give poetical expression to a mystical and
subjective mood. These men represent one extreme, as

William Crafts represents the extreme neo-classical. In all probability, Legaré would have disliked the work of Chivers, and even that of Poe, although he would have noted and approved the classical elements in Poe's critical theories—the insistence on unity of effect, the insistence that a poem or story must be a work of art, carefully designed and wrought by the maker, the conception of a work as being a whole. But Poe was almost untouched by classicism, save in this concern with form, and he is far removed from Legaré's position.

Timrod is not. His theories seem to be a fairly logical development from the criticism of Legaré. The essential characteristics of poetry, thought Timrod, "underlie the various forms which it assumes." But he differentiates between the "subjective essence" and the "objective form." There is a constant check, a refusal to give way to easy theories of composition: "I look upon every poem strictly as a work of art, and on the poet, in the act of putting poetry into verse, simply as an artist. If the poet have his hour of inspiration, tho I am so sick of the cant of which this word has been the fruitful source that I dislike to use it, this hour is not at all during the work of composition." But Timrod had a high conception of poetry, which he separated sharply from verse; he believed that a long poem, "without being all poetry from beginning to end, may be complete as a work of art," the intervening passages being composed of pleasing and skillful verse.

This represents a general loosening up, rather than an abandonment, of Legaré's classicism. Timrod is just as uncompromising in his demand for a unified work of art, but he makes a new and romantic distinction between verse and poetry. This seems a debatable question, and Timrod assuredly does not prove its truth; but he is more interested in proving that "if a poem have one purpose and the materials of which it is composed are so selected and arranged as to help enforce it," the result is one complete poem. Thus Timrod answers Poe; in his statement that each poem has its characteristic underlying form, he was answering not a romantic but a neo-classic critic.

William J. Grayson had presented, in an earlier issue of *Russell's Magazine*, his own definition of poetry. It was founded, he thought, on common sense and on reason. Poetry has been many things to many different people, and the craft of the poet has been magnified by philosophers, orators, and poets until it is something more than human. These commendations "do no harm if they are received with a discreet and proper spirit," adds Grayson drily. But the critics have busied themselves, of late, with making poetry "not only divine, but unintelligible" by so defining the nature of poetry that men are puzzled to know where "poetry or prose begins or ends." Now the critics talk of "prose poems and poetic prose, as if these terms were not as incongruous as the phrases, round square and oblong circle."

Individual critics give individual definitions: by their tests, certain writers "are not poets at all." One man would rule out the satirists, another the eighteenth century poets, and so on *ad infinitum*. Grayson quotes with approval Wordsworth's question and answer, put to a critic who thought "The Idiot Boy" unpleasing: "please whom or what? I answer, human nature, as it has been and will be. And where are we to find the best measure of this? I answer, from within." But each poet answers in that way; since tastes are different, poetry assumes a diversity of forms and applies itself to all subjects. "If there are 'Idiot Boys' there must be 'Londons,' and 'Rapes of the Lock,' and 'Elegies in Country Church Yards.' If we have Wordsworths, we must have Virgils and Popes also." To illustrate this point, Grayson cites readers who like, and who dislike such diverse works as the ancient ballads, Shakspere, Milton, the "Ancient Mariner," the "Vanity of Human Expectations," Gray's "Elegy" and Tennyson's "Maud." Grayson's command of salty and apt language makes these comparisons diverting, in both senses of the word, as well as pointed; he abandons the comparative method and launches a vigorous personal attack when he considers Wordsworth. "He was a sort of verse making machine all his life. He lived to manufacture verses. His morning and evening walks were taken to levy poetical black mail from every stock and stone, every shrub and flower, every bird and butterfly.—The daisy that to Peter Bell was a daisy and nothing more, was to Wordsworth a very different and much more important object—it was a peg to hang verses upon. ... If he visited a river, it was made to rhyme. If he returned again to its banks it was forced to do double duty. ... He looked on nature as a kind of poetical milch cow, which he was never tired of milking. ..."

Grayson objects to the manner, not the matter—the form, not the material—of Wordsworth's poems. As the minds to which poetry is addressed are varied, the forms and grades of merit must, naturally, be almost endless: "The great masters of song alone may occupy the summit, but every thicket and dell ... has its attendant melody." And the subjects are wide, not confined: descriptions of nature, delineations of "the passions that agitate the heart," the scourging of "the vices of their times," the treatment of wit, refinement, sense, and polished society, the poets who "rise to truth and moralize their song." Trouble comes only when "the critic has once set up his peculiar standard of poetry, founded on what he considers the invariable principles of art, and no one can tell at what conclusions he may arrive. Instead of sound and catholic taste co-extensive with art and nature, he substitutes some narrow judgment as limited as his own views. He excludes himself from the length and breadth of nature and poetry to wall himself up in some corner of their domain, insisting that there is nothing beyond his own boundaries."

If poetry can take all nature for its province, how can we determine what is poetry? Not by the nature of the thoughts expressed: "It is not beauty of imagery, nor play of fancy, nor creative power of imagination, nor expression of emotion or passions, nor delineation of character, nor force, refinement or purity of language, that constitutes the *distinctive* quality of poetry." These elements are shared with prose. Nor can it be found, as Coleridge attempts to find it, in any juggling with "best words." "If he had made the distinction to consist in the order, and not in the words, it would be nearer the truth. For certainly the 'best words' are as fully the property of fine passages in prose as they are of poetry. It is in the order . . . that the point of distinction is to be found." Grayson is so convinced of the necessity of form that he illustrates the differing rhythms of prose and verse by turning a prose passage of Milton's into verse, with results which at least indicate the point he is making.

Poetry is one "of the grand divisions of articulate sounds . . . there are but two." And the division which is poetry he would define as "the expression, by words, of thought or emotion, in conformity with metrical or rhythmical laws." Poetry and prose alike are "co-extensive with the limits of human thought and emotion. . . . It is true that there are subjects more suitable to one mode of expression than the other, and it would indicate a want of taste and judgment to mistake in the use of one or the other as the topic may

require. But the error would in nowise touch the validity
of the distinction between them." Thus, Lucretius may
have been injudicious in expounding the doctrine of Epi-
curus as he did, but his work remains a poem, and a prose
translation of it remains prose; the *Iliad* is a poem, not
alternate bits of poetry and prose, and a translation of it
may be one or the other; it can not be both.

"When from asking whether a book is a poem, we turn to
examine into its faults and beauties, the whole province of
inquiry is changed." The critic may term a poem verse,
or prosaic, as we term a man an ass, or effeminate. These
figurative expressions are necessary, but confusion arises
when they are applied to the category, rather than to the
merit, of a work. The chat at a corner, the plain talk of a
laborer, the slang of a pot house, are all prose; the doggerel
and extemporized stanzas are poetry. "A bad poem is still
a poem, the most excellent prose is still prose, and the landmarks must remain undisturbed by the conflicting parties."

Grayson referred to Samuel Johnson as "the sturdy old
master of vigorous common sense"; he looked upon himself
as an advocate, if not a sturdy one, of the same type of
thought. The point which he makes about "The Ancient
Mariner" is worthy of his critical master: we could believe
that the glittering eye might have held the guest after the
wedding, when he was "filled with wine and wassail," but
the lunatic eye would have caused a sober man "to run away
or call for the help of the nearest police officer." Such
poetry was not to Grayson's taste. Yet he is not objecting
to those tastes which prefer it, or insisting that this is not
poetry; he is simply, and sturdily, defending the wide realm
of poetry, which included a type that he did like: the neo-
classic. It is true that this is the precise kind the romantic
critics were ruling out of the realm of poetry, and Grayson's

essay thus becomes in large degree a defense of neo-classicism; but his own tastes were too broad and too thoroughly
tempered by romanticism for him to deny that the romantic
type was poetry.

In two sonnets, Grayson gives a fairly romantic picture of
the purposes of subjective and objective poetry. Through
the subjective, our natures can be "etherealized above the
dust and noise / Of earth's low thought"; through the objective, poetic melodies can "Impart new charms to nature,"
both by beautiful descriptions and by delineation of great
deeds. Poetry can exalt our joys, in bridal hall or national
victory, in thanksgiving for bounteous harvest or in saintly
devotions—whatever the purpose, "the voice of song im-
parts / A brighter smile to every bliss on earth." And the
poet receives his reward in the "Visions of beauty, and the
life and light / Of hope, and love, and joy, thy melodies
impart." If these quotations indicate that Grayson's sonnets have slight value as poetry, they indicate also that the
neo-classic critic was frequently caught up in the current
of romanticism.

But he is consistent in his dislike for romantic poetry,
which to him is "subtle and transcendental in its nature.
Every sentiment, reflection, or description is wrought into
elaborate modes of expression, from remote and fanciful
analogies. The responses of the Muses have become as
mystical, and sometimes as obscure, as those of ancient
oracles, and disdain the older and homelier forms of English
verse. . . . But the school of Dryden and Pope is not entirely
forgotten." Thus does Grayson preface his attempt, in *The
Hireling and the Slave*, to restore to favor the heroic couplet
and the didactic poem. Grayson knew that his theories
were not in style, that his poetry seemed old-fashioned even
to his friends, but he had "faith in the ancient classical

models, the masters directly or indirectly of all the grea
poets of modern times," and he could not be changed by al
the eloquence of a Timrod, or a Simms.

In his autobiography (which Professor R. A. Bass ha
allowed me to examine), Grayson enlarges without mate
rially changing the theories I have noted. Many of the
sentences from his earlier work are repeated. One valuabl
item does appear: he looks upon Horace's *Art of Poetry* a
the definitive theory, and he values Pope so highly because
"Pope comes nearest to the forms of classical eloquence.'
In occasional passages, Grayson's neo-classicism appears
to be formed directly on a study of classical models, but the
body of his work stems from the English or, it may be, from
the Latin critics; not from the Greek writers. He lacks the
philosophy of Legaré, and the wider understanding; if this
is traceable in part to Grayson's character, it is traceable
also, in part, to the closeness with which he follows a narrower critical doctrine.

Legaré represents, more ably than typically, the critica
thought of the South about 1830. His criticism helps to
clarify the early poetry and criticism of such a man as
William Gilmore Simms, when that writer was under the
influence of Dryden and Pope; it illustrates how such a poet
could, a few years later, fall easily under the influence of
Byron, then of Wordsworth. Embodied in this criticism
were the seeds of romanticism, which were held in check
not by the precepts of Horace or Pope but by the examples
of the Greeks. It was perhaps natural that these ancient
examples should wane, in the minds of other poets and critics, before the immediate and more comprehensible theory
and practise of Wordsworth and Coleridge. To Legaré,
Wordsworth's attitude toward nature did not seem revolutionary: the Greeks had loved nature as ardently and more

precisely. But the subjective associations, the casual circumstances, which he thought extraneous, seemed to Timrod and to Simms more important than the most accurate or the noblest description.

New concepts had come into the world, and they were not to be confuted or denied. It is worth noting that no Southern critic, after William Crafts, attempts confutation or denial: the more classical the critic, the greater his attempt to bring these into conformity with the established forms; the more revolutionary, the greater his tendency to deny value to form or, more often, its parallel but not identical element, objectivity. Southern criticism and Southern poetry reflect this mixture of romanticism and classicism. Any generalization which omits the one or the other paints a false picture. The criticism before 1830 tended to be classical or neo-classical, but it was strongly tempered by romanticism; after that date, the major emphasis gradually changes to a romanticism which, adhering closely to the tenets of unity and form, was tempered and restrained by classicism.

IX

Southern Towns and Cities

ALMOST fifty years ago Lord Bryce wrote that, with a few notable exceptions, American cities differed from each other chiefly in that some were built more with brick than with wood, and others more with wood than with brick. He missed entirely the local traditions and idiosyncrasies and the development of purely local products and specialties that gave character and individuality to European cities. Yet even Bryce's sarcastic distinction would hardly hold good today, when the processes of standardization have tended to make each town more like every other town, until differences in population remain the chief mark of distinction. But in 1880 there were few southern cities, and New Orleans was, significantly, among his exceptions. Even judged by the urban standards of that day, Nashville, Atlanta, Charleston, Richmond, and Memphis were little more than towns; Birmingham, a high vision wallowing in mud; and New Orleans, our one great city.

The reason for this lack of cosmopolitan development in the South is obvious. Before the Civil War, it was neither an industrialistic nor a commercial section. And its people were not only agrarian; they had, in addition, a localism that was largely self-sufficient. The town or city was a useful clearing-house, which disposed of money crops, such as cotton and tobacco, and which supplied, in turn, the luxuries that could not be made or produced. But even then, although in most cases the balance remained constantly on the side of the city, with the farmer and plantation-owner borrowing from year to year on his anticipation of future crops, it was only the financial balance, as measured

in dollars, that favored the city.   The true center of power,
the basis of the entire economic structure, rested on the land
and on the people who owned that land.   If cotton was not
king, in all sections, the power typified by cotton held dominion over the South.   The system was almost feudal, for the
ownership of land and of slaves carried with it duties and re-
sponsibilities to dependents, as well as definite claims upon
them.   The men living under such a system tried to avoid
buying any article that could be made at home, and every
plantation was in effect an independent manufacturing unit.

Whatever the defects of this system, the men produced
under it had little need for great cities.   But southern defeat
in 1865 ended abruptly a worn-out, yet human, way of life,
and it may be that both victor and vanquished have failed
to replace it with a better one.   Then, all was confusion.
Peace came, but without order.   The fields were laid waste;
guerilla bands harried many sections; irresponsible Negroes,
encouraged by Federal soldiers and accustomed only to
obedience, found the heady wine of freedom too much to
control.   The isolated farm was no longer safe.

The farmer had no choice.   In times of stress, men must
band closely together, and southern men in large numbers
moved to the town or city for safety and security.   Between
1865 and 1875, most southern towns doubled in size, although the new residents generally continued to think
of themselves as farmers.   Yet the type of farming had
changed.   For a time after the war, when cotton was fifty
cents a pound and other produce equally high in price, the
planters attempted to resume large-scale production.   But
taxes were disproportionate, workers irresponsible, and all
materials expensive—and prices soon dropped back to a
normal level.   Once a man could ride over broad fields in
the full pride of ownership, and direct a group of workers on

a communal project. Now each man wanted his own definite number of acres, to farm as he pleased. From this developed a system of tenant-farming, on the share-crop or money-rent basis, with each tenant farmer and small landowner quite independent. Yet his independence was limited and circumscribed; the self-sufficient farm community was a thing of the past. Now the farmer became dependent on town or city for farm implements, for articles of clothing, and, in many instances, even for food that he could easily have raised on his own land. For the first time in the history of the South, the agrarian community was subsidiary to the urban community.

This transition can be charted with reasonable accuracy. The farmer moved to the small town to escape the dangers of reconstruction, while he rented out his farm to poorer whites or Negroes; more often, he superintended the farm work by day and returned to town at nightfall. The sons of these men knew little of farming, and that little was unpromising. Farms, then as now, often failed to make enough money to pay running expenses, and the migration went on, from farm to town, and from town to city. By 1880, these younger men had acquired enthusiasm for other things. If money could not be made from raising cotton or tobacco, it could from the manufacture of products from those same staples. The South, men said, must be revived, "not with cotton in the fields, but cotton in the mills." Every town of consequence desired a cotton mill or a manufacturing plant of any variety.

In general, these industries came to established cities, rather then to newly founded towns. New Orleans, Louisville, Richmond, Atlanta, Memphis, and Chattanooga all gained rapidly, both in manufacturing and in population. At first, these new industries were chiefly financed by local men, and progress was heart-breakingly slow. In addition, not one of these cities welcomed industrialism with entirely open arms. A stubborn group of older men and women remembered an earlier and, it may well be, a better way of life, which had little to do with great factories or pushing businesses. But poverty will force most men into line, and—though Walter Hines Page at the turn of the century excoriated as mummies those who held out against new ways—soon the tide was all against tradition.

A few cities grew, almost overnight, out of nothingness. William K. Boyd, in *The Story of Durham*, traces briefly "certain well defined periods in its growth. These are the days of origin, down to 1865, followed by an expansion from a hamlet into a small manufacturing town between 1865 and 1881; then comes the transformation into a small city, a well defined period from 1881 to 1900; and, finally, there is the last quarter century, when industry became more diversified, government more complex, and new social institutions emerged." A less flattering chronicler has suggested that the city has ridden to renown on the shoulders of Bull Durham and Buck Duke. Beyond question, the story of Durham is the story of the tobacco industry, which, like the city, has advanced from infancy to such commanding position that its entrepreneurs can endow great universities.

Even more spectacular—the most striking, though the least representative—was the development of Birmingham. Least representative, because in that city alone was industrialism not at war with an older tradition: Birmingham was not founded until 1871, when the ordinary activities of the South were at a standstill, and it was planned from the beginning to be an industrial city. Men recognized the potential value of Alabama's immense natural resources in coal and iron, but for five years the new city floundered dismally along, until in 1876 Colonel J. W. Sloss proved beyond question that coke iron could be produced in Alabama. Yet vain efforts to interest northern capital failed time and again (for northern manufacturers refused to believe that iron, and later steel, of good quality could be made from this new bed of raw ore), until the city again seemed fated to remain small.

Then a new element entered into the life of Birmingham and, somewhat more slowly, into the life of the South. Northern capitalists were convinced of bright opportunities. In the 1890's, Andrew Carnegie, his associates, and his competitors bought into the Alabama companies, to give a literal, as well as figurative, truth to Birmingham's proud boast that it was "the Pittsburgh of the South." This was no isolated phenomenon: throughout the South, precisely the same development occurred in many and varied industries.

By 1900, the period of self-development had largely passed, and the era of exploitation had begun. The progress of southern industrialism, as long as it depended upon its own limited capital and resources, was necessarily snail-like. Men demanded more immediate results. Then started the campaign for northern capital, for new factories in every possible line of manufacturing. The chambers of commerce and allied organizations of business men lost no opportunity to paint in alluring colors the glowing advantages of the South, with its moderate climate, its cheap white labor, its abundant raw materials—the prospects were endless. This campaign among the cities culminated in bids that seem incredible: various places offered such concessions as freedom from taxation over a long period of years, free factory sites, and similar financial attractions for which no adequate recompense was ever received.

Whatever the ultimate profits and losses may have been, the tangible result was, more and more, to justify Lord Bryce's statement. The Richmond of 1870 was indubitably a part of Virginia, and Atlanta was definitely an integral part of Georgia. Each was dependent on the state for sustenance. But Richmond and Atlanta were definitely unlike in certain respects—in architecture and industries, for example. The result of the change sketched above has been to make Atlanta more like Richmond, and also, on a lesser scale, more like New York and Cleveland, but much less like Georgia. It has become, as far as its business is concerned, the representative of New York in the South, and it has striven for, and attained, much of New York's cosmopolitanism. In greater or in less degree, precisely that same development has occurred in every southern city.

The cities of the South have thrived almost unbelievably, but even this remarkable growth, when compared with that of certain other sections of the country, does not seem so great after all. Knoxville, in 1920, could advertise itself blatantly on automobile license tags as the 114% city—the growth of a single decade; Birmingham had grown from nothing in 1871 to 175,000 in 1920, and to more than 250,-000 in 1930. New Orleans, Louisville, Atlanta, and Memphis all had passed well beyond this same high mark, though only the first, at the turn of the century, had approached it. Bigness, for its own sake, had become a megalomania: at each census the various cities would annex surrounding towns, and make concerted drives for more inhabitants, in order that they might surpass rival cities. Yet Atlanta, though it may seem to us a metropolis, is smaller than Toledo or Columbus, and only a trifle larger than Akron; Birmingham and Memphis cannot equal Jersey City and Newark. Even New Orleans does not begin to compare in

size with a dozen cities scattered over other sections of the
United States.

There are several reasons for this lack of urban develop
ment. The South started late, and this initial handicap
has been hard to overcome. The small industries that ante
dated the Civil War were destroyed, and money was lacking
to revive or to replace these infant industries. But there
were less obvious, and possibly more important, reasons.
Although after 1900 the advocates of industrial progress
seemed to dominate the cities, there remained an older
more leisurely civilization that set little store by progress
that insistently held out for individual, as opposed to cor-
porate, growth. This attitude has been labelled prejudice
and has been subjected to bitter and fairly effective attack
from chambers of commerce and kindred organizations, but
it has never been completely uprooted. Men and women
prefer to trade where clerks know them by name, and at
least seem interested in them as individuals. Chain stores,
and any other store that fails to deliver its goods to the
purchaser's door, have found difficulty in securing patronage,
though they might sell goods a little cheaper than their old-
fashioned competitors.

This attitude has carried over into other, less superficial
aspects of business. For two generations it made men chary
of investing money in factories or intangible stocks and
bonds; accustomed to the ownership of tangible land, men
could not easily reconcile themselves to paper tokens, however valuable. The sons of gentlemen were educated for
the professions, and even today in the South the professional
man retains a faint dignity that has been completely denied
him elsewhere. Only a change in public opinion could bring
about the urban development of the South, and that change
was necessarily slow.

It was relatively easy for the commercial Northeast to shift from a mercantile to an industrial economy. But the South had never been capitalistic, although it had possessed a few shipping centers—New Orleans, Savannah, Charleston, and, partly southern, Baltimore—and it had to build up an entirely new set of values. After 1900 this conversion came rapidly, in part through the propagation of new ideas by such publicists as Walter Hines Page, but primarily and most effectively through the demonstration that financial prosperity could be achieved only through an industrialized society. In 1930 the city seemed dominant and continued to grow apace. This was the tangible symbol of the new South, and bitterly, that year, our cities fought for supremacy when the census counted heads.

But no one year gives an adequate compass: in discussion here, it seems better to treat the cities without exact regard to the immediate present, but in a more general time-sense, which may loosely be called "modern."

II

In what respect do southern cities differ from those of the North and the West? That, it seems to me, is a question that might reasonably be asked; it is a question that becomes increasingly difficult to answer. Before attempting such a task, it would be necessary to describe, briefly and pointedly, certain southern cities and to make some differentiation between them. For it is worthy of note that these cities differ radically among themselves, and it is no mean tribute that each name carries with it connotations and traditions that are peculiar to it.

At once the largest and most picturesque city in all the South is New Orleans—which, as Lyle Saxon has discerningly pointed out in *Fabulous New Orleans*, is in reality two

cities.   There is the old French city—the Vieux Carré—and
the newer "American city."   Here, more clearly than in any
other town, can one observe the incessant yet rarely noticeable struggle between progress and tradition.   For the two
sections pay allegiance to strangely dissimilar gods, and it is
with regret that one notices unmistakable signs of pre-
dominance of the god of business.

The streets in the old city are narrower; in the newer
section they frequently have a center drive, which is planted
with palms or evergreen trees.   Canal Street, the business
center, is neutral ground; in "old town," as it is frequently
called, the houses are predominantly French or Spanish,
closely joined together, with much graceful ironwork around
small balconies, and with inner courtyards.   The entire
atmosphere is leisurely and cosmopolitan: in part the work
of artists and Bohemians who inhabit the Vieux Carré, in
part the survival of French and Spanish family life.   Here,
too, are memories and realities: of Antoine's, Galatoire's,
La Louisianne, and older, not-quite-forgotten restaurants
that made of eating and drinking a fine art; the St. Louis
cemetery and cathedral; the old Ursuline Convent that
served also as an archbishop's palace; the great "dueling
oaks," that belong in spirit, if not in location, to the old
town—all these, and a score of blocks of houses, a few fine
government buildings, are relics of French and Spanish days.
Yet, as I write this, newspapers chronicle the doom of the
old and famous French Market House—*Halle des Boucheries*.
In a few months it will be torn down and replaced with a
new and up-to-date building.   Fire, also, has taken its toll,
in the old Opera House, and, caught between these twin
agents of destruction, the Vieux Carré seems fated, soon,
to disappear.

Yet the subtle forces of tradition permeate even the new

ity, with its wide streets and miscellaneous architecture.
Men work in leisurely fashion, and go out, each morning
and afternoon, for coffee that, according to legend, will help
o ward off malaria. And New Orleans bears the imprint
of river and of ocean. It is distinctly a Mississippi river
own, although commerce on the river has lost its economic
importance, and adds, today, little more than a touch of
olor and strangeness. But floods are ever-threatening,
and men can never forget that the city is often ten feet below
he level of the Mississippi, and dependent on levees for its
afety. Once, too, the great bend in the river gave to the
ity a rounded shape and the name of the "Crescent City"—
a name without meaning today, save that its principal streets
running north and south curve to follow the bend in the
iver. New Orleans remains a great seaport, a gateway for
uch southern products as cotton, grain, and lumber, and a
enter for imports from South America. But there is little
manufacturing:New Orleans, as much today as before the
Civil War, depends upon the surrounding country for its
upport. It is a clearing-house for the lower South.

Men have turned the brilliant social life of an older day
nto a first-rate tourist attraction. Mardi Gras has become
an institution, with its Rex, its Mystic Krewe of Comus,
Knights of Momus, and Crewe of Proteus. There are balls
and street parades, river carnivals, and both organized and
mpromptu revelry, but the ancient flavor has gone, to a
arge extent, in the modern effort to entertain visitors.
True, business stops while society plays ... but business
reaps in the end, one feels, a two-fold harvest. Yet in this,
as in so many other instances, the old and the new are in
combat.

Far removed from such conflict is Birmingham, city of
he new South. It is the one industrial center between

New Orleans and Atlanta, the center of the iron and coal industry south of Pennsylvania. The buildings are all of a kind: relatively new, with a preponderance of modern skyscrapers dwarfing the more ordinary store-buildings and the semi-classic governmental and institutional structures. Situated on the slope of Red Mountain, it escapes a monotonous regularity chiefly through this natural ruggedness of the terrain. For Birmingham is predominantly a child of the twentieth century, and it has no old traditions that cause men to regret the passing of old landmarks.

In physical location Richmond possesses one likeness to Birmingham: the capital of Virginia was originally built on seven hills, and once it was called the "modern Rome." But the hills, overhanging the James River, are small—and there, abruptly, the resemblance ceases. For Richmond, like New Orleans, is a blend of old and new; even the principal industry—the preparation of tobacco for use—far antedates the Revolutionary War. Few towns possess more definitely the intangible stamp of historical associations. The public buildings have one quality even rarer than tradition: they have architectural merit. The capitol building was designed by Thomas Jefferson after the model of the ancient Roman temple, the Maison Carrée, of Nîmes, and the later additional wings have conformed to the same general type. All the public buildings in Richmond have, in fact, conformed to this adapted classical style, and the statuary commemorating notable men of yesteryear adds to this impression of Richmond as a classical American city. Prominent landmarks and historic buildings recall memories of Washington, Jefferson, Marshall, Madison, Lee, and a veritable host of men only slightly less famous. One cannot easily forget such names, or forget that in 1730 Richmond was known as "Byrd's Warehouse", or that once it was the capital of the Confederacy. But Richmond is sorely divided, one group feeling that memories can be bought at too high a price, and striving desperately for business growth; the other prizing an older way of living that seems inevitably in conflict with modern progress.

"No city should be a museum, kept intact under glass." That statement was hurled at Richmond some years ago; with even more justice can it be applied to Charleston. Although it has an extremely fine port and is an important commercial city, this phase of its life has been rather largely neglected. All historic places and features have been carefully preserved: the Battery, with its magnificent view of the harbor and of Fort Sumter; wooded White Point Garden, with its monuments to great men of another day; the Powder Magazine, the Slave Market, and the old residential houses that recall days when Pringles and Heywards and Hugers ruled the community. Twelve miles from town are the Magnolia Gardens, perhaps the principal attraction to tourists, and certainly an integral part of the community. Like New Orleans, it possesses one of the few really important social events of the nation, but Charleston has retained for its St. Cecilia's Ball an exclusiveness that commercial prosperity has never tarnished. Here family is all-important, and relatives are counted to the "nth" generation; yet here, too, is a Gallic lightness of manner, and at times a fiery zeal bringing a recollection that Charleston is tempered with a large group of people of French Huguenot descent. That zeal once led the state into nullification and, again, led the South into a war. But today it seems dormant— primarily interested in preserving faded but imperishable glories.

Although Savannah was founded by James Oglethorpe in 1733, it seems to have less of history and somewhat more of humanity, than Charleston. The tang of the marsh is in the air, and the picturesque scenes native to any port town are constantly in view. For Savannah remains undeniably a small town, though an exceedingly busy port, and its air of leisurely dignity seems far more in keeping with Georgia than do the bustling ways of Atlanta.

Perhaps it is not by accident that two of our most prosperous cities have little connection with the agrarian South. Unlike Birmingham, Atlanta did not spring up over night. Before the Civil War the first name of the village, Marthasville, was changed to Terminus, because increasingly the railroads centered round that town. And Terminus in due time became Atlanta, the central goal of General Sherman, who described it as "the wrist of a hand whose fingers reach the five principal ports of the Gulf and South Atlantic coasts." During the days of reconstruction, Atlanta became capital of the state; since that time, its valuable central location and its easy accessibility have made it, in sober truth, the "New York of the South." For Atlanta also is new, with broad streets and a metropolitan air, and it has become a center of manufacturing as well as of distribution. Rural Georgia has little tangible connection with it, save to supply it with food, and the city quite evidently is not proud of Georgia. All emphasis is thrown on its fine buildings and educational institutions, and, above all, on the fact that Atlanta is the metropolis of the South and, basically, a branch of New York. Although a leisureliness, an old-time courtesy and gentility, pervades the atmosphere, the casual visitor is rarely allowed to forget, in his business contacts, that this way of life is less important than the city's commerce.

Compared with Atlanta, Nashville seems an overgrown small town, with narrow and out-moded streets, grimy old buildings, and the settled placidity of middle age. This, however, is only a half-picture. Once it was a frontier town, but those days are completely past, and long since forgotten; today it is "the Athens of the South," boasting of fine educational institutions and of grand old days, yet reaching somewhat reluctantly for new commercial projects. It has Vanderbilt, Peabody, Ward-Belmont, and Fisk: the four extremes in modern education. For Vanderbilt represents the old-time classical college that has branched out into a large university; Peabody, the modernized institution that believes men can be transformed into teachers if they are taught the correct methods; Ward-Belmont remains an outstanding boarding school for well-to-do young ladies; and Fisk is preëminent in the field of cultural education for Negroes. Here are four radically different schools, in a city that rebuilds the Greek Parthenon, and now puts on, through its Chamber of Commerce, a five-year plan to lure new industries from the North. A divided city, that prizes on the one side, Friendly Five shoes—and, on the other, the Hermitage. Like every southern city, it lives on inconsistencies: allows baseball on Sundays, yet forbids movies; prides itself on culture, but has no decent theatre and is shunned even by road shows; points with pride to historical tradition while it seeks the very things that, inevitably, must destroy the value and the validity of those traditions.

Memphis, like Atlanta, owes much of its development to the accident of location. It is the trade center for the upper Mississippi Delta and other less famous, but hardly less rich, valleys. Distinctly a river town in pre-Civil War days, Memphis retains a picturesque quality through its location on the bluffs of the Mississippi, and the dock and river-boats give it something of the appearance of a port town. No longer is the river an important commercial adjunct of the city, however; but railroads have kept it a focal point for trade in the old Southwest. Unlike most cities today, Memphis is directly dependent on the surrounding country, for practically all of its commerce and industry revolve around cotton and hardwood. It is the largest inland market handling actual cotton in the country and the greatest center for the manufacture of cottonseed products. An open city, with wide streets and many handsome buildings, it has remained a type of the old plantation center—and its attempt to rival larger cities in the North and the West received one tangible check quite recently when its newest skyscraper was sold at auction under the bankruptcy law. When the surrounding country is prosperous, Memphis thrives; when, as at present, the farmer and the planter are poverty-stricken, the city suffers in proportion.

There are other cities that might, with equal justice, be sketched in greater detail. The industrial cities of Chattanooga and Knoxville; the pleasant port of Mobile; the resort city of Asheville, and the tobacco town of Durham. But any sketches of this nature must be inconclusive and unsatisfactory. I have omitted, deliberately, the Texas cities, for Dallas and Fort Worth belong to the Southwest; and San Antonio, though a fascinating blend of Spanish, Mexican, southern, western, and military life, seems outside the scope of this discussion. For a similar reason, I have omitted Louisville, though it might well be labelled "southern"—Louisville seems clearly comparable with St. Louis, and far removed, somehow, from Memphis or New Orleans. With equal arbitrariness I have neglected with regret ancient and picturesque St. Augustine; without remorse the tourist cities of Florida. They represent a transplanted East. Some day this culture may bulk large in a study of southern life; at the present moment it is quite negligible. These arbitrary distinctions were unfortunate, but necessary, in any attempt to describe or to analyze the southern city as a type that is representative and that has become, in some instances, a section within the larger section that is the South.

III

Yet, when one takes a wider view of this group of cities, these distinctions seem less important than certain other elements that lead inevitably to the conclusion that southern cities have much in common. And the elements of kinship, not the differentiations, give to all, in varying degree, a certain character that may be called "southern" and that separates these cities quite distinctly from cities in other sections.

Most important is the amazing homogeneity of the people. Without undue exaggeration, Konrad Bercovici could write a book that dealt with many close-knit tribes of men, and title it *Around the World in New York*. But foreign colonies of people as yet unassimilated boil down, in the South, to one race: the Negro. (It may be well here to qualify slightly this generalization; there exist, of course, a few colonies, such as the Spanish Ybor City in Tampa, the Greek settlement at Tarpon Springs, the Portugese settlements along the Gulf Coast, and similar small but unassimilated groups. These colonies are too unimportant to influence any considerable portion of southern life.) And the Negro, though an integral part of the community life, does live, and apparently is destined for many years to live, in sections that are exclusively his own. The Negro has churches, schools, newspapers, of his own; to some extent, he has business houses that have strict regard for the color line.   Undoubtedly this is imposed upon him—quite often unfairly—by the white race; but the essential point here is that the Negro represents the one alien group of considerable size and influence in the South.

Only the Negro, however, constitutes a separate communal group within the larger community.   The South remains predominantly Anglo-Saxon.   This was not entirely through intention: for many years, after 1865, the various states made strenuous efforts to attract immigrants.   Virginia sent recruiting agents to Great Britain and Germany; a Southern Immigration Society, organized in 1883, attempted to secure immigrants from European countries. Even Chinese coolie labor was tried, but soon abandoned. Perhaps the most outspoken advocate of this movement was Henry Grady, who desired for Georgia one hundred thousand immigrants—and seventy-five thousand of these men he would place in the factories.   But immigrant wage-earners continued to prefer the North, and the movement failed completely.   Today such movements work more indirectly, in the attempt to lure industries to this section; and it is not by accident that Birmingham, most industrialistic of our cities, has by far the largest number of foreign-born residents.

The inevitable result is that we continue to value, as no city save Boston or San Francisco does value, tradition and family.   The power of wealth is rarely disregarded for long, even in Charleston, but each city has an aristocratic, though often poverty-striken, set of old gentlemen and ladies who refuse flatly to countenance certain people.   And men have been known, within the past ten years, to build great sporting clubs, primarily for the purpose of showing these dowager duchesses that, whatever the South may think, the world has moved forward, and does regard great wealth with proper awe. Yet in the slow but inevitable course of time these sturdy exponents of aristocracy also seem doomed; the entire course of life is set against them. They continue to exert, in some instances, a powerful influence; they add color and distinctiveness to a social life that is rapidly aping New York in flat monotony—even to the smart society columns in newspapers—but they are a remnant that soon will pass.

Included in this remnant is the one foreign element that has given something of tone and color to New Orleans and Charleston. In a sense, it is a mistake to think of the French in Charleston, or the French and Spanish in New Orleans, as foreign. They have been a part of these communities for always, relatively; they are quite unmistakably part of the grand tradition. Possibly for that reason these cities retain an element of light-heartedness that other cities lack. Somehow (perhaps through the influence of our Biblical defense of slavery) we came to adopt the American tradition of "work while you work, and play while you play." This adage and others like it have led the southerner to feel ashamed of leisureliness—the trait most often assigned to us by outsiders—and to feel that haste is a necessary part of life. The man of business in New Orleans must have a leisurely cup of coffee; in Nashville or Atlanta, his cousin will gulp a coca-cola. The noon meal has become lunch, and must be eaten hurriedly, often at drugstores.

This change in superficial matters has carried over into larger and graver affairs. On Sunday a man must attend church or go to some opposite extreme, such as playing golf or getting drunk. No longer can there be a middle ground that affords ease and pleasure. We must work or play; attend church or dissipate; but rarely, now, do we consider that conversation is an art, and drinking only a nectar that adds sparkle to casual talk. Yet even in this respect, the South, I believe, has gone less rapidly than the nation. We have tried valiantly to be swift, but we are not swift enough. The force of family ties does much to hold back this breakdown of leisurely living. Father and mother may go to church, while son and daughter play golf—but many families continue to regard the Sunday dinner as a delightful obligation when all the members must be present. This is a momentary check, I fear, and one rapidly disappearing, but one may be grateful even for delay.

For the cities have become swift and pushing; they have long since abandoned leisure as an ideal, and would have abandoned it in practice save for the incurable habits of an outmoded generation. These men have left an indefinable stamp; they have remained unregenerate. But one gets back, sooner or later, to the reason for this attitude: that they are not by nature cosmopolitan creatures; they were part of an agrarian tradition, of a tradition that valued local sections and local affairs, and they have given to each southern city a remarkable individuality.

It is natural and inevitable that each city in the country should have local traits and idiosyncrasies. Less natural is the fact that the city should be governed and given character by the country immediately surrounding it. This seems to me the one important factor that differentiates southern cities. With the single exception of Birmingham, they belong to the general sectional environment, and could not be transposed without being uprooted. This statement would be equally true of any old-line city: of Boston or Philadelphia, or the semi-southern Indianapolis. But Akron or Chicago might easily be in Michigan, and Detroit in Ohio or Illinois. The industrial city is a unit within itself. But the southern community has not yet been industrialized, and it retains the coloring of the surrounding section.

IV

For many years, the growth of the city seemed the death-knell for the small town. Once a local craftsman made wagons for the surrounding farmers; a shoemaker made shoes; a miller ground the wheat. Gradually these and many additional industries became standardized, until the local craftsman has practically disappeared. In the same interval, the city began to supply its inhabitants with electric lights, running water, sewerage disposal, and similar conveniences that made the small town appear, in contrast, glaringly backward and unprogressive. Today the processes of standardization have, strangely, made the town as modern as the city, for even the smallest places can have moving pictures, electric lights, radios, and filling stations. Usually, in farming sections, a single blacksmith shop remains, but it is dwarfed into insignificance by garages that repair farm tractors as well as automobiles. No longer is the small-town boy or girl subject to taunts on account of "country" clothes or manners. The town is no longer isolated. But this lack of isolation has resulted to economic disadvantage; men and women find it too easy to drive to the nearest city to shop, while they neglect the local stores. Boys continue to go to larger communities, because there is little chance for work at home.

Economically, the village has suffered, because it is directly dependent on the farmer. But it has suffered less than the city, because the floating population and, to a large extent, the laborers completely dependent on their salary checks, do not exist among them. Wealth may exist with less frequency than in the city, but poverty also is rarer.

The traveler in the South has a distinct impression that

our cities are, in many respects, overgrown small towns, and this, as I have tried to show, is often a virtue rather than a defect. But the town has, in turn, aped the city, usually with disastrous results.

The ideal picture is one of wide and shady streets, with old houses in colonial style, of wood painted white, or of aged red brick with decorous white pillars and façade. Somehow the business district remains a little obscured, except in that city peculiar to the South, the county seat. In these towns the county courthouse, a rectangular two-storied red brick building, with a monument to the Confederate dead occupying a clear space in front, gives a dignity to the small stores that surround it on every side. Here, too, is a park with green trees and grass, and inviting white benches on which old men sit and chew tobacco and spin long yarns of delightful yesterdays.

Too often this picture is ideal rather than real. The courthouse yard is likely to be littered with trash, the store windows to be dirty, and the goods displayed to be shoddy and ill-arranged. Too often the buildings in the business district are flat and tasteless, with a fourth of them derelict and deserted: the toll taken by the concrete roads that lead with increasing swiftness and directness to better-stocked places in some neighboring city. And the townspeople tend, like the city folk, to huddle together on fifty-foot lots, in small white bungalows, or in garish little stucco and ornamental brick dwellings. By an adaptation of the classic style, architecture in the old South evolved a large house of great dignity and beauty, but so far the small one-story or story-and-a-half dwelling has, it would seem, defied successfully all efforts to give it charm and individuality. Yet most of these houses are screened by vines, and they present, except in winter, a not unattractive front.

Perhaps the most notable physical characteristic that differentiates these southern towns from those of any other section is the presence of the Negro. Each town has its Negro section, usually given such expressive names as "Black Bottom" or "Nigger Hill." These titles might imply that the Negro is badly treated, but this most certainly is far from true. He is segregated, socially, but in all other respects he is a normal and, generally, a happy part of the community, with his own school and churches. For the small-town Negro, also, is not philosophical, and he remains unworried over subtle distinctions of race equality or of right and wrong. Enough for him that he is treated as a human being, with a consideration and courtesy that is rarely bestowed, in larger centers, upon the poorer class of immigrants.

There is another type of southern town, which has exact counterparts in many other sections of the country. Although relatively few in number, these purely industrial small towns of the South have received far more attention than any other type. Little of good can be said for our Gastonias and Scottsboros and Old Hickorys, where men exist rather than live, where row after row of drab and practically uniform houses stretch into a monstrous eyesore, where even existence depends upon the whistle of the factory, and where, until recently, men labored for ten or twelve hours a day for meager wages, and returned home each night too exhausted to value the few moments of leisure allowed them. Under a new régime such towns may soon disappear; at present, they exist, and cannot, unfortunately, be forgotten.

The manner of living in the small town is less attractive than in more urban communities, but the way of life is simpler and, in many ways, more pleasant. Here leisureliness and neighborliness are vital and real. No man is too busy to stop and chat, to loaf in the drugstore or courthouse yard. Such talk deals in the main with tangible facts, with weather or crops or business conditions or politics or sport. Gossip and discussion rarely aspire to the philosophical, though men at times are wiser than they intend to be. But at least the human relationship has never become mechanical.

In a novel that attacks the village, Sinclair Lewis describes a funeral where the corpse is taken to the grave in a wagon, attended only by a solitary mourner. The first part of that description might be true of a southern small town, and it need reflect no discredit on either family or community. But no family, however poor, would be thus neglected. Men and women would come to visit the sick, and to "sit up" with the dead body, until a decent burial had occurred. Sickness and death bring out the finest elements of small town people, for almost invariably they are kind and considerate.

The women have even greater leisure, and even greater preoccupation with small things. They are, in general, kindly to a fault, but they are concerned always with the affairs of other people. Gossip is ever among us, at the bridge table and the missionary society, and the person who strays in any manner from the conventional path is certain to furnish a topic of conversation—often condemnatory— to every inhabitant. Yet this gossip springs more often from curiosity than from malice. Recent novelists have tended to see too large the viciousness and meanness and lack of breadth of the small town, and too little its tolerant humanity. They have been impressed with the size of events, and have forgotten that the Fourth of July celebration, with its greased pig and amateur baseball game between two neighboring towns, is as important as the world series.

Unconsciously, our townspeople have made this distinction. Rarely are they troubled with great events. Life flows on quietly, yet not, for the most part, monotonously. The cares and concerns of little things, and above all of people, occupy the time of most of them. They have time to stand and stare, or to sit and chat. In a word, the life of the southern town is serene.

Part Two

X

Frances Wright at Nashoba
(1825-30)

FRANCES Wright early learned to juggle bright philosophical balls, tossing them into the air and catching them neatly, to the applause of even more skilled connoisseurs of the art. A protege of Jeremy Bentham, she talked on terms of equality with Francis Place, James Mill, George Grote, and John Austin. To her, Bentham was a modern Socrates, and the little group of philosophical radicals a nucleus that would reform the social, political and intellectual life of England. They talked almost nightly of government and utilitarianism, of the greatest happiness of the greatest number, of epicureanism as applied to modern life, of varied panaceas for economic ills—and in these theoretic discussions Frances Wright was not least among them.

This was strange company for a girl of twenty-five, but Frances Wright had flowered early, both mentally and physically. Born of orthodox Scottish parents in Dundee, in 1795, and reared under equally orthodox English relatives in London, she soon deserted religion for epicureanism. Conventional schooling and conventional pleasures were discarded at nineteen, for the purpose of writing a book on Epicurean philosophy, published in 1822 under the title, *A Few Days in Athens*.

For all her interest in the Greeks, when she came of age, Frances Wright voyaged, not to Athens, but to the United States. Philosophical ideals were of the mind, divorced from time and place; government, freedom, oppression, economics, poverty, were immediate, tangible. And Europe

was old, set in error. The west, ever the land of promise, beckoned—that land of changing institutions where
improvement might yet be made. It was a young land,
and much might be forgiven to youth.

Nor was Frances Wright disappointed, as were so many
Englishmen. From 1818 to 1821, with her sister Camilla
she traveled through the north and west. Frontier brusque-
ness, boisterous equality, crude manners were only outward
symbols of freedom; impassable roads, jolting stagecoaches,
and dirty, insectious hotels were trivial matters that could
be remedied soon. After the manner of all her countrymen,
from Captain John Smith to the most recent traveler, she
wrote a book on the subject: *Views of Society and Manners
in America*, (1821). What Dickens, Marryat, and Mrs.
Trollope attacked, she defended: the discomforts, the lack
of sophistication, indicated virility, as contrasted with European decadence. She was enthusiastic, uncritical: a de
Tocqueville might be conscious of tyrannical possibilities in
organized majorities and minorities; Miss Wright observed
only prosperity and democracy.

America, in turn, was kind to her. In New York she
made her debut as dramatist, with the production of *Altorf*
in 1819. This tragedy, with its theme of Swiss independence, was fairly popular and won favorable comment from
several critics. True, the prologue was doctored to titillate
American historical pride, but the drama was well above the
average play of that period. Although the blank verse is
at times straggly and the speeches lengthy and rhetorical,
the spirited action and theme of freedom were well suited to
the country's sentiments, and a published version met with
instantaneous success.

With the publication of *Views of Society and Manners
in America*, Frances Wright achieved recognition in Lon-

don. Not only Bentham and Place, but European radicals listened to her with interest. Her tall, rather masculine figure, her low, coarse voice commanded attention; her good sense held it. She was as radical as any of them, and perhaps as capable. More, the book won her the friendship of LaFayette, remembering America with more than faint nostalgia. She visited in his home, conversed with him by the hour, passed beyond him in passionate desire for freedom. Once he planned to adopt her, but his family objected, and the vague idea never materialized. As recompense, Frances and Camilla Wright were invited to accompany LaFayette on his official visit to the United States.

All her life Frances Wright lectured, wrote, and theorized on many subjects: philosophical speculation, economic and political reforms, woman's rights, free love, slavery, and education. Only once, for four brief years, did she desert the field of theory for the field of action. This abortive experiment was the Emancipating Labor Society at Nashoba, Tennessee.

On her first visit to this country, Miss Wright had avoided the south. She detested slavery so violently that she desired not even a glimpse of it. Now her attitude had changed, primarily through LaFayette. Many years before, he had attempted a gradual emancipation, a gradual education, of the slaves on his New Guinea plantation, an experiment soon ended by the outbreak of the French Revolution. Here was the germ of her plan:

She would establish, in the south, a colony to educate and to emancipate the slaves. But the work must be done gradually. Her proposed colony would be based on a system of coöperative labor, the slaves bought in whole families. Within five years, she figured, the labor of the slaves would pay for their original cost, including six per cent interest on the capital, and for their keep. In this period the older slaves could be taught a trade, taught at least to read, to figure, and to write; the children could be given a complete rudimentary education. Absolute and immediate abolition might be productive of great evil; this gradual emancipation, with careful teaching of the negroes, would benefit not only the slaves, but the white people. White immigrants would take the place of the negroes, who might be colonized in Haiti, Texas, or California, where they could work out a civilization of their own. Apparently it never occurred to Miss Wright that within a few years Texas and California would be integral parts of the United States, vital factors in the menacing issue of slavery.

Frances Wright sought advice from slave owners and abolitionists, visited the coöperative Rappite community at Harmonie, Indiana, and secured vast, though probably neither accurate nor definite, amounts of general information. Many men advised her: such diverse persons as Robert Owen, Benjamin Lundy, Chief Justice John Marshall, James Madison, and Thomas Jefferson. She even attempted to secure Jefferson's participation in the plan, but he declined, because of age.

The exact rules of the colony were to be purposely vague. Frances Wright planned for the colony to be the nucleus for complete abolition. She desired only a small colony, at the beginning; once proved successful, the experiment could be expanded easily. Lack of finances also compelled moderation: the cost of a settlement of one hundred slaves (the number planned) was estimated at $41,000. She had only $17,000 available.

Local tradition has it that Miss Wright and General La-Fayette, on the way from New Orleans, stopped at Memphis and together examined the site of the future home of the society. Like many traditions, this one is undoubtedly false. If General LaFayette had little to do with the location, Andrew Jackson had a great deal. In September, 1825, with an abolitionist named George Flower, Miss Wright came to Nashville in search of cotton lands in the upland cotton region of Tennessee. Jackson directed them to the newly acquired Indian territory around Memphis. Miss Wright purchased three hundred acres of Wolf River bottom lands in Shelby County, from William Lawrence and William A. Davis, friends and assignees of Andrew Jackson.

As the colony increased, additional lands were bought, until the estate contained 1,940 acres of land, thirteen miles from Memphis, on both sides of the Wolf River, and somewhat optimistically described by its owner as "two thousand acres of good and pleasant woodland, traversed by a clear and lovely stream." This was a poetic rather than accurate picture of the Wolf River and its malarial banks. Later, when the community failed to prosper, she described it more accurately as rolling and second-rate soil. The community was called *Nashoba*, the old Chickasaw name for wolf.

A few slaves were bought in Nashville, but friends had not been too generous with money. Miss Wright denied that LaFayette had contributed ten thousand dollars; the individuals had only their own funds to rely on. Both slaves and provisions were unusually high, and the total expense for the first year must not exceed eight thousand dollars. Only ten slaves could be purchased the first year. And one thousand dollars were needed for a small store; she had no desire to pay retail profits. A New York Quaker, Jeremiah Thompson, was requested to make the purchases

for her.   That worthy man made her a present of the first
goods, "in aid of thy good efforts."   Miss Wright had not
overlooked this possibility.

In February, 1826, the colony began to function.   Two
double cabins were completed; Frances and Camilla Wright,
George Flower and his family, took possession of one; five
male and three female slaves the other.   Soon the white
people were joined by James Richardson, a Scot who lived
in Memphis, and Richeson Whitby, recently a resident of
New Harmony.

That spring additional cabins were built, a five-acre or-
chard begun, and fifteen acres of corn and two of cotton
planted.   Clearing bottom lands, struggling with matted
underbrush and rotting stumps, is arduous work.   Frances
Wright, over-enthusiastic, toiled like a man, working with
the slaves from morning until night.   The result was a severe attack of malaria.   After a serious illness that refused
to go away entirely, she was forced to return to the healthier
climate of New Harmony.

Then came the slow, hot days of summer, when slaves
loafed on the job, and masters quarreled among themselves.
With the owner away, no single person was in control.
Somehow a wretched crop was harvested, but little profit
came from it.   Camilla Wright and Robert Jennings, an
educational theorist from New Harmony, labored to teach
both adults and children, with little success.

Miss Wright's continued absence led to a change in the
control of the society.   By a deed of trust, signed Dec. 17,
1826, Miss Wright changed the society from a personal
property to a trust, deeded to ten trustees, in addition to
herself: LaFayette, William McClure, Cadwallader Colden,
Richeson Whitby, Robert Jennings, Robert Owen, his son,
Robert Dale Owen, George Flower, James Richardson, and

Camilla Wright. Membership in the community could be secured by white people and free negroes after a six months' trial residence, on a vote of the resident trustees. The slaves were also deeded to the trustees, on condition that they maintain a school for negro children and that, when their labor should have paid to Nashoba a capital of $6,000, with six per cent interest from January 1, 1827, with enough additional to defray the expense of colonization, the slaves should be emancipated and placed outside the limits of the United States. Thus Nashoba was reorganized upon a co-operative, community basis, and each entrant must be considered individually, without regard to husband, wife or children over fourteen years of age.

Even these elaborate precautions did not satisfy George Flower. Remembering the queer visionaries of New Harmony, and interested in more immediate abolition, he soon withdrew.

The new ownership caused little change in the life of the community. The slaves continued to do the heavy labor, the cutting of trees and clearing of ground. They were put to constructing new houses for the additional slaves to be purchased in the spring. In her schoolroom Camilla Wright labored chiefly with children: she found the older slaves too shiftless and lazy, too incompetent mentally, to learn. And the school of industry prospered almost as little; accustomed always to having jobs given them, work carefully planned and supervised, the slaves refused to do work, even under the guise of schooling, on their own initiative.

In the spring of 1827 the New Harmony experiment was abandoned by Robert Owen. Frances Wright and Robert Dale Owen returned to Nashoba. Owen expected a miniature Utopia, "more cultivated and congenial associates than those among whom, for eighteen months past, I had been living." He found instead "second-rate land, and scarcely a hundred acres of it cleared; three or four squared log houses, and a few cabins for the slaves, the only buildings; slaves released from the fear of the lash, working indolently under the management of Whitby, whose education in an easy-going Shaker village had not at all fitted him for the post of plantation overseer." Here was neither cultured companionship nor philosophical leisure; it was only a wretchedly miserable community that had little need of him, or he of it.

And Miss Wright remained ill. Europe beckoned to them both, though Frances hoped to secure money and white recruits while she was gone. In May of 1827 they left Nashoba. Camilla Wright, Whitby, and Richardson were left to run Nashoba, with its complement of thirty-odd slaves.

James Richardson, probably from necessity as much as from choice, was forced to assume the leadership. Camilla and Whitby were honest, conscientious people, but easy-going, talkers rather than doers. Also, they were in love. James Richardson was accustomed to the south, understood negroes, and began to discipline the happy-go-lucky slaves rigidly. A strange combination of sensualist and materialistic philosopher, he wanted to discipline them mentally.

Thus began the era in Nashoba when "met the slaves" became a daily routine. A bewildering procedure it must have been for the ignorant negroes, forced one moment to listen to stern laws laid down for them to follow, and the next moment to listen to long discourses on the rights of free love, or to the metaphysical differences between slave and free man. One selection from the "Nashoba Book," kept by James Richardson, was sent to Benjamin Lundy for publication in *The Genius of Universal Emancipation*, (July 28, 1827). Probably no more provocative section exists in the entire book than this part, from which excerpts are given here:

Sunday Evening, May 20, 1827.

Camilla Wright and James Richardson, resident trustees. Met the slaves—Camilla Wright repeated to them how the work was to proceed in Mr. Whitby's absence. She also informed them that tomorrow the children, Delia, Lucy, Julia, and Alfred, will be taken altogether from under the management of the parents, and will be placed, until our school is organized, under the management of Mamselle Lolotte; that all communication between the parents and children shall, in future, be prevented, except such as may take place by permission, and in the presence of the manager of the children.

Saturday Evening, May 26, 1827.

Agreed, that the slaves shall not be allowed to receive money, clothing, food, or indeed anything whatever from any person resident at, or visiting this place, whether trustee, coadjutor, probationer, or stranger; and, that any article so received shall be returned to the giver in the presence of the slaves and trustees. If the giver be absent, the articles shall be destroyed by the receiver, in the presence of the trustees and the slaves.

Agreed, that the slaves shall not be permitted to eat elsewhere than at the public meals, excepting in cases of such sickness as may render confinement to their cabins necessary.

Sunday Evening, May 27, 1827.

Met the slaves—Camilla Wright informed them of the regulations agreed to yesterday.

Dilly having given utterance a day or two ago, to some grumbling at having so many mistresses, James Richardson stated to them, that it is very true they have many mistresses as well as masters, and that in all probability, they will soon have many more of both; as every free person who shall reside here, whether black, white or brown, will be, in some sort, their master or mistress; that this is just the difference between a free person and a slave; and that they can get rid of these masters and mistresses in no other way than by working out their freedom, when they will be transformed into masters and mistresses themselves, but that, in the meantime, they will gradually find out, that this multiplicity of superiors, so far from being a hardship, is of palpable advantage to them, in preventing them from being at the mercy of the temper of any one individual, and in rendering the concurrence of at least a majority of the resident trustees, an indispensable preliminary to the infliction of even the slightest possible punishment, for the greatest possible offense.

Friday, June 1, 1827.

Met the slaves at dinner time—Isabel had laid a complaint against Redrick, for coming during the night of Wednesday to her bedroom, uninvited, and endeavoring, without her consent, to take liberties with her person. Our views of the sexual relation had been repeatedly given to the slaves; Camilla Wright again stated it, and informed the slaves that, as the charge of Redrick, which he did not deny, was a gross infringement of that view, a repetition of such conduct, by him or by any other of the men, ought in her opinion to be punished by flogging. She repeated that we consider the proper basis of the sexual intercourse to be the unconstrained and unrestrained choice of *both* parties. Nelly having requested a lock for the door of the room in which she and Isabel sleep, with the view of preventing the future uninvited entrance of any man, the lock was refused, as being, in its proposed use, inconsistent with the doctrines so explained; a doctrine which we are determined to enforce, and which will give to every woman a much greater security than any lock can possibly do.

Sunday Evening, June 10, 1827.

Met the slaves—Stated to them that, as some of them have on two occasions broken the swing by using it in a riotous manner, they shall no longer be permitted to use it at all—we added, that they cannot be allowed to partake with us of any such amusement, until their habits shall become more refined than at present.

Wednesday, June 13, 1827.

Willis having reported that Henry declined coultering today, on the plea of pain in his knee joint, to which he is subject—we met the slaves at breakfast time, and told them that, though we did not doubt that Henry's knee gave him more or less pain, we did not have sufficient confidence in his veracity to trust his statement regarding the degree of ailment; that we would, therefore, take their votes respecting the capacity of Henry to follow the oxen today. From this vote we stated that we would exclude Willis, because he now acts as director of their work, and Maria, because she now cohabits with Henry. There were ten votes, five each way. We gave our opinion as the casting vote, in support of Henry's capacity to coulter (plough). He was therefore ordered to attend to it.

Sunday Evening, June 17, 1827.

Met the slaves—James Richardson informed them that, last night, Mamselle Josephine [quadroon daughter of Mamselle Lolotte] and he began to live together; and he took this occasion of repeating to them our views on color, and on the sexual relation.

Somehow the slaves failed to grasp these higher truths. The metaphysical security of unlocked doors, the added protection from numerous masters, eluded them. The germs of love and sex were proving troublesome, but the slaves were only bewildered by these large philosophical doctrines. Camilla herself proved incapable of following them, when talk became more than talk, and she and Whitby were married with all regularity and conventionality.

The publicity roused a hurricane. Free love and amalgamation of races were too much. Epithets like brothel became common; hot-headed southerners threatened fire and death. Only words came of it all. Safely married, Camilla Wright became more vigorous than ever in her denunciations of the marriage tie, declaring it a subtle and poisonous invention of the clergy. It was too much for the rank and file of Americans, but the theorists at Nashoba were overjoyed to return to the familiar battlefield of words, to neglect the stubborn and unfriendly soil.

One benefit resulted. Frances Wright, alarmed at so much unfavorable publicity, returned to the colony. On the voyage from England, however, she prepared a defense as inflammatory and violent as any previously issued. It was published without comment by the Memphis *Advocate and Western-District Intelligencer*, (Jan. 26,1828; signed at sea, Dec. 4, 1827), among others, under the title: "Explanatory Notes, respecting the Nature and Object of the institution at Nashoba, and of the principles upon which it is founded." She denied nothing. But these were her personal views; the trustees were not responsible for the principles that governed Nashoba. That government desired above all things complete freedom and happiness. In society they had little chance for either, under the tyranny of law. The United States offered political liberty, but that was less than half. Moral liberty could be found *nowhere*. No one could indulge in liberty of speech without incurring popular prejudice. Equality of intellect was never recognized, and an unequal division of labor doomed every person to a one-sided development. Yet "liberty without equality, what is it but a chimera?" She had sought such liberty, but had found it not. And Nashoba, at least, should attempt to prove that it could exist.

In the case of women, this tyranny was increased many times. The tyranny of matrimonial law, with its foundation in religious prejudice, hurt chiefly the most cultivated and talented women, who "shrink equally from the servitude of marriage and the opprobrium stamped upon unlegalized connections." Society must adopt a new attitude toward unmarried mothers.

These views were radical enough, but Miss Wright added a section in which she advocated the amalgamation of races. Emancipation could only be progressive, and with it would come amalgamation. Many southerners had dreamed of emancipation; some few had organized colonization societies or freed their slaves. So long as Miss Wright walked with care, they blessed her with words in lieu of money, but without forgetting that they were children playing on the edge of a volcano. Her defense succeeded only in alienating more the friends who had once supported her.

The *Notes* also announced several changes that were to be made in the government, as well as in the policy, of Nashoba. No more slaves would be bought, though planters who became members could bring in slaves, and free citizens of color were invited to become members, at a cost of two hundred dollars per year. This sum might be lessened to those capable of useful labor. Children would be taken in the school for one hundred dollars per year. All persons in sympathy with the colony were requested to send gifts, or to become members. The moral requisites for membership were few: an amiable and willing disposition, simple tastes, a high tone of moral feeling, and a liberal tone of thinking. Organized religion was to have no place in the colony, and religious doctrines would not be taught in the school. For religion would be substituted perfect liberty of speech and thought, and moral practice that had in view only human happiness.

With these high but impracticable doctrines, Miss Wright returned to Nashoba, early in 1828. She brought one notable recruit, Mrs. F. M. Trollope. However much Mrs. Trollope may have approved these theories, one glance at Nashoba was sufficient to convince her that more than theory was needed for happiness. Her picture of Nashoba, in *Domestic Manners of the Americans*, may be somewhat prejudiced, as she expected English comforts in this new land, but the description is undoubtedly authentic:

It must have been some feeling equally powerful [religious fanaticism] which enabled Miss Wright, accustomed to all the comfort and refinement of Europe, to imagine not only that she herself could exist in this wilderness, but that her European friends could enter there, and not feel dismayed at the savage aspect of the scene. Each building in the settlement consisted of two large rooms, furnished in the most simple manner; nor had they as yet collected round them any of those minor comforts which ordinary minds class among the necessaries of life. But in this our philosophical friend seemed to see no evil; nor was there any mixture of affectation in this indifference; it was a circumstance really and truly beneath her notice. Her whole heart and soul were occupied by the hope of raising the African to the level of European intellect; and even now, that I have seen this favourite fabric of her imagination fall to pieces beneath her feet, I cannot recall the self-devotion with which she gave herself to it without admiration.

The only white persons we found at Nashoba were my amiable friend, Mrs. W[hitby], the sister of Miss Wright, and her husband. I think they had between thirty and forty slaves, including children; but when I was there no school had been established.[1] Books and other materials for the great experiment had been collected, and one or two professors engaged, but nothing was yet organized. I found my friend, Mrs. W., in very bad health, which she confessed she attributed to the climate.

Probably any person accustomed to frontier life would have considered Nashoba fairly comfortable, and well equipped with the necessities of life. But it had made little progress,

----

[1] Apparently the conduct of the school was spasmodic. Robert Jennings, before his departure, and Camilla Wright, had given some instruction. Her bad health, mentioned above, may have caused its termination.

if any. Mrs. Trollope's description of the buildings and slaves would lead one to believe that few changes had been made since the first flush of enthusiasm. Disintegration came rapidly. James Richardson had gone before Miss Wright returned; Mrs. Trollope tarried only ten days; Robert Dale Owen only a few days longer. Richeson Whitby and his wife also left for New Harmony. After a spring alone at Nashoba, Frances Wright left the property and slaves in the charge of an overseer, and departed in June for New Harmony.

In that haven one could edit a newspaper in peace, could write of Utopian worlds without the constant reminder of one little Utopia's failure. For eighteen months the experiment received little attention, dragged to an end in poverty and misery. Memphians remembered her with some pity and affection; James A. Davis wrote of Nashoba in 1873, in his *History of the City of Memphis*, that it was one of the grandest schemes ever conceived by mortal man or woman. But somewhere Miss Wright had lost interest in the practical execution of her plan for gradual emancipation, and prepared to end the Nashoba experiment. In January, 1830, the remaining slaves were taken to Haiti, and placed under the protection of President Boyer. Robert Dale Owen, so long yet so casually connected with Nashoba, wrote of its end:

I have in my possession the manifest of the brig—appropriately enough it was the John Quincy Adams, of Boston—in which the little colony was conveyed to Hayti. It shows that by that act, thirteen adults and eighteen children—thirty-one souls in all— liberated from slavery, were transported to a land of freedom. I have also the letter of the president of Hayti (Boyer), dated June 15, 1829, in which, after eulogizing Miss Wright's philanthropic intentions, he offers to all persons of African blood whom she may bring to the island an assured asylum, adding that they will be placed as "cultivators" on land belonging to kind and trustworthy persons, where they will find homes, and receive what the law in such cases guarantees to all Haytien citizens, half the proceeds of their labor; all which he faithfully carried out.

Miss Wright herself accompanied these people and saw them satisfactorily settled. The experiment thus brought to a close cost her some sixteen thousand dollars, more than half her property.

The experiment had failed in every attempt that it had made. Frances Wright wrote that "for the first time she bowed her head in humility before the omnipotence of collective humanity." She died in 1852, before slavery ended in war. In the intervening years she would never again attempt to put into operation any of her radical visions. These visions might one day save a world, if others would only superintend their execution. Words were safer, less troublesome. For over twenty years, after Nashoba, she edited, wrote, and lectured, especially on feminism; married, and was unhappy in her marriage; received both adulation and scorn. But always she was content to point the way. More practical, pedestrian men must survey the route and smooth the road.

XI

Sut Lovingood

According to his own estimate, Sut Lovingood was a "nat'ral-born durn'd fool," and his mission in life was to raise "pertickler hell." At the beginning of *Sut Lovingood's Yarns*, George W. Harris describes his story-spinning East Tennessee mountaineer as "a queer looking, long legged, short bodied, small headed, white haired, hog eyed, funny sort of a genius"; he allows Sut to describe himself, more effectively: "I say, George, every critter what hes ever seed me, ef they has sence enuff tu hide frum a cummin kalamity, ur run frum a muskit, jis' knows five great facks in my case es well es they knows the road tu thar moufs. *Fustly*, that I haint got nara a soul, nuffin but a whisky proof gizzard, sorter like the wust half ove a ole par ove saddil bags. *Seconly*, that I'se too durn'd a fool tu cum even onder millertary lor. *Thudly*, that I hes the longes' par ove laigs ever hung tu eny cackus, 'sceptin only ove a grandaddy spider, an' kin beat *him* a usen ove em jis' es bad es a skeer'd dorg kin beat a crippled mud turkil. *Foufly*, that I can chamber more corkscrew, kill-devil whisky, and stay on aind, than enything 'sceptin only a broad bottum'd chun. *Fivety*, an' las'ly, kin git intu more durn'd misfortnit skeery scrapes, than enybody, an' then run outen them faster, by golly, nor enybody."

Sut was not, by nature, a political commentator. He was a Hallowe'en prankster who pulled his crude and often cruel practical jokes on every possible occasion, and who told of these exploits with a tremendous Rabelaisian humor, a fine regard for the effect of his story, and a callous disregard of the physical pain to his victims. Until 1861, Harris kept Sut close to home, in the Tennessee mountain region between Virginia and Georgia; not until Lincoln's inaugural journey did he allow Sut to roam into any other section.

The sketches on Lincoln, published in *Sut Lovingood Travels with Old Abe Lincoln*, follow closely the pattern evolved by Harris. They are oral stories, related by a man who can neither read nor write, and the style approximates speech. Harris frequently encloses a yarn within a slight framework, where, in contrast to Sut's crude and vivid speech, he talks with precise correctness. Here, Sut delivers a monologue, but he allows Mr. Lincoln a larger conversational part than he usually permits to other characters. Also, Sut talks more, and does less, than is customary. The wild prank of dressing Lincoln as a cross-barred man is in Sut's best manner, and the teller works up to this; but he depends more on anecdote and verbal wit than he did in the collected *Yarns*.

Sut lives in a fantastic world of his own creation. His world is at once fore-shortened, and highly magnified. By this treatment, the most ordinary social event becomes unique and peculiar: a dance leads, inevitably, to some trick which cripples half the dancers; a quilting leads Sut to make a horse run away, and kill the lady who gave the quilting; a sermon provides an opportunity for testing the effects of lizards placed in a preacher's pants leg. Fun is largely physical, and the greatest amount of fun is secured by causing a maximum amount of physical discomfiture to a victim —preferably dignified or conceited. Pain hardly exists, save as something humorous; it has no reality.

And conscience has no part in Sut's life: although he has made elaborate preparations to frighten a horse into running away, he says, "tarin down that lim' wer the beginin ove all the troubil, an' the hoss did hit hissef; my conshuns felt clar as a mountin spring." And Sut can answer, as to the cause of Mrs. Yardley's death: "Nuffin, only her heart stop't beatin 'bout losin a nine dimunt quilt. True, she got a skeer'd hoss tu run over her, but she'd a-got over that ef a quilt hadn't been mix'd up in the catastrophy." Harris deals with homely and localized events, but he has exaggerated his characters and incidents until they are far removed from a normal focus. Abraham Lincoln, in the sketches about his journey to the capital, is less a person than an animated clothes-horse, made to serve as the butt of Sut's jokes; he is consistent in the fictitious world, but the character has only the vaguest points of reference with the real person. To appreciate the art of George W. Harris requires a fairly complete and willing suspension of disbelief.

For Harris, on a small scale and within strait limits, was an artist. This is best revealed in his language. He followed the customary practice in misspelling words for comic effect, even when there is no point to the error; but his humor is not dependent on these mistakes. His superiority over his fellow-humorists can best be illustrated through his comparisons. They are apt, concrete, and homely; they spring immediately from the life of the mountaineer; they have poetic exactness combined with a far-fetched yet appropriate descriptiveness. Lincoln's legs go in "at each aidge sorter like the prongs goes intu a pitch fork"; "fools break out like measils"; and, from the *Yarns*, "yu might jis' es well say Woa tu a locomotum or suke cow tu a gal"; "sich a buzzim! Jis' think ove two snow balls with a strawberry stuck but-ainded intu bof of em."

Harris was a part of a wide-spread and popular group of writers, most of whom published anonymously, though a few became well known. These humorists produced a great body of literature which appeared mainly in newspapers and was widely re-printed; Mr. Franklin J. Meine

writes that "literally thousands of humorous frontier stories
and sketches went the round of the American press." A
few men gathered their sketches into books. Augustus
Baldwin Longstreet's *Georgia Scenes* (1835), the first and in
some respects the most notable, dealt humorously but realistically with the backwoods Georgia life. Longstreet's
example was followed by other able writers. William Tappan Thompson made of *Major Jones's Courtship* (1844) a
pleasant story of the bashful wooings of a good-hearted,
unsophisticated Georgia cracker. Johnson J. Hooper, in
the *Adventures of Simon Suggs* (1845), and Joseph G. Baldwin, in *Flush Times in Alabama and Mississippi* (1853),
describe an even rougher frontier life, and Hooper delineates
a shrewd and vulgar rascal. These books, because they
have a definite individuality, stand out from the rich welter
of early humorous writing.

None is more individual than the collected and uncollected tales of Sut Lovingood. Harris was unsurpassed at
the knack of telling a good yarn, and he permitted nothing
to get in the way of his story. He pointed no moral; he
did not attempt to present realistic or representative scenes
and characters; he was not squeamish in his language,
which was vividly racy, or in his attitude about sex. These
qualities have in the past been held to Harris's discredit,
and his work denounced as coarse. It may be, but it is
also lively and full of life, and it is superbly humorous.
As Mr. Meine remarks: "For vivid imagination, comic plot,
Rabelaisian touch, and sheer *fun*, the *Sut Lovingood Yarns*
surpass anything else in American humor."

George Washington Harris, Junior, was born in Alle-
gheny City, Pennsylvania, March 20, 1814. His father was
descended from a Sir George Harris, of Brentwood, near

London; his mother, Margaret Glover Bell Harris, had a son by a previous marriage who was working as apprentice in an arms factory in Pittsburgh when George was born. Soon after the war ended, Samuel Bell emigrated to Knoxville, Tennessee. By 1820, the Harris family had accompanied or followed him.

Knoxville had less than one thousand inhabitants. It was near the mountains, and on the navigable Tennessee River. Sam Bell opened a jewelry shop; early in life George Harris, whose total schooling did not exceed eighteen months, was apprenticed to him. Bell prospered and became locally prominent, later serving as mayor (1840–42, 1844–46). His apprentice presumably did well, and won some distinction for inventiveness: after the steamboat *Atlas* visited Knoxville in 1826, George constructed and demonstrated a miniature boat of his own. Before he reached his majority, he was captain of the *Knoxville*.

One incident from his river days has a particular relevance here. In 1838, Captain Harris was transporting the Cherokee Indians down the river, as one step in their removal west. General Winfield Scott was in command, and on one occasion, while on Harris's boat, he countermanded the Captain's order. Scott was six feet four, Harris only five feet six, but he delivered this ultimatum: "I am captain of this boat; my orders are going to be obeyed, and if you in any way attempt to interfere, my next order will be to place you on shore." No more orders were countermanded. Although the picture of "Old Fuss and Feathers," in the *Travels with Lincoln*, follows the traditional humorous account, Harris may well have taken a personal pleasure in drawing the long bow at the General's expense.

There is no definite record as to when or why Harris quit the river. He had married Mary Emeline Nance on

September 3, 1835, and to them six children were born. By 1840, he had become interested in politics, writing vigorous but ephemeral articles for the Knoxville *Argus* in favor of William Henry Harrison. In 1843 he opened a shop, and advertised that he possessed material, tools, and machinery for making "Jewelry and Silver Ware, Copperplate and Wood Engraving . . . Surgeons' and Dentists' Instruments . . . model Steamengines for Colleges" and similar items. Often he tinkered with mechanical things, making a churn turned with a handle, and inventing a railway switch that was widely used. Some of his work he described in the *Scientific American*.

In 1843, also, he helped to found the Young Men's Literary Society of Knoxville, and he began to contribute sporting letters to William T. Porter's *Spirit of the Times*. His first humorous sketch, over the name "Sugartail," appeared in 1845. It indicates the type of sketch which Harris was to write: he describes a mountain dance, at the home of a man who can "belt six shillins worth of corn-juice at still-house rates and travel—can out shute and out lie any feller from the Smoky mounting to Knoxville . . . can make more spinnin-wheels, kiss more spinners, thrash more wheat an more men than any one-eyed man I know on." Drinking, kissing, fighting, and practical jokes predominate, in this and later sketches, but not until 1854 does Sut Lovingood appear. After Porter's death, Harris contributed to other papers, notably the New York *Atlas* and the Nashville *Union and American*.

He gained fame as a raconteur. His friend Elbridge Gerry Eastman (successively editor of the *Argus* and the *Union*) told in print one of Harris's stories: of a catfish which got into a whisky jug and grew to fit the jug exactly. Another, which became famous, concerned a mountain wo-

man who ended her story, "I tell ye, Cap'n, this country
is fine on men and hosses, but it's Hell on women and cows."
He said that he knew men whose glances would addle eggs
and who could spit a blister, and he made free use of these
oral yarns in his written work. According to family tradition, Sut was based on a real mountaineer who carried the
chain when Harris surveyed the Ducktown copper mines
in Southeastern Tennessee.

Harris busied himself with many things, besides writing:
in 1844 he held some position with the postoffice department; he continued to work in metals; he built a glass
factory and was interested in an iron foundry; he contem-
plated editing a newspaper; and he served for over a year
(1857–58) as postmaster of Knoxville. For all his diversity
of occupations, he apparently prospered until the Civil War
disrupted his way of life.

Knoxville was strongly unionist (an East Tennessee convention met there in 1861 and petitioned for admission as
a separate state), and Samuel Bell wore an American flag
throughout the war; but Harris was a democrat and a secessionist. After Lincoln's inauguration, he wrote the sketches
describing how Sut manoeuvred Lincoln into Washington,
and, though good-humored, they reveal his feelings. So
he left Knoxville with his family and moved to Nashville;
then on to Chattanooga, where he worked in an armory;
after its capture, to Decatur, Alabama; and on to Trenton,
Georgia, where he acquired a partnership in a saw-mill and
where his wife, worn out by the hardships of war, died.

After the war, Harris drifted into railroading, and became
superintendent of the Wills Valley Road. In 1867 his one
book was published, and he began to contribute sketches to
Knoxville and Chattanooga newspapers. On October 19,
1869, he married Mrs. Jennie E. Pride, of Decatur. Un-

doubtedly, life had brightened for him, when, a month later, he went to Richmond to arrange for the publication of a second book. On the trip home, Harris evidently suffered a heart attack which prostrated him so completely that the train crew thought him drunk. At Knoxville, he was moved by friends to a hotel, where he rallied enough to recognize a brother-in-law and to murmur the word "poisoned" before he died, on December 11, 1869. No autopsy was performed, and it is possible that he was murdered; probably, he died of heart failure.

For all his varied and useful life, George W. Harris is remembered today because of Sut Lovingood. The "skeery," long-legged, whisky-drinking and yarn-spinning mountaineer is a slight but authentic creation, who is not likely to be forgotten as long as men like a salty character and a highly-seasoned humorous tale.

XII

Richard Malcolm Johnston

WHEN he came, somewhat reluctantly and well after he had passed the traditional three-score-and-ten years, to a modest summing up of his life, Richard Malcolm Johnston found that he remembered much of Middle Georgia in the years before The War. These memories stretched endlessly, but he was conscious that already they had under a thinly fictional guise formed the stuff from which some eighty stories and three novels had been spun. This old ground he traversed lightly; the new seemed flat and dull. As a result, the autobiography is brief.

The materials of his essential life are not scanty. For Johnston had known in his boyhood a small homogeneous world; as a young man he continued to revolve in and around that microcosm; and in later years he devoted himself to re-creating, through fiction, the old times and men of Middle Georgia. That he succeeded in his time is attested by the title loosely awarded to him by certain critics: "The Dean of Southern writers." If age counted, as well as achievement, the title remains as indication that men felt it well-earned; if the books which earned it seem less durable now, they had importance in their time and place.

In the autobiography, Johnston writes of men who figured but slightly in his stories. They were reserved for something better than a story-teller's casual handling: all his life, Johnston doubted the value of story-telling, and he omits much that a stricter artistic integrity would have felt was essential. Brief memoirs of Southern lawyers and statesmen from those early days when Johnston was himself a lawyer fill half the volume: men half-forgotten even in the towns where once their words crowded a courtroom were clear-cut in his memory. One authentic hero he had known, admiring not blindly but with a full perception of his defects, and this admiration for Alexander Stephens reflects credit on both men.

That these men were vital enough, and picturesque enough, to be remembered is plainly demonstrated in his pages. But forty years had gone since Johnston argued a case, or lived in the legal world which they illuminated for him. He had turned to teaching school and to writing books, and it was from his writing that recognition had come. But his mind retained little, it seems, of certain authentic writers of the same period, and of certain others who, whatever they lacked as artists, wanted nothing in picturesqueness and vitality. There is no word of Augustus Baldwin Longstreet, although Johnston was called an inheritor of the best traditions of Southern humor, and his first book of stories, published anonymously in 1864, was entitled *Georgia Sketches*. The parallel with *Georgia Scenes* is strong, in content as in title; so strong, in fact, that when taken with the ascription, "By an Old Man," they seemed to many persons to be indubitably Longstreet's.

And he was called, with justice, a local colorist. But of local color writers and writing there is nothing; of his own work in that field, a few pages. Not even Lanier, whom he knew well in Baltimore and with whom he sometimes played —for Johnston was an accomplished flutist—, is mentioned; and Thomas Holley Chivers, strangest and most appealing of Georgia poets, partially figures as the name of a fictional character in a novelette, in a way that may have significance. Mr. Thomas Chivers, as Johnston presents him, is a noted impromptu composer of whistling tunes and a capable farmer, with no relation to his famous living namesake.

Somewhere, possibly, Johnston had heard the poet's name; it seems inconceivable that he should be ignorant of it; but it seems, also, inconceivable that he would in the 1880's have so used that name unless it had sunk far into his sub-consciousness and ceased to have tangible meaning.

His autobiography, like his stories, is un-literary. Johnston was not. He taught in schools and in the University of Georgia; he read French and Spanish easily, translated educational articles from them, and wrote critical essays and text-books on English and Romance literature. There is a curious dualism in his published work, the dualism of an intelligently simple man. This dual quality, if one can so describe what amounts to the opposite pictures on one coin, seems at first glance strange in the work of an integrated person like Richard Malcolm Johnston, but it is easier of definition because more apparent in him than in complex and troubled characters.

It is possible for a man to set a reasonable estimate on his own worth, to hold to that estimate, yet be modest about himself and his accomplishments. In Johnston, the basis of that modesty was a quiet, unyielding pride. The roots of it were grounded in a consciousness of family which defied geographical change from Scotland to Pennsylvania to Maryland to Virginia to Georgia; in the feeling of being well-born, in an unquestioning sense of security and content-ment as a child. His father's people were Anglicans in religion, farmers always, and sometimes preachers, lawyers, and soldiers; on his mother's side, roughly the same history held good.

As a boy, Malcolm Johnston moved from Virginia to Hancock County, Georgia, in 1799; in a sparsely settled country, he embraced all the occupations common to his

226 SEGMENTS OF SOUTHERN THOUGHT

family. Massive in size, a natural leader, he prospered as
farmer, served as Judge of the County Court, and became
in his spare time a clergyman, after he abandoned the Episcopal Church for the Baptist. Before that, he was gay, a
lover of poker, fox-hunting, neighborhood dances; for his
religion Malcolm Johnston sacrificed cards, toddies, dances,
even Masonry. The new religion was bleakly stern, emotional, lacking in grace, but it was all-pervasive.

Richard, born in 1822, was too young for elation or grief
over this change. His mother, a woman of melancholy
temperament, approved. As it made the family more
closely a part of the community, his father's conversion
beyond question added to their prestige and sense of belonging. In a period when Georgia and the South generally was
turning from a transplanted and somewhat crude Cavalier-
Anglican tradition to the Baptist and Methodist versions
of frontier Puritanism, only the strong and independent
could hold out against this tidal sweep. Johnston drew
portraits of some of these in his stories: they were mainly old,
set in mind, and with influence waning as their voiced approval of cards and dancing, their habits of swearing and
drinking, or simply their stubborn opposition to common
opinion, made them seem loose and ribald and ungodly.

A man who whistled for the mere love of whistling and
of loosing his exuberant animal spirits could not regard
himself as worthy of "perfessin' " religion; but even the
notable and frequently noble persons who stayed outside
the fold lent their physical and moral support to the church.
Mr. Billy Downs, in "A Bachelor's Counselings," was typical; he was "as punctual at religious services as the very
deacons. Conscious of being a bachelor and a sinner, he
had never applied for membership, but he hoped, by the
use of other outward means, to make his case as mild as

possible at the final judgment, which naturally he hoped would be put off as long as possible." Johnston himself, at no slight financial sacrifice, left the Baptist Church; it is easy to attempt, in the light of his experience, to read in his works more approval of the independent-minded than is really there. He could say, truly, that he had written nothing which reflected on a religious faith: what he presents is acceptance, and that is probably what as a boy he felt.

The man could never accept, as the child could not, the prevailing system of education. At five, he went to an old field school, and his life for the next four years represented, at least in retrospect, a succession of incompetent, irascible teachers. They taught little and punished much; he records of one: "I think I must have gotten an average of at least a whipping a day, though I was less than seven years old." In his stories he describes picturesque punishments—the circus, in which children held hands and trotted round a teacher armed with a long switch, and horsing—but these were more sadistically brutal than appropriate to the offense. Fear ruled. The older boys might revolt and duck the master in a neighboring creek, or one might thrash him in fair fight, but the result was likely to be only a sterner and stronger man to run the school.

Harsh but just discipline he could pardon; severity as cloak for incompetence rankled, and remained vivid in his mind when he was old. In his first published story, "The Goose-pond School" (1857), he writes of one Israel Meadows, and of his ignorance and his delight in punishment. Over forty years later, he writes with passion in his autobiography about the man who was Israel Meadows. Such men made his most convincing villains: if he could not recollect them with tranquillity, he knew them so well that one accepts as real the characters he presents. In contrast,

Johnston sets a few young men, well-educated and honorable gentlemen, who minimize punishment, abolish espionage and tattling, and actually teach their students. These young men reading for the law are traced from men who had taught him, are in essence Johnston himself, living as he lived; yet he stays outside them, describing the man adequately without creating the character.

To talk of Johnston's boyhood days is to talk, also, of the most valid matter in his fiction. The purpose always before him was "to illustrate some phases of old-time rural life in middle Georgia." Evil men were there, along with good, but memory of most evil faded with time. The point is one of emphasis rather than lack of recognition. For dramatic purposes he introduced mean, grasping characters, shiftless men, drunkards, crooked lawyers, even a white widower who plans to make his comely negro housekeeper his mistress. Here, Johnston's solution is harshly melodramatic; a negro man kills his master and is acquitted of the murder. Evil was punished quickly and appropriately, with too much of poetic justice to be convincing. Only in his portraits of rascally teachers, more frequently New Englanders than native Georgians, does Johnston make the bad man come alive, as something more than the puppet of a plot.

Georgians were farmers and lawyers. Born on a plantation, Richard was intended to be the master of several hundred acres and of perhaps a score of slaves. The family was well-to-do, not rich. Social distinctions existed, but they were easily hurdled. Few men possessed great wealth; only the most shiftless, he writes over and over, were in absolute want: "there were almost none who could not, and who usually did not, make sufficient maintenance for themselves and their dependents out of a soil so fertile and a climate so salubrious." As he looked back upon it, that society seemed almost Utopian. The poor man had a feeling of freedom which led him to acknowledge readily a deserved superiority, and to rebuke and overthrow an undeserved arrogance. Lines of distinction were more closely marked in the towns, but here also the aristocracy was, Johnston thought, "of excellent type."

The Johnstons belonged. When the boys grew older, their father moved temporarily to Crawfordsville and then to Powelton, that his children might go to better schools. The older boy went to the University of Virginia, Richard to the newly-founded Mercer University (named for his father's friend, the Baptist preacher Jesse Mercer) as a member of the first graduating class, in 1841, of three students. A year of practical experience was sandwiched between school and college: a frail, dwarfish boy who knew little of farming, Richard was put to work in the fields the first four days of each week, and given freedom during the weekend only on condition that he spend his time out-of-doors. Either this discipline or belated growth worked well, for he soon passed the six-foot mark in height.

But his father's plan worked only in part. In theory, the life of a plantation-owner was the ideal way of life, and Johnston so described it in many stories. In actuality he found the labor irksome, and was relieved when the year passed.

Johnston has only kind but vague words to say about Mercer University; he is more explicit in his praise of Jesse Mercer, calling him "one of the wisest men the South has produced." He remembered the declamations, and some sense of self-reliance which he gained there, and he carried away as much interest, and better training, in the classics and in literature than he brought with him.

The death of one brother-in-law, the poor management of another, left the family in need of money. After graduation in 1841, Richard taught school, and in his spare time read law. Only four occupations were open to a gentleman: in the order roughly of their contemporary rating, they were farming, the law, preaching, and teaching. But preaching was not, at least for gentlemen, a gainful occupation: for his twenty years as preacher Malcolm Johnston received less than twenty-five dollars. And labor on a farm already well-manned and capably supervised could bring no additional return. Teaching was suspect as a permanent occupation but it made an excellent stop-gap. On that basis he entered into it; when he was prepared, two years later, to practice law, Richard abandoned teaching.

It is worth noting that business was not an avenue to distinction, or even a suitable occupation. The prejudice was negative rather than positive: planters frequently owned a part-interest in stores, and storekeepers who did well bought plantations and were readily accepted; they might be acceptable as sons-in-law and social equals before they owned land. Johnston records the prejudice and the easy way in which individuals could overcome it, just as he records the ease with which a "poor white" could become a famous lawyer and politician. An appropriate figure with which he describes the society is that of a wall made by "the natural fitness of things, along which is many an open gate for going in and coming out." In *The Widow Guthrie*, Seaborn Torrance has attained recognized leadership at the bar because of "the pleadingest mouth I ever heard" and great industry mixed with adroitness, although he came from a poor family; Duncan Guthrie is rapidly sinking, for all his wealth and position, to his natural level of legal mediocrity.

In the fifteen years before 1857, Richard Malcolm Johnston alternated between the place of teacher, which he liked, and that of lawyer, which he liked in part. After the first few days, when disciplinary problems perplexed him until he won over the recalcitrant pupils, a school-room seemed an ideal place, save for one fault: it led no-where. The court-room held endless promises, and he listened long to them. But the scholarly lawyer was at a disadvantage. The laurels went to the orator, the pleader, the masterful handler of juries and of crowds. Although a diligent student of law, and quickly recognized as masterly in preparing a case, Johnston lacked the yet more valuable knack of swaying men with his voice. It is clear that he was deficient in showmanship, that he disdained trickery, and, above all, that he did not intuitively and psychologically rise to an unexpected situation. Lawyers and listeners thought well of him and said that he would make an excellent Judge; but for that day this was, as Johnston knew, a qualified praise. He ran for office and was defeated; when he was offered a Judgeship in 1857, he declined it.

There were compensations. The lawyers were circuit-riders, traveling in light gigs from county-seat to county-seat, stopping at pleasant small-town hotels, and spinning constant and lengthy stories. They made delightful companions, and they were hospitably entertained by the towns-people. In the course of a season's work, Johnston saw every part of middle Georgia, every type of person, bad and good. This exact knowledge based on continued and necessarily close observation gives his work validity as social history, after certain qualifications are made. If the accuracy of his dialect was questioned, Johnston *knew* its correctness: he had used it in oral stories with audiences that would tolerate no errors. He knew that among women, "even of the humbler sort, dialect is less pronounced than among the men"; and that men who knew better used it deliberately, some eminent lawyers being so fond of it that "they preferred it often, not only when in sportive moods but when incensed by resentment." The author knew, what readers find hard to accept, that dialectical consistency exists only on paper and that even the unlettered exaggerate or minimize peculiarities of speech according to the occasion. ·

The story flourished. Tall tales, closely realistic sketches, expanded anecdotes, humorous and pathetic stories were in demand; the manner of telling was as important as the matter. Judge Longstreet had created something of a stir when he wrote down a few stories and in 1835 published them in a book, *Georgia Scenes;* but Longstreet was exceptional. Men who could hardly write their names were famed as story-tellers, and most men who knew anything of traditional literature enjoyed and told similar stories but thought them too commonplace, and possibly too vulgar, to be written. In an article, "Middle Georgia Rural Life" (*The Century*, March 1892), Johnston gives an excellent description of this pleasant method of passing time, and of its wide influence.

From first to last, uneasiness about the value of writing and publishing this type of work tempered his pride in accomplishment; in the Preface to his first collection, published anonymously, he writes: "These sketches . . . were written for the sake of my own entertainment, in the evenings when I had nothing to do." This might be read as a modest fore-stalling of criticism, until it is connected with one of his reasons for seeking, at the age of seventy-three, a government job: "I did not like the idea of continuing at story telling down to the very grave." Something of ra-

ionalization is here, to conceal from himself the undeniable
fact that he needed money which his writing no longer provided, but even taken as rationalization it is significant.
He himself believed the statement, for he doubted the ultimate value of such work: an old man who soon must meet
his God had better be out of it.

By 1857, he had written "The Goose-pond School." It
was published in *Porter's Spirit of the Times*, and widely
reprinted by Georgia newspapers. But in the same year
he was elected Professor of Belles-Lettres at the University
of Georgia, and he states that he wrote no more of these
sketches before the Civil War. Apparently he regarded as
more appropriate to his new position such essays as "The
Education of Youth," in the *Southern Cultivator* (1856),
and "Religious Intoleration" in *De Bow's Review* (1857).

These essays are good enough, without being excellent.
The statement on religion relates significantly to his life.
As a boy he accepted evangelical religion without questioning it. As an older man writing fiction and even autobiography, when he was removed in time and place, and had
removed himself from the controversy by joining the
Catholic Church, he could view the religious strife and
intoleration tranquilly. When he was in that strife, part
of the region and aware of straitening, crippling dogmas,
he was personally troubled. The earlier leadership of the
planters had given way to the driving leadership of professional preachers, sincere enough but ambitious for their
particular faith even when they were not ambitious for
themselves. The earlier acceptance of religion as faith
had gone, and with it tolerance, to be replaced by a concept
of religion as being almost solely the property of one de-
nomination. Sect was arrayed against sect. What had
begun as an individual's right to shape his own creed and

beliefs was rapidly hardening, by the 1850's, into a narrow dogmatic theology. State and section suffered, and continued to suffer as a result, but Johnston himself was rapidly moving away from the Baptist Church. His change in thought is revealed more concretely by his refusal of the presidency of Mercer University, shortly before he accepted the Professorship.

For a man of thirty-five just entering upon the teaching of literature, Johnston's qualifications are not impressive. Evidently his reputation was greater than the tangible products of his career as lawyer, teacher, and writer would reveal. "The Goose-pond School" has distinction in the field of writing, but Johnston was selected before its publication, and there is no proof that colleagues or students knew of his writing it. Though few of his stories surpass this initial attempt, he seems to have felt that such work reflected on the dignity of a Professor. During his three years in Athens, he abandoned creative writing to deal with formal literature and to write a pleasant and graceful, but unimportant, history of the English Classics.

University teaching was respectable, a career for a gentleman. The one phase of it which he actively hated was the requirement that teachers spy on students, and report them for lapses of conduct. His philosophy of education, always tenuous and sketchy, grew out of irritations with the system as he found it. Men in authority could not expect students to behave as gentlemen when they were not so treated. Johnston was convinced that only respect for individuals could produce men of intrinsic value. His espionage took the form of social calls, but even in that form the purpose of his calls troubled him. It violated the code of conduct by which men should live; essentially, it was dishonorable. The implications of this attitude or belief carry over, then, to a larger theory: the purpose of education is to train young men to be honorable, upright gentlemen, who respect others because they respect themselves. Mental discipline is important, but secondary; a great part of his energy went into teaching an appreciation of literature which would lead to a finer perception of life.

Not all persons can profit much from this system. The theory is aristocratic, and assumes the existence of a natural, fluid aristocracy which exists by virtue of character and intelligence. Education becomes a wide and open gate in the figurative wall that Johnston talked about; it becomes also a scale in which people are weighed. Learning becomes assimilation, not accomplishment or acquirement; it teaches one not *to do*, but *to be*. The man who holds and lives up to this theory, as Johnston did, makes an admirable teacher, and for this phase of his life and character there can be no quibbling: it is worthy of admiration at all times and in all places, wherever found.

Life in Athens he found pleasant, socially and professionally. In a small school he could know every student by name, and stop on his way from class to chat with little groups of boys; in a small town, he could raise chickens, work in his garden, and exchange frequent social visits with his friends. His wife played the piano, Johnston the flute, and music enlivened many quiet evenings. The surface of life was infinitely pleasant.

Not far below that surface, for every thoughtful Southerner in the years just preceding 1860, were uncertainty, stringent questionings, boiling fears and hopes. By temperament optimistic, Johnston recorded the bleak pessimism of Alexander Stephens in a journal, but he hoped for some reconciliation of sectional difficulties, and thought that war and secession could be avoided. Aware, through conversations with Stephens as well as through his own thinking, that more than slavery was basically being attacked, that a way of life was threatened, he held to the position of a mild Unionist, but an outspoken one. Certain Athenians—notably Howell and Thomas Cobb—were leaders in the movement for secession; people were nearly unanimous for it.

Feeling that even among a quick-tempered people he was excessively hot-headed, Johnston attempted always to put guards upon his tongue, without notable success: his anger in politics had almost led on occasion to duels which had been prevented by his friends; in social life, to a hot dispute with Aleck Stephens over a hand of whist that did not stop their games, but Johnston as a precaution never again played as his partner; in the schoolroom, to sharp reprimands which were followed, when he thought his words unjust, by open apologies before the entire class. Avoiding controversy when possible, he held to his convictions, and refused to join a civic demonstration in favor of secession, although warned that he would be the lone exception, and subject to insults. No trouble came, but he soon resigned from the dwindling University.

During the war, Johnston ran a private boarding school on his plantation in Hancock County. For the first time, he could try freely his theories of education: the students were treated as honorable gentlemen, and taught as though they wished to learn; they were given a large degree of freedom, allowed to play cards and have dances, and made to feel responsible for themselves. What Johnston desired was to give each student a disciplined, ordered mind, to inculcate a self-discipline which was largely prevented by the older method of external rules and punishment. Relatively few could acquire this, but true education will always be the possession of a limited minority. His training centered in individual values, and was meant to develop gentlemen rather than scholars or successful men. What he aimed at seems valid even now, when that conception of education has almost disappeared: only as it vanishes do we recognize the value of what has been lost.

The school prospered. It did not take all of Johnston's time; he served as Aide-de-camp to Governor Joe E. Brown, earning the title of Colonel which had been given to him some years earlier, and he wrote more sketches of middle Georgia. In 1864, his second book and first collection of stories was published in Augusta.

After the war, the plantation seemed remote, dangerous, almost worthless; the freed negroes troublesome and undependable. If his stories of negroes are mainly idyllic, his factual recollections were unpleasant. A boarding-school could be moved easily, and in 1867 the Johnstons moved to Baltimore. Forty boys moved with the school, and for six years, he notes, the undertaking "prospered as before." When he joined the Roman Catholic Church, the number of students dropped off: Protestant families hesitated to send boys to him, and Catholic families did not replace the loss. By 1883, he had ceased to be a teacher, and become a professional author.

This change had come about slowly, almost by accident. Henry Turnbull, editor of *The Southern Magazine*, reprinted his early stories and encouraged Johnston to write more; in 1871 he published nine of them as *Dukesborough Tales*, by Philemon Perch. The magazine could pay nothing, the book little. And other literary work brought but slight financial return: in collaboration with Dr. William Hand Browne, he expanded and revised his work on the English Classics into *A History of English Literature* (1872); with Browne's help, he wrote a biography of Alexander H.

Stephens (1878); he allowed the publication of some articles and commencement addresses. Only the life of Stephens has lasting value; it is a performance in full dress, with the usual defects of the authorized biography, and Johnston was too much a part of what he wrote about to form reliable judgments; but he knew Stephens as only a close personal companion can know a man, and he had kept letters, recorded conversations, and had started his preliminary work on the memoir as early as 1858. Although far from definitive, the biography is an indispensable source-book.

Not until 1879, when he was fifty-seven years old, did Johnston sell a story to a magazine. Sidney Lanier, who may have taught in his school and who planned a lecture-series with him, was largely responsible. It was Lanier who read the stories, sometimes aloud with the author, and suggested refinements and corrections, Lanier who persuaded him to submit "Mr. Neelus Peeler's Conditions" to *Scribner's Magazine*. In 1883, Henry M. Alden and the firm of Harper's brought out an enlarged *Dukesborough Tales*, on which the name Richard Malcolm Johnston appeared as author. His sketches and stories appeared frequently in magazines; his collections of them, and his novels, appeared with almost annual regularity.

He had drifted along, until the full tide of local color caught and swept his work into a belated popularity. Although he had continued to write in the frontier-humor pattern, Johnston belonged at heart with the local colorists. He spans the transition. Longstreet wanted to present typical figures, even using the argument that truth to life justified vulgarity and profanity. So did William Tappan Thompson, who wished "to present a few more interesting specimens of the genus Cracker." Johnston made use of several basic situations employed by Longstreet and Thompson; following in their steps, he may have borrowed from their material, but it is equally probable that he had heard similar oral stories many times, that he was re-telling the same incidents but drawing on other sources. These humorists presented localized, realistic portraits which were heightened, exaggerated, sometimes distorted, but their work was firmly bedded in what Henry Watterson has called "the local tone." Only G. W. Harris cared for boisterous fun and gargantuan practical foolery as an end in itself; he is farthest removed from Johnston's early position. Yet, if they were concerned with a locality, with strangely picturesque characters, and with dialectical peculiarities, their primary interest was in the humorous effect of a particular tale.

The distinction is less in the purpose than in the product. The local color school was gentler, more refined, and more intent on preserving a record of something fast disappearing from the earth than in catching something which seemed likely to remain alive. This change can be traced in the successive editions of *Dukesborough Tales*, or in a comparison of *Georgia Sketches* (1864) with his novel, *Old Mark Langston* (1883). As a crude but vigorous artistry waned, sentimentality triumphed. The characters are washed: the structure and logic of the novel almost require a meanly evil Doolana Lines, but the author remarked that she pleaded with him until he changed her into a sweet woman. This testimony to kindliness denies art; it robs much of his work of any ultimate reality. And it serves also to reveal his deficiencies as humorist and novelist. When writing of a fisherman who shoots a heavy gun-load of salt pork into the buttocks of a thieving neighbor, of a shiftless hunter who trades a well-loved watch-dog for twenty dollars and accepts as payment two hound pups, or of boys gradually nerving themselves to revolt against a master's petty tyrannies, Johnston seems to let the story work itself out naturally and without interference. Generally the author is omnipresent, not only in his frequent use of a personal narrator—usually a boy named Philemon Perch—but in his own character as commentator and guide. Destiny moved without logic at Johnston's will.

His method of writing is partially responsible: "In the start I usually had only one or two characters in mind, and none or little thought as to how the story would end." This method, or lack of it, could give the same air of spontaneous development which one finds in the concealed artfulness of a well-told oral tale, and some of these stories—"The Goose-pond School," "Mr. Bill Williams Takes the Responsibility," "Parting with Sailor," and a few others—have this character. But the method leads also to overworking certain devices which come to mind as pertinent because they have proved effective before. In Johnston's case this was particularly true, for he began to write regularly long after his mind was set, with the inevitable result that his characters and situations are repeated over and over.

Thus, in a few instances death is used effectively, not for tragedy but for pathos. Death, sudden and fateful, can be accepted as part of life until it becomes simply a convenient *deus ex machina* by which the author gets rid of one character in order to marry the survivor to a more worthy bachelor or widow. Although pathos abounds, the stories end happily and most often romantically. Johnston enjoyed writing love scenes, but he wrote badly, as a rule, about them. Probably they are true to life, in that they are stilted, flowery, and unnatural, as people often are under stress of emotion and embarrassment. As fiction, these

episodes try the patience of the reader more than his credulity. That is enough.

In general, the early stories (written before 1880) are
better than the later ones. The author gained something
in expertness; the stories become more refined and more
explicit. These are doubtful gains. The Longstreet-
Thompson tradition had in it coarseness but it had also
vigor and life. The Southerner writing for a Southern
audience, and writing as amateur, could leave many items
to the understanding of the reader; he could afford to work
implicitly. From the beginning, Johnston's purpose was
"to illustrate characters and scenes among the simple rural
folk of my native region." This was Longstreet's purpose
also, and Thompson's, as their prefaces plainly show. But
an audience which was as ignorant of that native region
as of some remote and savage land required that oddities
and types be pointed out to them. For this purpose, Johnston introduces into *Old Mark Langston* not only a Vermont
schoolmaster, who belongs there, historically, but his
Catholic sister. Outsiders comment on local scenery,
manners, customs, and Johnston works them hard through
conversations and letters home. It was a typical trick of
the local colorist, employed with monotonous regularity
because it was so easily made effective. The author frequently breaks the narrative to comment on typical or
contrasting qualities; some of his best characters, in the
guise of shrewd old philosophers, work more legitimately
toward the same end. Essentially, Johnston represents
the author as teacher, not the author as artist.

His material ran thin. In Johnston's hands, it was better
suited for stories than novels. But another reason for his
failure with sustained work is that plots were necessary,
and the lawyer-novelist turned back to improbable legal

cases: forged wills, double kidnappings, mistaken identity, and over-convenient deaths. The full-drawn characters are transcripts from life, sufficiently real without much existence as persons; the plots strain credulity to the breaking point. *Old Mark Langston*, which deals with Dukesborough, is weak enough, but does present a locale; *Widow Guthrie* and *Pearce Amerson's Will* are set in larger towns, and lose even the interest which accrues to implausible but accurate local color romances. These were products of his professional days, written when he could not afford to forget "the perspective of a check," and they reveal too clearly all his defects as a writer.

Products of that period, also, were his one book of travel and his three volumes of literary essays. *Two Gray Tourists* records the summer visit of Philemon Perch and Major Rawls to England and Northwestern Europe. Perch, of course, is Johnston; he tells conversationally, with much use of dialect and anecdote, of art galleries, castles, homes of authors, and scenery. In contrast is the ingenious and ingenuous Georgia farmer, who called the guillotine a *gulletin* because "it went through a fellow's gullet in a jiffy," but who has also a native shrewdness and wit. These innocents abroad have something of humor, and they give some freshness and sparkle to the description of an uneventful tour, but that is all that can be said in their favor.

The essays were originally lectures, most of them delivered at Catholic schools. They supplemented a meager income: one pleasant anecdote tells of Mark Twain lecturing with him one night, and refusing to take his share of the proceeds, as the Johnstons were hard pressed for money. Of these hundred-odd literary and social essays, thirty-two were collected. Only the uncollected "Middle Georgia Rural Life" adds to our knowledge; the other social studies

supplement but hardly strengthen the ideas better presented in his fiction. The literary essays survey thinly but
pleasantly the whole world of literature: ancient and Amer-
can philosophy, Irish lyric poetry, Goethe, Baronne de
Staël, Shakspere, George Eliot, and other unconnected subjects. Surprisingly, Johnston reveals a fairly complete
misunderstanding of Elizabethan drama; appropriate, in
the light of his own work, is his conclusion that all Thackeray's artistry does not compensate for his failure to encourage
"higher and braver thoughts." He thought of fiction,
first, as being valuable for instruction; only this end justified
its existence. Here is the other side of the coin. Essential
values in fiction were to Johnston non-essentials: he felt
compelled to make the story something other than a story
before he could be happy with it. Even so, fiction was
suspect. Essays worked directly; they were a suitable
occupation for a scholar and a gentleman. That part of
his work which means something, he could not believe in.

The last three years of his life were spent in preparing,
as a clerk in the Bureau of Education, garrulous yet valuable
reports on the Old Field Schools of Middle Georgia. Close
kin to his stories, they describe the games, customs, methods,
all the minutiae of school-life, with such loose exactness
that they are mines of social history unrefined. And in
those last years, before his death in 1898, he wrote his
autobiography, received an honorary degree from the
University of Georgia, and prepared a justification to be
published posthumously of his joining the Catholic Church.
As the autobiography amply proves, he had removed from
Georgia physically and in formal religion, but his mental
and emotional life were deeply rooted in the land he had
left.

Richard Malcolm Johnston's work divides neatly into two

classes. He set more value upon the scholarly than the creative because he had no doubts about the worthiness of doing that kind, but the text-books, essays, and lectures, though they had an immediate value in their own day, were of transitory rather than enduring worth, and they have sunk into the limbo which holds so much replaceable work. Even the biography of Stephens survives as a contemporary source, not as literature. And with these sunken craft on which he set much store have gone also most of the ones he could never regard without troubled scruples, and it would be foolish to attempt to revive them. His novels and the majority of his stories have some value as a part of our social and critical history: they reveal the manner in which local colorists were the heritors of the earlier humorists, and they describe one part of a life well worth living. They serve as texts, and there is irony in the fact that it is this portion of his work which has the greatest historical and scholarly value. A few stories—certainly less than a dozen—may continue in their own right, barely discernible above a choppy surface which even now threatens to submerge them. They deserve to remain. If they are tales and sketches rather than stories, if they have the natural growth of expanded oral incidents with small aid from art, if they give one part of life instead of a whole, these stories re-create within their slight translated world a few humorous, pathetic, simple, vital characters, a little town in middle Georgia, and a culture which grew out of a way of living.

XIII

Mark Twain as Southerner

THERE is abundant justification for a new life of Mark Twain. But Stephen Leacock's *Mark Twain*[1] is not a full-length protrait based upon all the available information; it is only a rough thumb-nail sketch, that could have been written as well ten years ago as today. Mr. Leacock has relied almost entirely upon the compendious but uncritical biography by Albert Bigelow Paine, and the interesting but highly imaginative "psychograph" by Van Wyck Brooks, *The Ordeal of Mark Twain*. He has, apparently, not even consulted any of the recent research in the background of American frontier life, or of American humor; research that should change greatly our present conception of Mark Twain as a thwarted artist. It may be, for lack of time, that Mr. Leacock could not have consulted Bernard De Voto's excellent study, *Mark Twain's America*, but he could easily have familiarized himself with the many earlier studies that De Voto used so intensively.

The results secured from compounding Paine's personal biography and Brook's attempt at psychoanalysis are at times startling. Mr. Leacock presents Mark Twain according to the conventional present-day view, as a fine novelist and humorist who was, at the same time, a frustrated artist. The real man, Samuel Langhorne Clemens, appears but rarely, and that man might have said momentous things to a world sadly in need of them, had he not been stifled by an American Victorianism that was far more deadly than the original. The man was swallowed up in the Legendary

[1] *Mark Twain* by Stephen Leacock. New York: D. Appleton. 1933.

245

Mark Twain, who spoke always in character and who could not escape the deadly label of "humorist" when he most desired to be serious. Mr. Leacock notes, pointedly, that he wrote only of the West, or of Europe as seen through western eyes; not once did he write of the abuses of his own day or of the New England in which he lived. Yet, though "Mark Twain's nearest and dearest thoughts were spoken only in a murmur, and the world laughed," Mr. Leacock concludes that this was, after all, for the best, since it leaves the priceless heritage of the legendary Mark undefiled and imperishable.

One could hardly ask for a more fundamental misconception either of Mark Twain or of his work. He was, essentially, a child of the Southern frontier. His best novels represent emotion recollected, if not in tranquillity, at least in nostalgia. He was never at home in New England; the only civilization in which he could have lived normally had been destroyed by the Civil War. Yet Mark Twain had so little personal philosophy that he could see in that older civilization only a tyrannical and slave-holding oligarchy, which he could not value. It was not the artist, but the man, who was uprooted. The artist could reconstruct, as no other has ever done, a life that had gone forever; had this life continued, with Sam Clemens as an integral part of it, he might never have been aware that here was literary material, or that he had any reason for writing. Whatever artistic instinct he had was really free only when he wrote of days fondly remembered, but completely gone.

And he did not fail to satirize his own age. True, he did not write directly of New England, but his satires on old England, though circumspect in method, are satires on the nineteenth century as well as satires on the sixth or the twelfth centuries. Always his fundamental purpose was to

confront privilege with humanity, and the basic outlines of
that injustice are timeless. Apparently he realized that
indirect satire may often permeate farther, and in the end be
more powerful, than any direct attack can ever be. So he
lashed out against tyranny in many ages; but the beast,
though it might have many heads, remained always one and
unchangeable. He attacked the tyranny of chivalry, of
slavery, and of religion; of any organized system except
industrialism, one is tempted to say, over the individual.
But he was content with the superficial realization that *here*
was tyranny; he lacked the disciplined mind and the personal
philosophy to examine the true defects of any system. For
that reason, his later tracts against religion, which he valued
so highly yet feared to publish, seem an old story many
times told before ever Mark told it.

Fortunately, the submerged philosopher in him remained
for the most part submerged. He had an intuitive gift
that no philosophy can equal: the gift of telling a story
through characters who live as individuals in their own right.

These individuals were not devoid of humor. To them,
as to Mark Twain in his formative years, humor was a part
of life. But it was something far different from that of the
cap-and-bells jester, or the smart wit of sophistication; it
gave savor and gusto to every-day affairs. This frontier
humor consisted only in part of tall tales. One element,
too little recognized, should not be overlooked: these infinite
exaggerations were founded, almost always, upon a literal
reality, though little of truth would linger in the final
legend. Mark Twain made of the tall tale a work of art,
but he was master, also, of this literal humor: *Innocents
Abroad* contains little else. He saw things exactly as they
were, upon a flat surface; the rounded and figurative values
that tradition or belief might give to objects had no value

in his eyes. He had lived too long among a people who made traditions ever to understand persons who live by them. The realities on which he embroidered grotesque legends were to him realities, and nothing more.

This attitude, I believe, rather than any frustration in a born artist, explains the personal discontent of Mark Twain in his later life. But there were contributing factors. He needed deep friendships, and he received adulation; he valued the individual, and the nation made of him a type. Sympathy, in time of trouble, may be valuable, but it can never replace understanding. And Mark Twain had cut himself away from the life which he understood, from the people who might have understood him.

His humor was little solace, for he could share it only with the world, and not with old cronies. And he lacked a personal philosophy that might have shielded him in loneliness: always, Clemens the man, and Twain the writer, veered with lightning suddenness from buoyant optimism to darkest pessimism, from complete confidence to deepest distrust of himself and of all that concerned him, from heady schemes to save the world to a judgment that men were "the damned human race." He hated every system that involved tyranny, from monarchy to slavery; yet, crowning irony, he was completely ensnared by the subtler slavery of industrialism. With easy optimism, he would save a world, one moment, through prosperity, through education, though mental healing, through almost anything; he would damn a race, next day, past all salvation.

But if Mark Twain could not integrate himself to a new life, he could remember, magnificently, an older one. The indirect satires and the direct, vicious attacks seem well on the way to oblivion, but Huck Finn and Tom Sawyer and the days on the Mississippi give evidence of being vital for

many generations yet to come.   Samuel Clemens might not
understand the world, or be able to change it; Mark Twain
understood one small portion of it, and that intuitive knowledge has far more value than ratiocination can ever have.
When he attempted to widen that horizon, he lost everything; within his narrow limits he was, first personally and
later artistically, supreme.

XIV

Sawney Webb: Tennessee's Schoolmaster

W HEN a fifth son was born to Alexander Smith and Cornelia Adeline Stanford Webb, on November 11, 1842, the parents were yet undecided as to a suitable name. The father and close male relatives had previously been honored, after the family custom in the South; the name of the boy's maternal grandfather, Richard Stanford, congressman from North Carolina (1797–1816), had been bestowed on an older brother. Some name must be had, and the child was called *Sawney*; probably as a compliment to his father, for Sawney is a Scottish diminutive of Alexander, a name already given to the fourth son. Duly a few weeks later the baby was christened William Robert, as a matter of record; in fact, he was Sawney, and through the changing years he remained Sawney Webb.

When he began to teach, immediately after the Civil War, he became Old Sawney, and the name in turn became a legend. By the inflection of old, schoolboys indicated whether the term was used in affection or in irritation. By 1900 his appearance justified the prefix, but by that time man and legend, in the public mind, had become one. Eventually they were one, for legend only spread through the country the lengthened shadow of a personality. And that person did not merely represent an institution; he was the institution. With high appropriateness, Webb School had become known far and wide as "Old Sawney's."

The distinction was deserved. Graying men looked back with nostalgic pride to Old Sawney's as to something set apart, which incorporated within itself the old-fashioned virtues, tangible and intangible, that a hurried world was rapidly discarding. That in itself was enough. But discerning men knew also that Sawney Webb had helped greatly to renovate the system of education in the old Southwest, and that his work continued to have vitality and influence after he was dead. The man and the legend survive, along with the work that he did, and it may not be out of place in this era to recall the ideas and ideals of a man whose work refuses to crumble under the grinding pressure of changing customs and fickle generations.[1]

II

Sawney's early life was simple and pleasant—the first three years on a farm near Mount Tirzah in Person County, and after 1845 in the small town of Oaks, North Carolina, with congenial brothers and sisters for playmates and the wide freedom of a farm for playground. When Sawney was seven years old, his father died. As a youth, he realized only that some vital part was missing from life, and from this sense of loss came a later resolve that he would at all times be a father to the boys under him. By the time of his father's death he was in school, under a sixteen-year-old

[1] Relatively little has ever been published about William R. Webb. He is mentioned in state histories and histories of Southern education, but he has been, in general, undeservedly neglected. One article by Randolph Elliott, "Old Sawney's," appeared in the *Atlantic Monthly*, Aug., 1920. William Robert Webb, Jr., has prepared an article, as yet unpublished, entitled "My Father and His Ideals of Education." Mr. Webb of Bell Buckle, Tennessee, and now Principal of Webb School, has in typescript seven volumes of speeches delivered by his father to the students of Webb School, and manuscript copies of two speeches which Sawney Webb made at Peabody College, Jan. 29-30, 1923. He also possesses a large file of newspaper clippings and similar items of information that otherwise would be almost unobtainable.

sister who taught the equivalent of eight modern grades. The schoolhouse was a log cabin, with backless puncheon benches; the boys split wood for the stove, made the fires, and brought water to drink from a spring nearby; the girls swept the floors. But the teacher, in young Sawney's opinion, was perfect: "When she saw her pupils were tired, she could tell a beautiful story, or read a beautiful poem, and I never saw a little boy leave her school that did not have a love of good poetry and good English . . . though Uncle Remus had not been published, we knew all about Brer Rabbit and the Tar Baby."

It was ideal for a young boy, though perhaps better in reminiscence than in actuality. But the scope of teacher and of school was definitely limited, and his mother felt that a growing boy needed the supervision and the training that only men could give.

In 1856, when he was fourteen years old, Sawney entered the Bingham School in his home town of Oaks. It was an excellent preparatory school and, for that day, expensive. Mr. Bingham would accept no paper money, though in his neighborhood wild-cat banking flourished; on the first day he required seventy-five dollars in gold as payment of tuition for five months. Bingham's was old, even then, as American schools go. Robert Bingham had graduated from the University of North Carolina that year and had returned to aid his father with the school. Robert was young, strict, and scholarly, yet with a dynamic energy and a readiness to engage in boyish games that made him the idol of the students. He was admired by town people, and particularly by young girls; in that day the teacher who had his own Academy was considered a successful and admirable person, and one to be both imitated and envied.

Perhaps young Sawney was even more impressed with

bearded old W. J. Bingham. That gentleman taught Latin, and Sawney told his own "boys" later that "I have been there months at a time and not heard a single boy miss declining a word. I was a little kid, one of the smallest in the class, and I would watch the old man sitting back and smiling like he was eating peaches or Georgia watermelons. I never heard him stand and lecture boys. His theory was that the boy knew. When a boy ever missed declining a word, he thrashed him. He warmed him up, I tell you. He wasn't mad. He thrashed a boy, all the time looking nice and sweet like he was doing the nicest job he ever did in his life. . . . That's the only school I ever saw when thirty or forty boys, in a log cabin, knew their lessons every day— never missed."

For four years Sawney studied Greek, Latin, Mathematics, and English. No other courses were given; no others, men felt, were needed.

In the fall of 1860, Webb entered the University of North Carolina. He liked the school and the scholarly atmosphere of Chapel Hill, and he liked even more his Professor of Mathematics, Dr. Charles Phillips. The University seemed large, with 376 students, and it had a new dormitory for men, though most of its buildings, even then, were "hallowed with age." President Swain was economical: each student had to provide candles for his room and wood for his fire. Usually the students would take turns in this, but once two students could not agree as to whose turn came next. Somehow the word "liar" passed between them. A duel followed. One boy was killed. Sawney Webb had no direct connection with the affair of honor, then, as a custom, almost passé in the South; but it made a lasting impression. He would tell this story with approval on rare occasions to drive home points to his own students; more frequently he would refer to that "field of dishonor" when he talked of the sanctity of human life.

But the University, like the South, was troubled and unquiet. Men talked more often of the results of Lincoln's election than of Latin, religion, or love. Classwork went forward uncertainly; the present seemed too all-engrossing for either future or past to matter very much. Sawney tried to keep his mind free of these troublous doubts. His own people, and he with them, believed in the Union.

When the holidays were past, he found that a few students from Georgia and South Carolina had not returned. Rapidly the states seceded, until on February 4 a congress of delegates met at Montgomery, Alabama, and elected Jefferson Davis president of the newly organized Confederate States of America. The students, the entire South, were on fire with excitement. Each night, it seemed, he must say tense farewells with some new-found friend or acquaintance, departing to join his state's military forces. Yet he continued to hope; years later, he wrote of his thoughts in the spring of 1861: "I didn't believe it was justifiable. For my life, I can't see that, if Mr. Lincoln had met Mr. Davis as Davis requested and gone over their troubles with commissioners from both sides, they couldn't have come to a peaceful settlement. . . . I never had been a secessionist. I had read about them. All my neighbors and kinfolks were for the Union. But Mr. Lincoln said: 'I want 75,000 troops' in response to Mr. Davis's request for peace. 'Here, you—Tennessee, North Carolina, and Virginia—must furnish your part of the troops to subdue the South.' We were the South. All my college mates were hurried out to battle, and there was something wrong when the college boys met on the fields of Nashville and Chattanooga."

Sawney Webb hurried out, in company with his mates. A few days before Sumter was fired upon, late in April, he too said brief good-byes and departed to join the "Alamance Boys" in Company H of the 15th North Carolina Volunteers. Before the company departed for Virginia, Mr. Thomas Ruffin gave a barbecue—and made a vigorous speech. Sawney enjoyed most of the occasion, but of one feature he disapproved completely: liquor was consumed freely, to an extent that some of his friends must be carried or helped back to the camp. A few days later, when he was elected supply sergeant of the company, he remembered that dinner. It had crystallized in his mind an earlier conviction, that any alcoholic drink was, in its very nature, evil. Almost his first act was to refuse to supply liquor with meals. His comrades protested, but Sawney was adamant. Finally the officers effected a compromise by appointing another man to distribute liquors.

The Alamance Boys had expected to fight; they found instead that their chief occupation, for twelve long months, was to dig. Sawney once told his students, humorously, that he had wielded pick and spade all over Northern Virginia. Soon enough the time for fighting came. For seven days the battle continued. On the final day, at Malvern Hill, on July 1, 1862, the company was pushed into the front line. In the earlier battles they had suffered comparatively little, but Malvern Hill took a deadly toll: by nightfall, 70 per cent of the company had been killed or wounded. Sawney Webb had been shot three times, and one wound by a minnie-ball through the shoulder continued to trouble him intermittently all his life. Although he lacked four months of being twenty years of age, he was elected next day first lieutenant of his company. But he could not hold the office. For brief intervals he would return to active campaigning, that summer and fall, but his wounds refused to heal satisfactorily. He returned home to recuperate and to help with the lighter tasks of farming.

In the fall of 1863 he reëntered the University of North Carolina. Only sixty-three students remained, and of these almost half had seen service and were temporarily unfit for campaigning. Eleven men, nine too old to fight and two who had returned with ruined constitutions, made up the faculty. But the school had steadily refused to close. And at Chapel Hill there was Dr. Charles Phillips, "a university in himself"; and there was also a military unit that Lieutenant Webb could assist in military drill and tactics. For a few months he returned to his study of Latin and Greek and mathematics; one dreary night he took down and read Cicero's essay "On Friendship." Almost it seemed too much that men should be in preparation for battle, when such noble sentences *proved* the essential kinship of men. But reflection could aid him or any man very little at that time; the "weather-vane" in his shoulder, which throbbed heavily in damp weather, was constant reminder that he had spilled his blood on a hard-fought battlefield.

Soon, he knew, he must risk that chance again. Early in 1864 the South prepared for a last desperate thrust which *must* gain independence, and every man was needed. Even the "seed crop," as Jefferson Davis called the young men, must be thrown to the wind. Sawney could no longer march and dig and fight with the infantry, but at least he could fight, . . . and he rejoined the army in Virginia as adjutant of Company K, 2d North Carolina Cavalry. As one of Jeb Stuart's men, he took part in almost every notable battle during the Virginia and Petersburg campaigns, as

well as countless cavalry skirmishes, and at Namozine
Church he commanded the right wing of his regiment. It
was his last fight. Three days before Appomattox, Sawney
Webb was captured. When General Lee surrendered, he
was en route to prison in New York.

Temporarily these last prisoners were placed at Battery
Park. One day Sawney and a companion waded out into
the ocean, and to the dismay of the sentinel suddenly dived
around the end of the parapet which projected into the
water. They escaped safely, then separated. All day
young Webb wandered around the city. When curious men
or soldiers asked what he was doing in New York City, he
would reply calmly that he was an escaped Confederate
prisoner from the Battery. No man could believe such a
tale; he was derisively laughed at and unmolested.

Sightseeing palled on him. Peace, he knew, was near at
hand, and he would be put in irons if captured, and perhaps
imprisoned permanently. He decided to return to the
Battery. At the entrance were several fruit stands, and
behind one of these the sentry must march. As he passed
this point Sawney stepped over the line; when the sentry
returned, the uniformed Confederate asked permission to
buy some fruit. Indignantly the sentry pushed him back,
with a profane command to get to his quarters, since the
hour of freedom was past. The escaped prisoner returned
voluntarily to his bunk and his absence was unnoticed.

A few days later all the Confederates were offered their
freedom if they would take the oath of allegiance. When
Sawney refused, with most of his fellows, he was removed
to Hart's Island; but after the surrender of General Kirby-
Smith, in July of 1865, he was released. Sick in body and
in spirit, he returned to his mother's home at Oaks, North
Carolina.

The section to which he returned was sorely stricken. Four years of war, of enemy occupation, and of inflationary prices had ruined almost every family. Once Sawney had planned to be a lawyer; but now four years of his life had gone, and his younger brother John was ready for college. He felt old. A veteran of twenty-three must look after his younger brothers and sisters. Yet there was pitifully little that he could do. He could farm a little; but his neighbors were all doing that, since they possessed no money to spend on food. His old teacher, now Colonel Robert Bingham, could provide a small amount of teaching for him to do; but the Binghams were themselves all teachers, and the school, though it had many prospective students, made little money.

Dr. Charles Phillips remembered the boy who had studied at irregular intervals under him, between campaigns, and who had once seemed so promising. In the summer of 1866 he helped Sawney to secure a position as teacher in the Horner School at Oxford, North Carolina; and he insisted that the young man complete his college work. Chiefly through Phillips' insistence, the University of North Carolina had made arrangements for its students, who had served as Confederate soldiers and who could not possibly return to do the necessary residence work, to complete the course by a liberal system of correspondence work and special examinations. In 1867 Webb received the degree of Bachelor of Arts; in the following year that of Master of Arts, although he was never after the war officially a student in residence at the University.

Later, he said that he had been "shot into the schoolroom." It was his niche in life. For four years he taught Mathematics and Latin and Greek, to find amazingly that he enjoyed teaching and enjoyed working with boys. Already his character was fully developed. Horner's school was Episcopal and gave dances and card parties. As a strict Methodist, Webb did not believe in, or at least did not indulge in, such worldly amusements. As teacher, however, it was proper and right for him to be present. He attended all these entertainments without participating in them, yet without making the boys feel that he was priggish, or the local Methodist minister feel that he was less devout.

But teaching in another man's school was not entirely satisfactory. And local conditions were even less pleasing. He resigned in 1870 and set out for Tennessee, which under Governor Senter was the quietest and least troubled of the Southern States. "My reason for leaving North Carolina was the unsatisfactory political condition of the State. The carpetbaggers and native thieves, with the help of the Negroes, dominated and controlled the entire State of North Carolina. I had had four years of war and five years of reconstruction taken right out of the heart of my young life." He had figured out that the one thing for which Southern people would always spend money was education, and he was more than reconciled to life in the schoolroom.

It seemed at first that Tennessee had no need for him. Teachers of a sort were plentiful and the cities and larger towns were invariably well supplied, in most cases with genteel but impoverished ladies, or with ex-soldiers broken in body and glad of any chance to make a respectable living.

Finally he located a school in the village of Culleoka, in Middle Tennessee, where the trustees, though fearful of his youthful appearance, were willing to give him a trial, after he had successfully passed an impromptu examination in mathematics. He could establish a private institution, Webb School, and they would support him with local students.

Webb had definite ideas of the type of school that he wanted: to prepare boys for college. When he announced this plan to his patrons, one man laughed derisively and remarked that "we expect to raise here only cornfield hands." It was an ambitious project, far more ambitous than it appears today. For education in the South was in chaos. In slave days the sons of rich men were privately tutored or went to schools on the seaboard, or in the East, and not rarely, in England. A few universities had been established west of the mountains; and some of these, like the University of Nashville, had attained a respectable size and had done good work. In general, these universities had succumbed during the war, and in most instances they had not been reopened by 1870. When Webb began, he could find "no institution of higher learning west of the mountains. Every college, so-called, took all ages from ten-year kids up. There were no public schools in the State to speak of; there were private schools, but as far as I could find out, there wasn't a single, solitary school that confined itself strictly to preparatory training, when I under-took the idea then. The schools that were in existence published a curriculum that would make the modern college curriculum look like thirty cents, for they had everything that anybody wanted, including navigation, ... but they had just a small faculty. On one occasion at a teachers' institute I talked in favor of a school strictly preparatory for college, and one old gentleman said he was very much interested in it, and would be glad to receive some of my students in his college. I said, 'My friend, where is your college?' 'Beech Grove.' 'How many members are there in your faculty?' And he answered me, 'Well, uh—one.' He had a college and he was the only member of its faculty."

Webb's beginning was modest enough. His schoolroom

was the basement of a church, damp and gloomy, with green moss growing on the dirt walls, so that after a rain "we swept it with a spade." The building had no sanitary conveniences; and it remained persistently cold, in spite of roaring fires. The library contained exactly fifty dollars worth of books, purchased by Webb. His students were as poorly equipped intellectually as his buildings were physically. The students were at first insubordinate and had to be quelled by corporal force; they were accustomed to reading the Latin without regard to the quantity of the vowels, and the teacher the year before had read the translation back to them.

It was slow, discouraging work, but the young teacher met, in addition, the disapproval of the parents. In opening the school, he announced that students could go in and out as they pleased, when not reciting, and might study out-of-doors if they preferred, so long as they kept up in their work and did not create too much confusion within the room. Soon the patrons met and demanded a stricter discipline, but Webb refused and offered to resign, saying that "before I would imprison innocent children, I would quit the profession of teaching; I would rather make my living plowing on a steep, rocky hillside with a blind mule." His resignation was not accepted, and he continued through the years his outdoor type of education.

Somehow the school progressed and secured additional pupils, largely through the efforts of Sawney's good Methodist friend, Bishop Payne.

The year 1873 was a big one for him. That April he married Emma Clary, once his younger sister's roommate at college. That year also his brother John, "the greatest scholar I have ever seen," Sawney often said, joined him in the school. Now he was more content with life. Few people anywhere, he had come to believe, think as teachers think; they were interested in the tangible matters of life, in the price of bullocks and lands and crops, in the weather, and in local personalities. Such conversation was pleasant enough in its way, but it was not sufficient and he had spent many lonely days in Culleoka, until he was driven for recreation to working the most difficult problems in mathematical journals. By such work he could occasionally be of impressive aid to his less tutored neighbors, and could gain a reputation for scholarship; but he could not be satisfied as a person. Now all that was changed. He felt himself a man of position and of family and he had a trusted brother to help him with his school.

But his school that fall threatened to disintegrate—1873 was a cholera year. Panic had seized the South until men would scarcely venture out-of-doors. In Nashville that fall Sawney and his young wife walked ten blocks without seeing a human being on the street; in Culleoka, with a population of two hundred, he saw eighteen people die within a month. He helped to nurse the sick and somehow he escaped the disease, but his school was postponed of necessity until January. Then his boarders returned in greater numbers than ever before, and the two brothers returned to work. The character of his school had changed; it was predominantly a boarding school, with only a sprinkling of local boys.

He had outgrown the church basement. A new schoolhouse costing about $1,500 was built on six acres of ground. To build, it was necessary to borrow money at 10 per cent. This led to one of the most dramatic incidents in his career: one day he owed a thousand dollars, and he had no money. "I was out in the garden hoeing beans when a Chinaman whom I was educating to be a missionary to his own people came in great excitement and said there was an Indian chief and a tribe of Indians at my gate. Chief McCurtin of the Choctaws was there with twenty-three boys. I feared the social effects of having such a large percentage of my students Indians, and so I made arrangements with Mr. McCurtin to take eight—enough to fill one boarding-house. He paid me $250 in greenbacks for each Indian, making two thousand dollars, the largest sum of money I had ever received at one time. So after dinner I called for my thousand-dollar note and handed over the greenbacks as if it were a matter of no moment." Often when he wanted to point the moral of courtesy to his students, he would tell this tale, and explain that McCurtin brought the boys to him because once in Louisville Sawney had gone out of his way to take a stranger to his destination.

It was his last financial hurdle. The years flowed peacefully by, bringing always more students, and bringing to Sawney personally, in the course of time, eight children. There was only one matter to vex him, but that tried him sorely: liquor. He had fought it in the army, but to no avail; now it threatened to undo all that he could do in the schoolroom. Merchants *would* sell beer and whisky to his students, try as he might to prevent it; and at last his patience gave way. He precipitated a local fight on the question, but lost; and that year of 1886 he moved his school to the little town of Bell Buckle, where local option prevailed.

He had only to move in the physical sense. For Webb School had become, even then, a *traditional* institution; and its students followed Old Sawney.

And he was no longer penniless. He had $12,000, enough to put up a fine building or two; certainly enough, in the Tennessee of 1886, to make a fine display. But Sawney

Webb was not a typical American, given to the doctrine
that a good "front" is the first essential of success. He
valued homelier and less obvious virtues; and he thought that
buildings were for use, that they were only *a part of the tool*
of a good institution. Far less valuable as display, but in
his estimation far more essential, were books. So he spent
$2,200 upon sturdy wooden buildings; he spent $400 for a
library building, but in it he put $8,000 worth of books
carefully and painstakingly selected by the two brothers.

There was never any question of the school's success.
The educational team of "Sawney and Johnny" continued
to thrive mightily. Although new teachers were added
from time to time, John Webb taught the seniors entirely,
and he gave life to languages often spoken of as dead.
Sawney Webb taught various classes, mostly mathematics,
but he was primarily an administrator. For forty years he
remained in the tiny village of Bell Buckle, teaching boys
of the 'teen age. In that period he produced no scholarly
books; except for a few relatively unimportant side-excursions into politics, he did nothing except to run a preparatory
school for boys. It seems a quiet, humdrum way of life
that would never present much opportunity for positive
achievement; yet Sawney Webb was known throughout the
land, and Webb School was father, or older brother, of
many scattered and lesser known institutions.

III

Personality contributed in large degree to Sawney's
prestige. He looked distinguished and picturesque, with his
short, stocky body and his heavy gray-bearded head. Each
Sunday afternoon, and on many mornings supposed to be
given to class work, he spoke to his boys. The speeches
were inspirational, exhortatory, often impromptu; but they

were alive. He would stand before them, with his narrow black string tie under his left ear, and the third buttonhole of his black coat attached to the second button, and talk on every subject known to man: the biographies of great men, the announcements of new scientific discoveries, school events, current happenings, and the Civil War. But above all he delved into his own memory for stories of great men and great days. Somehow he could catch up an audience of boys and hold it with wit, humor, and the dramatic flair of a born *raconteur;* and he made each story carry the principles of clean living and of great deeds. After boys had grown into men, they spread the stories of Sawney Webb, until his maxims and his personality were known and felt in regions far from Bell Buckle.

He made of teaching a drama in miniature. Not only were his speeches calculated to awaken interest and ambition in his students; but his method of teaching competitively, so that each student sought daily to lead the class, kept the scholastic air electric with excitement. Equally dramatic were his punishments, when the calm, sad-voiced Sawney would tell some youngster, "You have been on that problem two days; if you do not have it tomorrow, I shall have to whip you"; or the actual though infrequent whippings that did at times become necessary (for he had the greatest contempt for what he called the "moral suasion" theory of pedagogy); or best of all, when he could invent some punishment worthy of the *Mikado* to fit some unusual crime, as when he made one boy who had run off to go fishing try his luck for hours with rod and hook in a rain barrel. Legend tells of a "classical cow" which kicked violently when a small boy, stationed immediately behind it, missed a Latin verb or Greek noun, in the sessions held for refractory students after school was over; and not until years later did it become generally known that a canny master had taught the cow to kick when he milked with only one hand. Such stories grew and multiplied with the years, until the body of authentic and fictitious legend surrounding Sawney Webb was in truth something to conjure with. Yet what boy, or what group of men, on seeing and hearing him, could doubt that these stories were true?

With the skill of the born teacher, he used every device available to hold the attention of students. But these devices were only the trimmings, the outward apparel that attracted most attention because most obvious. Inevitably, there was a deeper, sounder reason for the success of Webb School, and for Webb's own popularity and influence.

He was a master of the essential theories and practices of education. That alone may sound easy and simple, but such mastery is given to few men. Sawney's school had one purpose, and only one: to give a boy the mental training and discipline which comes from a reasonable and fairly exact mastery of the humanistic subjects, specifically Greek, Latin, English, and mathematics. With such mastery must come also development of character, an evolution not merely of boy into man, but of boy into gentleman, in the old and best sense of that word; but even this development was by its very nature incidental. A boy could be encouraged to build and strengthen character, but no man could build it for him. The primary purpose of education was to infuse in boys a love for learning, to permeate their lives as well as their minds with the nobility and grandeur of classic literatures.

Perhaps some idea of his intention can be given from his conception of mathematics in a school. For him, it was neither an abstract science nor a business convenience; it was an art which through its severity of form approached nearest to perfect beauty. Yet small boys struggling with algebraic formulæ could not be expected to grasp this severe beauty; they must first learn the subject, by force and corporal punishment if necessary. This was a last resort; before that, the teacher must put all his skill and knowledge, all his dramatic individuality, to the effort of kindling young animal minds into realization that here was indeed some dim but attractive art that might some day be appreciated in its entirety. Under his hand the subject and the class were both alive.

That idea of knowledge he carried into other fields. To arouse intellectual interest and curiosity, to mold character, to infuse ambition—these were the purposes of his general talks. They were *applied* education. They gave an immediate, practical, and yet a philosophical point to the minute drudgery of day-to-day work. And he carried his precepts into practice: for example, his constant admonition "never do anything on the sly" (which later became famous as "the only *Don't* in his gospel of *Do*") was reinforced and made real by his early inauguration of the honor system.

But he never confused this need for intellectual curiosity with the requirements of the basic curriculum in his school, or in any school. Only the tried and certain courses had a place there. Often men would tell him that their sons must have stenography or geography or even telegraphy; often in the later years, when college entrance requirements had become standardized, college presidents and governing boards would write that he must teach chemistry or physics or history and must use an English grammar. Steadily he refused, for he believed that teachers commonly undertook too much. "A man spreads very thin when he spreads himself over the whole earth. . . . When I turn out students, they at least can pass the examinations in these subjects;

they know them." And it is on record that some Webb students offered for college entrance and passed the examinations in history solely on the basis of reading done in the school library. His students won honors at Harvard, Yale, Princeton, and Vanderbilt with such regularity that one eastern college president remarked, "The best students we get come from a small school in Tennessee known as 'Old Sawney's.'" Because his studies were definite and in a large way related to life, the student prospered; and the school became famous.

Undoubtedly Sawney Webb would have gained recognition in almost any place, at almost any time. But the misfortunes of the South contributed to his own fortunes as teacher of a private preparatory school. When he came to Tennessee he founded a school that was peculiarly his own and highly individualized, though it served as model for many a similar school throughout the South; the standardized requirements of a later period would have hampered, though they could hardly have destroyed, the value of man and teacher. With the growth of the public school system has come the inevitable decline of the private school; with the education of the millions has come a softer and more varied curriculum which trains boys for vocational work, for leadership (in the Y. M. C. A. sense of the word), and for a hundred other things. Organized extra-curricular activities which Sawney had rejected have generally become at least as important as the formal studies. But in these varied processes mental discipline has gone by the board; to a large extent the old idea of a cultured, humane gentleman as the finest product of education has gone with it. Stenography has replaced Greek, and manual training is reckoned more vital than Latin. That day Sawney Webb lived to see, but in his own school he would not permit such changes. A proud bulwark against superficial ideas of progress, Webb School remains classical and faithful to the noble conception of an older, less hurried day.

That explains another more subtle reason for his popularity. Sawney Webb was the apotheosis of a type long revered in the South, and now almost completely gone. He was the schoolmaster. Dotted over that section of the country were many other schoolmasters, less famous but no less respected locally; for almost every county had its own renowned academy or "college." These men too were individualists, and their methods of teaching seemed vicious and antiquated to the professional educators who were busily attempting to make teaching a science. They taught in many cases with a sternness that made the rod omnipresent, and that makes a softer generation shake its collective head; but at least they taught. In most cases such men knew their subjects, however little they might know methods; to them Latin and Greek and mathematics were vividly real, and students who could not be persuaded of that reality were quickly forced at least to learn the subjectmatter. Only the strong survived educationally; but the survivors possessed disciplined minds and sound, if often limited, knowledge. Each man set his own standards, but good teachers could and did draw students from the public schools; and the incompetents drifted into other kinds of business. In general, they were colorful men, and they shaped the thoughts and lives of many of their students. Of this type Sawney Webb was preëminent, but men in other sections could understand and admire him the more because he was only a greater personification of a wellbeloved local person.

IV

There are only a few additional facts to record. Webb's niche in life, as he himself said, was the schoolroom; and he stepped out of that niche rarely. But a man's business was also with life, and sometimes the progress of events seemed to call for more direct and immediate action than teaching permitted. On such occasions Sawney Webb became a political orator, stumping the State for principles that he believed to be just. When Tennessee seemed likely to repudiate its debts, he took an active part, advocating with all his power the payment of the debts in full. In 1886 he canvassed the State in favor of the prohibition amendment to the State Constitution; and in 1913 he became a member of the governing board of the Anti-Saloon League, a position he held until his death. Always he fought for temperance, to the point of deserting the Democratic party in order to support the dry and Republican Ben W. Hooper against Governor Malcolm R. Patterson.

Twice he received political honors. In 1896 he campaigned vigorously for sound money, at a time when William Jennings Bryan threatened to sweep an emotional nation off its feet; and he was a delegate to the old-school Democratic convention at Indianapolis which nominated Palmer and Buckner as presidential and vice-presidential candidates. Seventeen years later he was unexpectedly elected United States senator to fill the unexpired term of the late Robert Love Taylor. Webb had made no effort to secure the place, and his unanimous election came as a complete surprise, since John K. Shields had already been elected for the regular term, and Governor Hooper had previously appointed Newell Sanders to the place. When the Democratic Senate and House in joint convention ignored the Republican Governor and his appointee, Webb succeeded Senator Sanders, although he was formally elected to succeed Taylor.

As senator, he served for a month and a day; but he

enjoyed that brief interval of public life immensely. He introduced one bill, to prohibit desecration of the flag, and made one notable speech in favor of the Webb-Kenyon bill (named for Representative E. Y. Webb of North Carolina), which prohibited the shipment of liquor into dry states. He also made a eulogistic speech on his predecessor. But, his month of service over, he returned to Bell Buckle without regret, and with no ambition to hold other political offices.

These chores were appropriate interludes, hardly more important to him than his attendance of educational associations, and certainly no more important than thrice serving as member of the General Conference of the Methodist Episcopal Church, South. He valued such honors as they deserved to be valued, yet always mindful that they were incidental; and he was equally proud of the honorary LL.D. degrees which Erskine College conferred on him in 1919, and the University of North Carolina in 1922. It seemed to him that being a good schoolmaster implied also being a good citizen and a good churchman, but a man was naturally gratified when such qualities were recognized by other people.

His son, William Robert, Junior, joined him in the school in 1897, after his graduation from the University of North Carolina. Gradually Sawney gave up teaching, until he became in fact as well as in name the headmaster; after 1908 he had little to do with the routine conduct of the school. But he continued to make speeches to the students, and he was also in great demand as a speaker in other localities. For his many lectures on temperance he received, he once said, only a pocketknife as payment; but he had never learned to value money as the sole recompense for his services, and he spoke as readily and with as much en-

thusiasm in the smallest hamlet as in Nashville or Chattanooga. Many times his name was suggested for some
political office, but Sawney steadily refused every induce-
ment.

The years rolled peacefully on. Only the death of his
brother John brought great sadness to him. The children
were a constant source of comfort: all of them were pros-
pering moderately, as he would have wished, and several of
them in Tennessee and California were carrying on his
ideas of education. He was content with life. And Sawney
Webb had become a tradition in the State, and in less
degree throughout the South. He was the schoolmaster of
Tennessee and recognized as the State's unofficial "first
citizen."

Death ended that contentment on December 20, 1926,
after a brief illness. He was eight-four, a good Christian;
and he was not afraid to die. A few days before his death
he dictated to his son Will a final message to all "his boys,"
and that farewell expressed tersely and characteristically
his philosophy of life: "Give the boys my love, and tell
them to lead a large life. A large life is no piffle, but one
that makes the world better because you have lived. If
the world is better because of you, you are a wonderful
success. If it is worse because of you, you are a miserable
failure. When you come to the end, you'll find that the
only things that are worth while are character and the help
you have given to other people. The first step in the
development of character is loyalty and obedience to your
parents, your teachers, and your God. And don't forget—
never do anything that you have to hide."

XV

Walter Hines Page and
the South

A T THE turn of the century, southern men in abundance called Walter Hines Page traitor and yellow dog. He was betraying publicly the shame and ignominy of the South, its poverty and backwardness, and for this he was damned as a modern Judas. A publicist, a liberal in a land peopled by conservatives, he left his birthplace to preach back at it from the section that in no remote yesterday had despoiled it. So Southerners believed, and they excoriated him.

Then came the triumph of liberalism, in so many ways also the triumph of industrialism. Men came to believe that, if cleanliness could only prevail universally, Godliness would take care of itself. Here Godliness represents tradition, that part of the past which is worth being made a part of the present. Any change must necessarily be an improvement, any breaking down of traditionary idols must be progress. This idea permeated through the South more slowly than through other sections: indifference defies almost all weapons. Once it conquered, Walter Hines Page took his rightful place as last of the new Southern heroes, in the line that included Henry Grady, Ben Hill, and Sidney Lanier.

Today, when liberalism has collapsed, when the ideas, the conquests of Page and all the Pages seem empty mockery, when the world seeks vainly for new panaceas, this place seems less deserved. A new evaluation of Walter

Hines Page, and through him the movement which he represented, must be made.

In his way, he was as great a romanticist as his distant cousin, Thomas Nelson Page. Their careers paralleled in remarkable fashion. Almost the same age, they died almost at the same time, shortly after the end of the world war. Each was a distinguished literary man. Walter had served as Ambassador to Great Britain, Thomas as Ambassador to Italy. Here the superficial resemblance ceases, abruptly.

For Thomas Nelson Page was descended from a proud Virginia family, a gentleman and a cavalier. His own period seemed ignoble and squalid. With nostalgic yearning he turned in memory to "the sweetest, purest, and most beautiful civilization" that this country had ever known. In the end, the Before-the-War of his imagination assumed more reality to him than the tangible actualities of his own day. His life went in an effort to recapture and to interpret this lost civilization, and he succeeded in the grand manner. However false they may be, *Red Rock* and *In Ole Virginia* recall much of that glamour and charm, that romantic aristocracy, which we associate with the old South.

If the novelist looked to some yesterday that was gone, Walter Hines Page looked just as yearningly to some tomorrow, working and planning for a day he felt must dawn. Past glories of Virginia extended but remotely to North Carolina. What small glory reached the state did not include that branch of the Page family. They were no grand gentlemen, living in the grand manner. Allison Francis Page was a prohibitionist before prohibition became of national importance, a sturdy Old Testament prophet in a land that honored the gentleman, an owner of a few slaves who abhorred the institution of slavery. A strict Methodist, he forbade card-playing, dancing, even the theatre. In addition, he was a Unionist during the Civil War.

The son suffered from this in school. Born in 1855, he received the sketchy training common after the war. At twelve he was transferred to a private academy, and he writes: "The son of a Confederate general, if he were at all a decent fellow, had of course a higher rank at the Bingham School than the son of a Colonel. There was some difficulty in deciding the exact rank of a judge or a governor, as a father; but the son of a preacher had a chance of a good social rating, especially of an Episcopal clergyman. A Presbyterian preacher came next in rank. I at first was at a social disadvantage. My father was a Methodist—that was bad enough; but he had had no military rank at all. If it had become known among the boys that he had been a 'Union man'—I used to shudder at the suspicion in which I should be held. And the fact that my father had held no military title did at last become known."

Such a school would hardly endear tradition to one whose family was beyond even its outermost circle. His experience at Bingham, as much as any subsequent examination of facts and of conditions, determined his attitude toward the old South.

Strangely enough, this man who was to live so much for the future began his career by delving deep into the past. After a distinguished undergraduate career at Trinity and Randolph-Macon, where he specialized in Greek, he received one of the first fellowships given by Johns Hopkins. For two years he studied Greek under Basil Gildersleeve, but that great teacher talked too much of Southern needs: the man who taught him scholarship also taught him to be dissatisfied with it as a life work. Though he wrote to a young lady, "learn to look on me as a Greek drudge, pounding into boys or men a faint hint of the beauty of old Greekdom," he had not the taste for academic life. A colleague justly decided that "Page was most interested in that one of the main tenses which we call the present."

But teaching, once begun, is difficult to leave. A degree has pecuniary value only in the academic market. The summer of 1878 he taught in the University of North Carolina, and might have taught Greek a lifetime, had he been offered a position. No offer came. For want of better, Page taught English in the Louisville Male High School the following year.

It savored too much of the cloister. Life, and journalism, beckoned in the shape of a small Louisville magazine that imitated the *Nation*. But youthful enthusiasm, untutored talent were not enough, and the *Age* barely survived the year.

During this period he formulated the policy that he was to pursue until death. One tangible result was an article, published in the *Atlantic Monthly* in May, 1881, called "Study of An Old Southern Borough." He portrayed a sleepy North Carolina town inhabited by Southern Gentlemen, living in the past, unconscious of the present. They read Horace, Vergil, Addison; above all, they read Sir Walter Scott, and patterned their conduct on his bookish notions of chivalry. In contrast to these idlers Page pictured the new order that had arisen: young men who advocated a burial of dead issues, a united country. These young men envisioned a South that would realize to the full its industrial and agricultural possibilities; as a first step in that direction, they desired a free, modern educational system.

Though the essay was written when he was twenty-four,

it expresses completely and accurately the man's ideas
thirty years later. He belonged to a hopeful generation
that believed a millennium close at hand. All wrongs, all
sorrows could be corrected by three agencies: education,
industrialism, and science. To him education was not an
end in itself, but a means to an end. Yet his thought
processes, apparently, were never concerned with where this
means might lead. The primary purpose of culture was to
increase material prosperity, to equip mankind for more
rapid progress. And he measured progress with the yard-
stick of industrialism: more money, more factories, bigger
businesses, constant activity. Leisure must be paid for by
hard work, and under no conditions could proper work be
done well in a leisurely manner.

Without hesitation or doubt, he started to remake the
South in his own image. The sad truth that a literate
population can be more invincibly ignorant than an illit-
erate one never penetrated his optimistic but superficial
philosophy. That prosperity, like poverty, may degrade
and cheapen as easily as it may ennoble, never occurred to
him. If science could hasten the tempo of life, could get
more things accomplished in briefer time, then it must be
good. Surely man could not have too much of good. His
section lacked these benefits of modernity, so he wanted a
South modern in education, in thought, in industrialism, in
agriculture, in everything. A change, any change would be
for the better. He had scant sympathy for tradition; he
had suffered too much from its dead hand in school days.

His faith in journalism never wavered, and through
journalism he learned that ceaseless repetition will in the
end soften the hardest head. After a newspaper apprentice-
ship in St. Joseph, Missouri, he represented New York
newspapers in the South, a free-lance reporter. His letters

and articles repeat his old conviction. The past was gone; it must be decently interred, and forgotten. Jefferson Davis was a glorious relic of the past, but a drag on the slow wheel of progress. Although he admired George Washington Cable and Joel Chandler Harris, the youthful prophet cried for a literature that would deal with the present rather than with the past.

These articles won him a short-lived place on the editorial staff of the New York *World*, then more of a magazine than a newspaper. With the advent of Joseph Pulitzer, he resigned.

Once more he returned to North Carolina, to found the Raleigh *State Chronicle*. The venture soon failed, as did all his southern ventures. Not only were his direct, homely truths—more accurately, half-truths—unpalatable, but a vulgar strain that occasionally emerged under stress hampered the effectiveness of his work. He called the older conservatives mummies, and labelled one of them Thothmes II—the equally sensational King Tut of the nineties. Whether the tradition be good or bad, he mocked and jeered it unmercifully; enough that it came from a by-gone day. "What North Carolina most needs is a few first-class funerals."

And again, "It is an awfully discouraging business to undertake to prove to a mummy that it is a mummy. You go up to it and say, 'Old fellow, the Egyptian dynasties crumbled several thousand years ago: you are a fish out of water. You have by accident or the providence of God got a long way out of your time. This is America.'"

Yet Walter Hines Page could never understand the true cause of his unpopularity at home. Any means were good if they accomplished an end. His judgment of men was the new judgment: a man's worth can be estimated by what he achieves. He had no patience with the standard that valued *being* more highly than *doing*. Once this lack of achievement was made plain, he could not understand why these leaders were not summarily overthrown. He judged them not by what they were, but what they did—or failed to do. But his campaign, which might have thrived on anger, wilted under indifference. The South, wiser than it knew, temporarily denied him leadership.

Page returned to the North, to edit in succession the *Forum*, the *Atlantic Monthly*, and *World's Work*. After many brilliant starts, he had found his life work. The dead hand of past policy weighed little on him; the dignity that prevented editors from soliciting manuscripts never deterred him. Most magazines were atrophied, suffering from dry rot. Few had any definite purpose.

Walter Hines Page felt that each issue must be timely, immediate. His ideal was a glorified newspaper, prepared with greater care and leisure. The fiction and poetry must have distinction, but they were of secondary importance. The best man for each job must be secured: no more talented literary tuft-hunter than Page ever lived—nor one more particular about his game. Reputation must be supplemented by first-class work. Newcomers were welcome, but only if they could compete with the best.

Among the pale reproductions of English magazines, and among those living on past glories, his periodical stood out. His own magazine, he insisted, was first and always edited to give a complete and rounded picture of the American people. Defects must be pointed out unsparingly; progress must be lauded. The numbers were carefully planned in advance, so that each month's issue would contain articles on politics, economics, education, manners; in short, on any and so far as possible on every matter of contemporary interest.

Although Page sought out contributors, commissioned articles on many subjects, he believed that his obligation ceased when he paid for the article. If he thought it poor, it was never printed. And his editing was dramatic. Once he commissioned articles from some of the most prominent men in the country, on the first year of Cleveland's second administration. None satisfied him. He threw them away, and wrote an article himself. The same love of flattery that was to betray him in England dogged his editorial days: after calling in an associate to hear and to praise one of his articles, Page would often tear it up, with the comment that he could do better.

Vainglorious, perhaps, but effective. His assistants became imbued with some of Page's enthusiasm. They too believed that the periodical was the greatest and best means to educate the people. This aim Page constantly worked to attain. "I am running a forum, where the best minds of the country can meet and address the people." All the people, for his magazine must be "intelligible to the Kansas farmer's hired man's thirteen year old daughter."

Not only must it be intelligible to her, it must be immaculate enough not to shock her finer sensibilities. One young lady, whose style he admired but whose stories seemed beyond decency, insisted on writing about themes better left alone. One day he had a long talk with her, and she left his office in tears. "I have tried every other method with that young lady," he remarked, "and now I have spanked her." What benefit resulted will never be known.

He had no conception of literature for purposes other

than propaganda, improvement, and, far below these, amusement. Writing intended for adults should have no greater robustness, no intenser vitality, than juvenile stories. How thoroughly Page would have approved of clean moving pictures! Religious and sex topics were taboo. Sex should not be discussed publicly, under any circumstances, and religion was a topic ill suited to the magazine field. He refused a *Life of Jesus* by Louise Imogen Guiney on that ground.

The clean, romantic novel with its spotless heroine was better literature than any subjective psychological story. Added benefit, it pointed a moral. Subjective thinking was alien to his nature. He felt rather than thought, and his emotions were always right. None the less, this, like sex, was a subject better left untreated. Enough that he was right. If he could only stir others as he had been stirred himself, all would be well.

Since his efforts to reform the South from within had failed, he made a persistent effort to reform it now from without. Almost every issue contained an article on some phase of southern progress or southern backwardness, written by him or by such able people as William P. Trent, Edwin Mims, Ellen Glasgow, and Mary Johnston. One month he would arouse heated antagonism by an article on lynching, the next gain approbation by praising North Carolina's progress in public school education.

Most of his articles were sensible, highly intelligent, but too often they rubbed old wounds with salt. Whether people agreed with him or not, they had to listen to his vigorous statements. Somehow, he felt, the intellectuals of the nation must be awakened and they could never be awakened by flattery. A man patently wrong needs kicking, not caressing.

He roused other sections, as well. When war with Spain was declared, the cover of the *Atlantic Monthly* bore the American flag, unfurled... the first time that staid magazine had worn such spirited colors since the Civil War. Brahmin Boston was pained at this bad taste, openly flaunted. Disapproving of the war in general, it naturally frowned upon this particular manifestation of imperialism. Page supported the McKinley administration in as unpardonable and useless a war as history can show. He was easily duped by high-sounding phrases about democracy and the rights of the common man. His work with the *Atlantic* was over, and in 1899 he resigned.

After a brief experience with Harper's, Frank Doubleday and Walter Hines Page established the new firm of Doubleday, Page & Co. Primarily, Page's work in the new firm was to edit a magazine. The title, *World's Work*, reflected his own major interest in life. It soon became almost a part of him. All the plans and experiments made with the *Atlantic* and the *Forum* were shaped for this new publication, and in it carried to full fruition. Always it must present America, vital, and picturesque—and, though never written down to an audience, it must never become too literary for the average man.

I doubt if any magazine ever wielded greater influence. The flaws in the liberal program were not then apparent. Granted the original premise, that education and industrialism would bring happiness and prosperity to all, no flaw can yet be found with it. Unfortunately, no method has yet been found to teach intelligence, and without intelligence literacy has no value. Even more unfortunately, no method has yet been found to curb and to direct industrialism. Instead of sane and healthy growth, Page and his fellow liberals encouraged a gigantic and ruinous exploitation. But Page was no economist. He saw the defects in our civilization, at least the obvious ones, and he believed in the easy, popular reforms of the liberals.

Often he hammered at the South. Twice he raised the hurricane. In 1897, in a speech before the North Carolina State Normal School for Women, Walter Hines Page had talked about "The Forgotten Man." A fine, apt title, that he used with telling force again and again. Only in the South did there exist a forgotten man: one in every four who would receive no education, no chance in life. Aristocratic and sectarian systems of education alike passed him unheeded. The old civilization, in failing the commoner, had failed.

The South listened. Under the leadership of Page, Edwin Alderman, Charles D. McIver, Edwin Mims, James H. Kirkland, and others, the South made great strides in education. One phrase, and one alone, silenced all enemies— "professional Southerner." Soon it came to savour of blackest ill-repute.

New business, new factories, concrete roads, great universities came rapidly. Bustle succeeded leisure. Smoke-laden air told of new Pittsburghs in the land of tradition. Farmers became factory-hands, and their daughters mill-workers. The millennium approached on fleet wings.

Somehow the results have gone awry. Though today we have more millionaires than ever before, we have a hundred times more poverty-stricken, miserable individuals than in the days of backwardness. Though our property values have increased enormously, never were our states so heavy laden with debt. Though schools abound, we have no leaders to put alongside Jefferson, Jackson, Calhoun and Lee. We prefer to honor the Cannons, the Heflins, and the Longs. It is all very confusing.

From this confusion a few unmistakable truths emerge
The new industrialism was not a normal growth, dictated by
local needs and fostered by local men. Outside capita
exploited the South because of cheap labor and cheap re
sources. The resulting fungus proved more deadly than any
growth of old Confederate Colonels. An indigenous indus
trialism might have worked for good; this new order intensi
fied old evils without removing one of them. Machines
bred machines. Farmers turned factory hands were worse
than forgotten men; inevitably, as new machines replaced
human labor, they took their place on the industrial scrap
heap.

The farm was no refuge. Scientific farming required large
capital, huge money crops. No longer was the farmer
sufficient unto himself. Taxes alone demanded more cash
than a year's maintenance had previously required. The
farmer had become a cog in the system. The result—
overproduction. But there was overproduction everywhere
Too many farmers, too many laborers, too much food
clothing, machinery. . . and too much starvation and suf
fering. The agency that promised deliverance had over
whelmed us.

Education failed, for the same reason. All men must be
educated. Yet relatively few people could endure, much
less digest, the rigorous diet that intellectual education
demanded. Then education must be made non-intellectual
Soft minds, incapable brains, must be fed pre-digested
pabulum. And courses in brick-laying, bee-keeping, foot
ball coaching, housework, the teaching of teaching—these
and a thousand similar absurdities replaced foreign lan
guages, literature, mathematics, and history, until the trade
school overshadowed and outranked the college. Instead
of educating individual persons, we tried to teach teachers

who could not teach, train leaders who could never lead. How could they, when they could not even be taught to think? But the glorification of mediocrity grew like rank weeds, until today it has swamped us.

Fortunately for Page, this confusion and its natural result came not in his day. The path remained clear, to his view. He reenforced his articles and speeches with an anonymous novel, *The Southerner*. Chapters of it first appeared as a serial in the July, 1906, issue of the *Atlantic Monthly*, under the cumbersome title, "The Autobiography of a Southerner since the Civil War," by Nicholas Worth. The book appeared in 1909, as *The Southerner*.

The early life of Nicholas Worth paralleled closely that of Page, as I have described it above. Worth remained in the South, however. And a young man, born of parents sympathetic with the Union cause, had little opportunity when opposed to the three ghosts that dominated Southern life. These controlling forces responsible for southern degradation were: the ghost of the Confederacy, the ghost of religious orthodoxy, the ghost of negro domination. Everywhere the young hero found his progress blocked by wraiths from the past.

He is driven from the educational field when he tries to educate negroes as well as whites. He can make no headway in politics because of Confederate Colonels who appeal to sentimental prejudice at the expense of reason. At last he turns to managing a cotton mill, convinced that the true salvation of the South lies in economic progress.

Not autobiographical in fact, the novel is surely autobiography of the spirit. It was intended less for fiction than for propaganda. Page desired to overcome obstacles that he himself had encountered, and this novel was only one more chapter in his fight.

He followed the novel with an attack on hookworm. Convinced by Dr. Charles Stiles that the microbe of laziness was eradicable, that it was physical rather than spiritual, Page campaigned almost fanatically until he secured aid from Rockefeller, and until the disease was known and recognized as one dangerous to human life. In the ultimate analysis, his fight against hookworm may well prove the most useful work of his life.

These were avocations. His practical work in the world remained that of editor and publisher. He felt that publishing was more than a business, and he printed a brochure called *Confessions of a Publisher*. When George Bernard Shaw attacked it as the most blatant of American hypocrisies, as embodying the Rotarian ideal of "service with a profit," it received wide attention. If any hypocrisy existed in him, Page remained unconscious of it. The pamphlet simply stated his deepest convictions: "The writers of good books are among the benefactors of mankind, . . . the publisher is the partner, the helper, of the author, and the servant of the public." Page thought and wrote in platitudes, but he believed in them, also. Mankind could be lifted from its own stupidity only through the untiring zeal of faithful servants, a constructive program for democracy required unselfish labor on the part of united and high-minded men—such cant phrases possessed real meaning for him, and he worked untiringly in many causes.

No man could doubt his personal honesty. He had secured, and helped to administer, many of Rockefeller's charities; in *World's Work* he published the *Random Reminiscences* of John D. Rockefeller. When these articles were appearing, newspapers secured proof that the Standard Oil Company had at least one Senator on its payroll, to whom its officials suggested desirable legislation. Page made no effort to side-step the issue: the November, 1908, number contained a chapter of the oil king's autobiography, but it also contained a long editorial denouncing his oil company. Rockefeller had something of greatness in him, for Page continued to help direct his foundations.

To honesty was added kindliness. When his friend Alderman was stricken with tuberculosis, Page wrote him a long, chatty letter each week. His direct charities were unobtrusive, but personal. His larger reforms have failed, not for want of good intentions, but because they replaced evils by greater evils. Too often, the noblest schemes for social uplift result in nothing.

In 1912 he campaigned for Woodrow Wilson, long his friend. After Wilson's election, the energetic publisher embarrassed the president-elect with plans for multitudinous reforms: particularly in education, agriculture, conservation, rural credit. Somehow he just missed a place in the cabinet, perhaps because he desired to do too much. There were some obvious reasons. Bryan had first claim on the Department of State. Page's campaign against pensions disqualified him for the Interior, in the eyes of politicians, and he did not much want the portfolio of Agriculture. In the end Wilson appointed him Ambassador to England.

His work as ambassador needs small attention here. But in the short period before the war, several incidents occurred that help to clarify Page's general attitude. One is his impression of Europe. That continent, like the South, lived too much in the past; it had become "rotten, tyrannical, and yellow-dog," not worth exchanging for Moore County. The Latin races were slippery and immoral. As a good democrat, he hated monarchies; as a good American, he distrusted a civilization that preferred tin tubs to modern plumbing. Only to England and Switzerland would he grant worthiness, and Switzerland after all was a small place.   In one letter he describes a magnificent reception, and concludes, "all for His Majesty of Denmark, a country with fewer people and less wealth than New Jersey."   Only bigness could have greatness.   The future of the world belonged to America.

England he loved, with some reservations.   The monarchy, since it ruled in name only, did not trouble him, but the lack of opportunity and the subservience of the lower classes seemed heinous.   Court receptions and social gatherings fascinated him.   Soon he learned the art of transacting diplomatic business on week-end parties.

He saw, as all men saw, the superficial evils that bestrode the land, but he believed them superficial.   England's poor needed the same remedy he had prescribed for America's forgotten man: education and prosperity.   The anomaly, that his recipe for prosperity in the South, industrialism, had even then ruined England, never entered his mind.   A few reforms, and fundamental rightness of character would soon lift England from the mire.   In an England headed rapidly for economic ruin, the saddest thing to him was "the servile class."

When war began, this feeling of peaceful security deserted him.   Though he distrusted France and Russia, he distrusted Germany more. . . and he had come to love England. From the beginning he felt the Allied cause a just one, a war for democracy.   Germany's violation of Belgian neutrality, Germany's submarine campaign, horrified him.   He believed implicitly the Allied propaganda about German atrocities.

For Walter Hines Page had never learned to be a passive spectator.   Emotionally, he felt England to be in the right, and he became her strongest partisan.   He would have gone to any length to prevent war; once war was declared, he "waged neutrality" to the embarrassment of his own country. Once we entered the war, he made an ideal ambassador. No man could have done more to cement friendly relations between England and America, or work with more zeal and energy for victory.

After the war, he returned to North Carolina, worn out, utterly weary, to die within the year... as surely a casualty of the war as any soldier killed by enemy rifles.

It was better so. Walter Hines Page died triumphant, universally admired. He had lived to see the South progress, to be recognized as one of the great forces in that progress. The nation too had advanced, in the way that he had pointed out. Finally he had played a great part in a war that had saved democracy, and that perhaps would end all war.

He had seen visions, and for a few brief moments these visions gave promise of attaining reality. Then came disillusionment. The visions were mirages, leading deeper into deserts void of oases. He had been a greater romanticist than Thomas Nelson Page. At least the novelist looked to a period that could be simplified, romanticised, without harm to the present. But Walter Hines Page had lived for the future, had promised in that future a better world. No man could ever have believed more implicitly in his own pronouncements, could have worked more enthusiastically for their adoption. Such faithfulness, wherever found, must be admired. But he pinned his faith to education and to industrialism, and these have betrayed him. The South, no less gullible, believed and followed him, and the South has reaped the consequences. However honest, idealistic, unselfish, Walter Hines Page's purposes may have been, his program has proved as worthless as any pieces of silver to a condemned man.

Part Three

XVI

Eugene O'Neill's Symbolism

Old Gods for New

WHEN Eugene O'Neill's play, *Days Without End*, was produced, the New York dramatic critics were quite evidently bewildered, and were exceedingly frank in voicing their disapproval. Perhaps their dislike for O'Neill's subject-matter was to be expected, since the critics in most cases are flip gentlemen eager for a wisecrack or an epigram and they were nurtured in the iconoclastic school of realism. But the bewilderment (only too apparent because it was never admitted) is a sad commentary: from the evidence of the reviews they might never have seen or read an O'Neill play before. They seemed to have no conception of the intricate, varied symbolism which runs though his dramas, and which differs only in kind from that in his latest play. Instead of criticising the validity of this symbolism, one typically pontifical remark was that "somebody should tell Mr. O'Neill that a crucifix is a beginning, not an end."

A crucifix may be either beginning or end; it may have and does have many meanings to many different people. But as symbol or reality it is never cheap; it is not a subject for meaningless epigrams. In this play the crucifix gives a meaning and a direction to life, in precisely the same fashion that O'Neill has previously used other philosophical symbols to give life an inner meaning. And Eugene O'Neill does not value it lightly, in this theatrical presentation of religious emotion.

To O'Neill, such distortion need not be surprising, for no

playwright has suffered more from interpreters who refused to allow him those qualities which they lack in themselves. They made of him a realist. Such an interpretation was not completely unjust or untrue; it was only half-just, half-truth. O'Neill had all the trappings of realism, but he had something more: a mysticism which was, at base, only a washed form of religion. By his use of sociological and psychological symbolism, and in large part concealed by the crude vocabulary which a fashionable realism demanded, this mysticism, this essentially religious element, remained subdued. But to the careful reader it was ever-present, although in the successive plays it seemed ever-shifting, as though the dramatist's subconscious mind had sensed the futility of each particular symbol once he had embodied it within a play.

Yet, as long as these symbols were modern—that is, as long as they were rationalistic or sociological or mechanistic, when they set up as gods something which could never be God—they were either accepted or unnoticed. In 1931 the discerning Joseph Wood Krutch could see this modernity and approve it: "They, better than any other, represent the 'world view' of today, and they, as a matter of fact, constitute the only inclusive theory of human conduct which would not render any drama based upon it anachronistic or 'poetic' in the very sense that O'Neill is most anxious to avoid. . . . The greatness of his plays lies in the fact that they achieve a grandeur which their rational framework is impotent even to suggest. Man, deprived of the importance which Religion conferred when it made him important to the universe as a whole, here raises himself by his own bootstraps, and by the very strength and articulateness of his passions asserts the dignity which a rationalistic psychology denies him."

What Mr. Krutch refuses to admit is that O'Neill in every play adopted a mythologic or pseudo-religious symbolism which would give man importance. Man does not raise himself by his own bootstraps into importance; he is given importance by philosophies that are as irrational as religion. As long as the dramatist used these modern and artificial symbols, his work was accepted as serious and searching explorations of the human mind and soul; when he returned to the verities, for precisely the same purpose, his work is sneeringly dismissed as "sophomoric."

It requires only a brief study of O'Neill's symbolism to realize that this adoption of religious mythology was logical and inevitable, that it differs only in degree from his previous use of rationalistic philosophy as the framework for his plays, and that it has kept Eugene O'Neill the artist from being drowned in the same well of self-pity which has closed over such realists as Sinclair Lewis and Theodore Dreiser.

II

With the advent of science came the seeming need for a new symbolism. The day of mythological gods and heroes was past; even the moral order no longer carried a vital power. For a new day a new and fresh power was needed, and it was found in the scientific laws which, men suddenly discovered, were the true if inanimate rulers of the universe. Writers could not accept the myths of yesterday, as Herman Melville recognized when he wrote that "great geniuses are a part of their times, they themselves are the times, and possess a corresponding coloring." But he was in part ahead of his time, since we in America did not grasp the scientific and natural symbolism in *Moby Dick* until long after Melville was dead. He used a form in which the people of his day could not believe: he took for a springboard into the exploration of the unknowable soul, not an outworn mythology, but the sea and a man's relentless search for a white whale. Nature became the tragic force, and Moby Dick the *deus ex machina*. Ibsen made of heredity a tragic force, in *Ghosts;* Hauptmann made of social pressure and economic want a similar force in *The Weavers*. Gone in these plays were the great men who suffered from Nemesis, when pride had grown too big for a finite universe, gone were they who wove their own undoing through one false step which led on to another, and on eventually to destruction. Men became toys in the hands of a natural, scientific fate, or of an economic law which was equally inexorable. They were but pawns who strutted on the stage of life, and the dramatic pawns which reflected life could no longer joust even with the minor gods.

For this small creature was the new symbolism created. Man must not be portrayed as ennobled, but realistically, as only a trifle above the animals. Dramatic conventions followed the conventional scientific thought of the day.

O'Neill also has followed these modern conventions, and in the effort to express them in drama he has run the gamut of these symbolisms. In the early one-act plays he placed man against nature. He wrote of *The Moon of the Caribbees:* "the spirit of the sea—a big thing—is in this play the hero. ... Smitty in the stuffy grease-paint atmosphere of *In the Zone* is magnified into a hero who attracts our sentimental sympathy. In *The Moon*, posed against a background of that beauty, sad because it is eternal, which is one of the revealing moods of the sea's truth, his silhouetted gestures of self-pity are reduced to their proper significance, his thin whine of weakness is lost in the silence which it was mean enough to disturb, we get the perspective to judge him—and the others—and we find his sentimental posing much more out of harmony with truth, much less in tune with beauty, than the vulgarity of his mates." Man must, according to this conventional idea, be reduced to a state where only vulgarity is decent, and the noble savage alone is in harmony with nature. This was an idea that O'Neill was to use in later plays, but never as successfully as in *The Moon*. The idea is old, older than Rousseau, although it has been posed, especially in the new literature about the negro, as modern. Essentially, it denies grandeur to man until he becomes again close kin to the beasts of the field. Such men can struggle, at best, inarticulately; the drama, unfortunately for such subjects, is articulate conflict. Man beginning to think may be a fit subject for sociological or psychological investigation, but he is too weak stuff for drama.

But the subject fascinated O'Neill—as in turn most contemporary substitutes for religion have fascinated him. (Perhaps the most significant indication of their weakness is the rapidity with which capable minds have adopted and abandoned them). He tried again in *The Hairy Ape* to dramatize this theme: "it was a symbol of man, who has lost his old harmony with nature, the harmony which he used to have as an animal and has not acquired in a spiritual way. Thus, not being able to find it on earth nor in heaven, he's in the middle, taking the 'woist punches from bot' of 'em.' This idea was expressed in Yank's speech. The public saw just the stoker, not the symbol, and the symbol makes the play either important or just another play. Yank can't go forward, and so he tries to go back. This is what his shaking hands with the gorilla meant. But he can't go back to 'belonging' either. The gorilla kills him. The subject here is the same ancient one that always was and always will be the one subject for drama, and that is

man and his struggle with his own fate.   The struggle used
to be with the gods, but is now with himself, his own past,
his attempt 'to belong'."

Thus O'Neill attempts to dramatize one phase of evolution.   He sees clearly the eternal subject for drama, but he
attempts to restate it in impossible modern terms.   Man's
struggle continues to be with whatever gods there are, or
whatever gods man may create: ultimately, perhaps, with
himself.   Man's place in the universe has long puzzled, and
will long continue to puzzle, the strongest minds; it is tough
meat for philosophical and religious thought.   The process
of evolution, the problem of man's place in the world, may
be *a part of drama*, but it is not drama.   Human beings
may and do symbolize qualities, characteristics, states of
being, but they are not within themselves symbols.   And
the hairy ape is a symbol.   He is never a person, never
conscious of himself as an entity; he is only a missing link.
It would be as fitting to declare that the gorilla who flings
himself against the bars of his cage is a great tragic figure
as it would be to call O'Neill's hairy ape "tragic."   For
tragedy requires nobility and comprehension, not weakness
and feeble-mindedness.

Yet it is amusing to see critics who hailed that play now
damn *Days Without End* as sophomoric.   The ultimate
symbol is the same, and the ultimate longing: man's desire
to find a satisfactory spiritual peace, a place 'to belong' in
this world.   Apparently, when stated in scientific terms,
the idea is revolutionary, and marks O'Neill as a great
thinker; when stated in terms of religion, the idea becomes
laughable.   Perhaps a more careful reading of the two plays
will demonstrate that it is the first idea which, if not absurd,
is at least not a fit subject for the drama.

In *The Hairy Ape* O'Neill has abandoned the more valid

part of *The Moon*, the tragic loneliness of a pitiful man against the sea, of man's weakness in the face of an element he cannot control. For all of O'Neill's analysis, the person, not the sea, makes *The Moon* a dramatic success, as persons will always make or break plays. And in one other one-act play he wove the struggle of a man (always *a man* against nature, never as in *The Hairy Ape*, *man* against nature) against brute nature into a high drama, *Ile*. Here is a man obsessed with an overwhelming idea. A tight, hard-fisted, just New England sea captain who has failed for the first time to secure his quota of oil is faced with mutiny, and with the prospect of a wife going slowly insane, but in spite of all, when the ice breaks and the whales appear, the captain turns inevitably to the chase. The background is deliberately meager; all the overtones, the true background, are in the struggle shadowed forth rather than expressed between man and his ancient enemy, nature. As in all great plays there are two conflicts: the internal struggle in Captain Keeney between pride and compassion; the external struggle between a captain and his crew, a husband and his wife, a man and the universe. Because he is above all else the primitive man, the proud hunter, he makes his decision, and relentlessly, with nature a *deus ex machina* as inevitable as the Greek gods, tragedy results.

Æsthetically, *Ile* is artistically sound and well handled. It is modern in form, lean and spare in structure, with no surplus matter and no sentimentality, but with an almost classic restraint in writing and in characterization, as though the author were reluctant to approach the catastrophe. But the play succeeds because of the captain: if not a great protagonist, he is at least a dignified one, and his tragedy is not tinged with the pathos which surrounds the tragedies of little men.

One quality the play lacks: elevation of language.   The speech remains prosy when it should have sweeping movement, color and grandeur.   This is a defect common in all the plays, and felt more keenly in later, more complex characterizations, but in no play is this inability to handle language more obvious than in *Ile*: there are moments here, and later, when the flexible power of a mighty and tumultuous blank verse would take speaker and auditor alike away from prosiness, away from the too real present, into an inner, more comprehensive reality.   But O'Neill has always been too much the modern, too much concerned with portraying through changing symbols "that self obsession which is the particular discount we moderns have" ever to get away from wordage into the deeper region of language. His distrust of poetry is only too obvious, and he has remarked that we "have endured too much from the banality of surfaces," but he has too often given us prosy characters mouthing prosy speeches for him to complain too bitterly of surface realities.   And he has done it, as in *The Hairy Ape*, in the name of art, forgetting that such prosiness is sure indication of the surface type rather than of the revealed individual.   Even when his characters are most fully realized—as in *Ile, The Great God Brown, Mourning Becomes Electra*, and *Days Without End*—they suffer from a wordy, groping inarticulateness.   This is sometimes appropriate to comedy, as O'Neill proves in his magnificent recollections of his youth in *Ah, Wilderness!*   But tragedy demands something better.

This leads me to believe that a discarded dogma of Aristotelian criticism may well be revived to meet a modern need.   One cardinal tenet of that academic criticism was that a tragic protagonist must be a great personage, so that his own fall would shake the world, or at least a portion of it.

Today the pomp of kings has gone, and the mighty have fallen, but the old rule has not quite lost its power. The tragic protagonist, though he be a street sweeper, must be individualized until within himself he has elements of greatness. It is not enough that he shall be part of a social order, a communist or capitalist or seaman—in other words, a type. The type may be useful in propaganda, but in the drama he or it is dead weight. And the protagonist must be given an innate nobility for a second, less obvious reason: he must be an articulate person. As long as realism demands that a stoker shall speak like a stoker, a street sweeper like a street sweeper, and a college boy like a Broadway columnist, then they cannot be considered subjects for any drama which seeks higher levels than the most pitifully obvious statements of cause and effect. Such persons may have emotions of sufficient depth, but the tragic and dramatic figure must do more than feel; he must express his emotion to an audience. Contrary to all the tenets of realism, emotion is not expressed simply through words; emotion is language, and the two must be subtly fused into one. Without this fusion, the actor talks about, but never reveals, his emotion.

This problem of expression is peculiarly important with Eugene O'Neill because he has so often tripped over it. Time and again he has tried to explain to the public, through letters to newspapers or to friendly critics, precisely what he intended a play to mean. Yet he has consistently refused to put into the mouths of his characters a language which would carry his shades of meaning. In one of the least successful of his plays, *Welded*, he has the lover-artist Michael tell Eleanor that he wishes to express his feelings, but that he can only "stutter like an idiot." This is begging the question. There are emotions too deep and too complex for expression, but the dramatist must manage to imply, must in general express these emotions in language which carries a rounded meaning.   It is all very proper for a Penrod, or an ordinary mortal, to stutter at such moments, but seventeen is a ludicrous age, and the ordinary mortal remains inarticulate most of his life.   But the artist Michael, or the Hairy Ape, or the Cabots in *Desire Under the Elms* are not intended to be ridiculous personages; they are simply inarticulate persons groping for words at the moments when clear poetic expression is vitally needed.   Great dramatists have achieved this necessary theatre before; to be reckoned as great, dramatists must again achieve it.   In O'Neill's case this is the more necessary because he has often refused to allow his symbolism to be an underlying current felt under the smooth surface of an otherwise straight-forward drama—the manner in which Chekhov used symbolism— but has attempted to make symbolic the action, the characters, and even the artificial devices of the theatre.

These obvious devices need little attention, for they have received many examinations—apparently on the theory that great subtlety must be hidden in this experimental stage technique.   One obvious attempt at symbolism was the division of each act in *Beyond the Horizon* into two scenes, one indoors and one out, to suggest a tide-like rhythm in the lives of the characters.   O'Neill has experimented also with symbolic names for his characters (in *The Great God Brown*, for example), and with the use of masks, of asides which revealed thought, and even, in *Days Without End*, of two actors to play the dual personality of one person.   Such experimentation, for all the fanfare of publicity which has surrounded it, is basically superfical.   It indicates that the artist's discontent with his basic subject-matter is carried over to discontent with his medium.   But the medium was not a primary fault; the essential faults were in muddied expression, and even more in that the artist had settled upon no point of view, that he had no philosophy of life.

He had, indeed, a great many philosophies, which reflected many contemporary points of view. One idea which became exceedingly popular was that man achieves immortality through his children. O'Neill made a slight use of it in the climax of *Welded*; he made it the underlying motif of *The Fountain*. Ponce de Leon searches fruitlessly for youth, and at last, when he has given up hope, he finds a vicarious immortality in the youth of his nephew. The intellectual idea was simply the wish-illusion of fearsome generations, the outgrowth of a scientific philosophy which denied the possibility of God yet felt the imperious need of some substitute to fill His place. O'Neill dramatized this concept of immortality—but, in spite of some excellent writing, the intellectual framework is so absurd that Ponce de Leon's vicarious salvation at the end is hopeless *tour de force*.

Yet the play might, one feels, have been a great one, if O'Neill had retained throughout the play the motif which he explained in a note on the program: "The idea of writing a *Fountain* came on finally from my interest in the recurrence in folklore of the beautiful legend of a healing spring of eternal youth." Unfortunately, folklore came into conflict with a modern philosophy, and the philosophy prevails, until near the conclusion de Leon rationalizes (in a manner which seems strange when contrasted with the theme of the play) his belief: "One must accept, absorb, give back, become oneself a symbol." This is the best affirmation that O'Neill's philosophy at the time would admit. Certainly it had nothing to do with the folk-consciousness of which he speaks; instead of writing out of that, he has attempted to combine the simple with the esoteric.

Time and again, he has attempted to explain simplicity

with a false profundity. Twice he took the negro as protagonists, and in his hands the customary noble savage idea took a queer turn. In *The Emperor Jones* a half-savage is pitted against savages. But the romantic noble savage delusion has one advantage: it emphasizes the individual person. Although the intellectual content, when reduced to outline, is fairly meager, the portrayal of the obsessed Jones has a majestic dignity that makes the performance impressive. Once again the antique yet never old theme of man against the universe holds the stage. Man in queer and tattered garments, semi-ridiculous, but after all a man. When such a character appears in a reasonably good play, we recognize immediately that the underlying symbolism is, in the final analysis, far less important than the play itself.

What we also realize is that, for the dramatist as well, the symbolism must be subordinated. In *All God's Chillun Got Wings* the surface play can never get started, it is so heavily weighted with propaganda. Freudian interpretation of sex dominates this play of miscegenation. The "noble savage" motif can hardly be said to appear for the simple reason that nobility, in the larger sense, never appears. But the negro is portrayed as noble: he has the necessary characteristics but he fails to achieve life. Like most sociological tracts the play is concerned with types. But the type is an abstraction which exists nowhere. By a dramatic rendition of what happens when black marries white it might be possible to adumbrate the entire problem. But for O'Neill, the problem, not the person, is the play. He is not content with adumbration; he desires to state the facts clearly. Here, as elsewhere, the symbolism is the real play, stalking the stage, and forcing the puppet actors to deep around it. What he feared was literal realism, but his fear betrayed him into such over-writing that inner and outer realism alike are gone.

Freudian symbolism of sex bulks large in the later plays of O'Neill. Sex and religion become in his mind inextricably intermixed. *Desire Under the Elms* is a weak and melodramatic study in sex obsession, and unusually shoddy in language. But *Mourning Becomes Electra* is a grave, dignified, and successful attempt to jazz up a Greek tragedy, by motivating the action with psychological complications and endowing each character with repressions or frustrations or fixations, until the dramatic struggle becomes "a conflict between puritanism and healthy love." Much of this psychological symbolism also motivated *Strange Interlude* and *The Great God Brown*, though in these plays a more dominant motif was the religion of art. According to this belief, the creative power, some vague part of nature, would perform the age-long functions of religion.

It is around this theme of creation that O'Neill comes nearest to integrating his philosophy. To him, the fountain was a symbol of life, tossing its little drops high in the air. They had myriad shapes and colors: some were caught in the light, others dully dropped back, or burst into a miniature rainbow of light. It did not greatly matter. The essential thing is life: more drops must be propagated that more drops may be tossed into the air. The same basic theme governs *Strange Interlude*. Men and women are shells, acting a part, growing to other people, then away from them, but under and above all is life, taking care that new individuals shall be brought forth. Men and women cannot resist forces stronger than themselves, cannot tamper with the laws of nature; any attempt to do so results in tragedy. As the old people prepare to go off the stage, always there is the son of one couple, the daughter of another, to take their places. The cycle is complete, never broken, never ceasing.

And with what strange finality does this Freudian interpretation recall the older, simpler rites of the Greeks, when men made sacrifice to the goddess of fertility and the song of the goat gave the name *tragedy*. In denying importance to persons, O'Neill goes back unwittingly to the oldest of religions (disguised as the newest of science) to give some meaning to life.

These plays are too confused with symbolism to take on life. In *The Great God Brown* the little drops of water become all-important, at least to themselves, and the play receives importance through them. Men play upon one another, wear masks to the world, but underneath those masks the souls grow, warp, shrivel, rot. We become a part of others, and others become a part of us, but all without understanding, as we grope in the world's half-light which blinds us more effectually than any darkness. The light which O'Neill can see has little illumination, and offers no insight save for a creative force which the characters "do not clearly comprehend." O'Neill defines his purpose as showing "the mystery any one man or woman can feel but not understand as the meaning of any event—or accident— in any life on earth." Significantly, at that time O'Neill endowed Cybele, the pagan earth mother, and Dion with this mystical element—but the mysticism is present, and in such a way as to accentuate the importance of individuals.

The play might be satisfying, but the philosophy behind it was not. "The playwright today," wrote O'Neill, "must dig at the roots of the sickness of today as he feels it—the death of the old God and the failure of science and materialism to give any satisfying new one for the surviving primitive

religious instinct to find a meaning for life in . . . ." It led
him to search through many mythologies, even led him in
Dynamo to envision a man who saw a new god in the whirling
wheels of machinery and the weird power of electricity.
Although the play deals with religious mania, the implication
is obvious that religion is dead, and that man must create a
new religion to take its place. It is a dramatic statement of
the sentence quoted above.

But when a man searches too intensively—and, in
O'Neill's case too extensively—for the meaning of life, he
may miss life itself. The mythology of the Greeks may be
outworn, but it served to give a purpose and meaning to
life, and to reveal humanity underneath. That is all the
Christian mythology, or Brahmin or Norse or even Freudian
mythology, can accomplish. Joseph Wood Krutch praises
O'Neill most highly because "his dramas have nothing
archaic about them. They do not seek the support of a
poetic faith in any of the conceptions which served the
classical dramas but are no longer valid for us. They are,
on the contrary, almost cynically 'modern' in their acceptance of a rationalistic view of man and the universe. Yet
he has created his characters upon so large a scale that their
downfall is made once more to seem not merely pathetic
but terrible."

In all save the final sentence, this criticism misses the
point entirely. To call O'Neill's view of life rationalistic
is to mis-read the plays. True, he did not accept the Christian mythology until *Days Without End*; what he did was to
create, or at least to borrow, a dozen pseudo-religious mythologies and symbolisms which are as irrational as ancient
myth. If ever any man viewed life through the spectacles
of mysticism, that man was Eugene O'Neill. His realism,
in the final analysis, is limited to dialogue, and realism

hampered rather than helped him.　And the lack of a unified point of view, the inability to find a purpose in life—what Krutch calls his cynical modernity—has simply led him to minimize the individuality of his characters, to substitute a jumpy and involved series of chaotic modern faiths for a single clear and ordered faith.　What Krutch forgets, what O'Neill has too often forgotten, is that this faith, meaning, or complex (whatever name may be given it) is at most a background.　It is the skeleton framework, not the completed structure.　It never appears distinctly; it simply *is*. And the playwright has attempted to find too many frameworks on which to hang his characters, without ever believing in any one of them.　This affects the single play only when the idea is basically sound, and overpowers the dramatist, or when it is absurd, and the play is patently unconvincing.　But it does affect vitally the entire body of his work, and in O'Neill's case the fact seems apparent that his shifting allegiances philosophically have marred many single plays, and have removed the cumulative effect of a continued and unified effort.

III

To get back to the original point, why have the critics almost unanimously damned *Days Without End* as "sophomoric," as "an emotional binge," and as "collegiate theorizing."　In the past they have justly acclaimed O'Neill as the greatest American dramatist; now they turn upon him with a fury which is, perhaps, not altogether explained by their verdict that *Days Without End* is a bad play.

Actually, when examined without bias, the play is well up to the high standard of O'Neill's better plays.　It has the same strength and the same weaknesses.　It lacks the tautly compact and the classic perfection of *Ile*: a play possessing a valid symbolism that portrayed nature as representative of God, and that achieves magnitude despite its small compass; it lacks the close unity of *The Emperor Jones*; above all, it lacks the spaciousness and the comprehension of *The Great God Brown*. In that play a mind can walk about, can explore itself while observing exploration in the character's minds, and can identify itself with those characters emotionally. *Days Without End* has a more restricted emotional compass; the framework is more rigid.

But the basic ideas in all the plays differ in terminology rather than in actuality. Once again Eugene O'Neill is attempting to give a meaning to life, but he has found that meaning in the Catholic cross, not in the fountain or the dynamo or the sexual delta. O'Neill has not even abandoned his modern psychology, for in this work he makes use of dual personalities and of Freudian psychoanalysis. He uses these dubious sciences, however, in the attempt to explain a man's recovery of his faith, and in that, it seems, he has proven himself sophomoric. Yet the old strength is here: the ability to reveal man and woman is just as apparent as in *Strange Interlude*; the same old fear of literal realism has led him into an intricate and closely-knitted plot, and into portraying John Loving as two characters on the stage, a device which sometimes seems a superficial means of attaining profundity; the same ability to handle pure emotion artistically. There are also the same weaknesses of over-writing and of occasional faulty expression, but they are all elements which have appeared before.

It may be that O'Neill has portrayed the liberal thinker of the last decade a little too exactly, in the early part of John Loving's characterization, for these gentlemen's comfort. Possibly the picture sketched of Loving by Father Baird is in part O'Neill's own spiritual autobiography, but that is a point I am willing to leave to the professional psychoanalysts. One thing is sure: many men did go through approximately this spiritual evolution:

... I was the heathen to him and he was bound he'd convert me to something. First it was Atheism unadorned. Then it was Atheism wedded to Socialism. But Socialism proved too weak-kneed a mate and the next I heard Atheism was living in free love with Anarchism, with a curse by Nietzsche to bless the union. And then came the Bolshevik dawn. ... He was particularly delighted when he thought they'd abolished love and marriage, and he couldn't contain himself when the news came they'd turned naughty school-boys and were throwing spitballs at Almighty God and had supplanted Him with the slave-owning State —the most grotesque god that ever came out of Asia! ... I knew Communism wouldn't hold him long. ... Soon his letters became full of pessimism, and disgust with all sociological nostrums ... what do you think was his next hiding place? Religion, no less— but as far away as he could run from home—in the defeatist mysticism of the East. ... But the next I knew, he was through with the East. It was not for the Western soul, he decided, and he was running through Greek philosophy and found a brief shelter in Pythagoras and numerology. Then came a letter which revealed him bogged down in evolutionary scientific truth again—a dyed-in-the-wool mechanist ... I enjoyed a long interval of peace from his missionary zeal, until finally he wrote me he was married. That letter was full of more ardent hymns of praise for a mere living woman than he'd ever written before about any of his great spiritual discoveries. ... He seems to be fixed in his last religion. I hope so. The only constant faith I've found in him before was his proud belief in himself as a bold Anti-christ.

This "hide-and-go-seek" mental career does not precisely parallel the dramatic production of Eugene O'Neill. But there are some unusual similarities: he made the sea a god in his early one-act plays; he wedded atheism to revolutionary propaganda in *The Hairy Ape*; he put more than touches of anarchism and of social reform into such plays as *The Emperor Jones*, *All God's Chillun Got Wings*, and *The First Man*; with his mechanistic philosophy he created God from the dynamo; he made use of sociological nostrums in some plays already mentioned, and particularly in *Desire Under the Elms*; and he made the creative life-force carry the underlying purposiveness of being in *The Fountain*, *Strange Interlude*, and *The Great God Brown*. Of all the contemporary panaceas, the "Bolshevik dawn" alone seems to have left him unmoved, and something of Sovietism might be read into his comedy *Marco Millions* with its portrayal of Marco Polo as the original Babbitt—but this would be, at best, a strained and probably unjust interpretation. No injustice is needed to show that O'Neill's mental evolution has resembled that of John Loving, or that he has made each nostrum into a pseudo-religion.

And O'Neill was not alone. The critic and thinkers of his era did exactly the same thing. But they have remained stationary, continuing to preach the same gospels from the same soap-boxes. This they do in the name of rationalism, but the essential fact is that each belief is a panacea which acts temporarily—perhaps in some cases permanently—as a substitute for religion. Not one of the ideas is truly rational. Each gives to men a reason for existence, but none was satisfactory to O'Neill for very long. Yet he could not believe, with his character Loving, that "we are all the slaves of meaningless chance"; he belonged instead with the idealistic John who felt that "a new savior must be born who will reveal to us how we can be saved from ourselves."

Only the words in this plea are new. Always, Eugene O'Neill has expressed his temporary theory of the infinite beyond the finite; he has simply changed from the terms of philosophy to the words of religion. *Days Without End* is a sincere and moving play, as fine in conception and execution as any of the plays except *Ile* and *The Great God Brown*, but it has been condemned by men who refused to accept these words without perceiving that it has the same basic symbolism which animates all the other plays. It gives meaning to life through religion, but it expresses, after all, the immediate philosophy of Eugene O'Neill.

XVII

Portrait of Lavengro

A Biographical Essay on George Borrow

I<small>T IS</small> a fortunate fact that we cannot see ourselves as others see us; even more fortunate, perhaps, that others cannot see us as we see ourselves. In the history of literature only a few men have mirrored themselves for the world to gaze upon without first making certain that the glass was concave or convex. Montaigne and Pepys wrote in the most intimate manner about themselves; most authors have written with careful expurgations, with skeletons closely hidden in dark closets. It has been more seemly to doctor the accounts carefully, to present only one side of the coin.

George Borrow belongs to this second class. Almost everything he wrote was about himself: like Montaigne, he was most interested in himself. But Borrow also had a flair for dramatics; in him, as in Napoleon, there was a good bit of the poseur. Consciously or unconsciously changing the facts when it pleased him to do so, he told the story of his life not exactly as it happened, but as the creative artist in him felt it should have happened. Yet this picture Borrow presents of himself, touched up though it is by a master hand, is authentic and intrinsically honest. For a man reveals himself in everything he writes: if within himself there is validity and intellectual integrity, his work will have in turn worth and beauty. Something of these Borrow had, and something of them he caught in his books. But the true thing, the essence of the books, was Borrow himself—one of the strangest characters literature has ever known.

Above all else, George Borrow was a man. Six feet two, perfectly developed physically, and trained from childhood in the art of boxing, he was a worthy antagonist for any man. But if any person needed to be so equipped, he did, for this friend of bruisers was quick-tempered, prejudiced, intolerant to the nth degree. Not all his combats were physical: the same man who in youth found a supreme delight in battering down the Flaming Tinman, champion of a province, in middle age received equal pleasure from less successful attacks on Sir Walter Scott and the Roman Catholic Church. With his superb physical energy was combined a not unnatural tendency toward drifting, a desire to be ever on the move. A vagabond by instinct and by training, more a gypsy at heart than many a Romany Chal.

Combined with these, stronger than the physical self he gloried in, George Borrow possessed also the instincts of a scholar. *Lavengro* is sub-titled: The Scholar, The Gypsy, The Priest. They represent three different persons; no one thing would have insulted Borrow more than to be labeled a priest. Yet he partook of the nature of all three: characters highly incompatible, standing for different things. So did he. The author of *Lavengro* was a man divided against himself: a man of learning whose scholarship was neither academic nor profound, a philologist with a gift for tongues but no love for systematic labor; in short, a scholar tainted with gypsy. Yet as gypsy he was equally tainted with learning, made dissatisfied by ambition. And he was just as much the priest. No other point of view and no other religion were so nearly perfect as his. All men think this; it is the peculiar vice of the reformer and the priest that they are not content with thinking so themselves, but they must try to force all men to think as they do, to assume their thought-garments and cast away the original ones. In

America Borrow might have founded a new religion or led a crusade against slavery; in England, when he loosed his intolerant fulminations, he merely lost his popularity. Since his death, however, a cult of Borrovians has established itself—his works are read, admired, and quoted; his followers are proud of their cultishness.

My own introduction to the work of George Borrow came, not uniquely, in a rather dramatic manner. I suppose that I had heard the name in a survey course, but it had meant no more than the names of Theodore Hook, Marjorie Fleming, or Monk Lewis. Then one day in English 5, at Harvard, Professor Charles Townsend Copeland, after the usual preliminaries in getting just the right amount of light and ventilation in the room, read from *Lavengro*:

I now wandered along the heath, until I came to a place where beside a thick furze, sat a man, his eyes fixed intently on the red ball of the setting sun.

"That's not you, Jasper?"

"Indeed, Brother!"

"I've not seen you for years."

"How should you, brother?"

"What brings you here?"

"The fight, brother."

"Where are the tents?"

"On the old spot, brother."

"Any news since we parted?"

"Two deaths, brother."

"Who are dead, Jasper?"

"Father and mother, brother."

"Where did they die?"

"Where they were sent, brother."

"And Mrs. Herne?"

"She's alive, brother "

"Where is she now?"

"In Yorkshire, brother."

"What is your opinion of death, Mr. Petulengro?" said I as I sat down beside him.

"My opinion of death, brother, is much the same as that in the old song of Pharaoh, which I have heard my grandam sing—

> Canna marel o manus chivios and puv,
> Ta rovel pa leste o chavo ta romi.

When a man dies, he is cast into the earth, and his wife and child sorrow over him. If he has neither wife nor child, then his father and mother, I suppose; and if he is quite alone in the world, then he is cast into the earth, and there is an end of the matter."

"And do you think there is an end of man?"

"There's an end of him, brother, more's the pity."

"Why do you say so?"

"Life is sweet, brother."

"Do you think so?"

"Think so!—there's night and day, brother, both sweet things; sun, moon, and stars, brother, all sweet things; there's likewise a wind on the heath. Life is very sweet, brother; who would wish to die?"

"I would wish to die—"

"You talk like a gorgio—which is the same as talking like a fool—were you a Romany Chal you would talk wiser. Wish to die, indeed!—A Romany Chal would wish to live forever."

"In sickness, Jasper?"

"There's the sun and the stars, brother."

"In blindness, Jasper?"

"There's the wind on the heath, brother; if I could only feel that, I would gladly live forever. Dosta, we'll now go to the tents and put on the gloves; and I'll try to make you feel what a sweet thing it is to be alive."

This "wind on the heath" episode seemed to me then, and seems to me now, one of the finest passages in literature. In the people of that day, in our own grandfathers and grandmothers, there was a toughness and hardiness, a love of life simply for the sake of living, that seems to have disappeared, in large measure, from among us. Elemental beings found their pleasure in elemental things, in existence, and in the moon, the stars, and the wind on the heath.

It is this restless personal quality, this intensity, which attracts readers. Borrow reveals himself—and the integrity behind this fiery intolerance, which sometimes alarms us in contemporaries, inevitably attracts us with magnetic force to writers of an earlier day, whose opinions can no longer do harm. Here is no structural art, no objectified form; it is not as an artist that Borrow must be judged. Although he dramatizes and heightens, he remains personal: fiction is employed only to buttress fact. A slow writer, a conscious artist, Borrow barely enters into the domain of art with a whole book. Whether fiction or fact, the dingle episode with Isopel Berners is properly objectified, for all its personal nature, and his unerring vignettes of character with their selectivity of detail reveal his strength. Even the dry craggy humor grows mainly out of idiosyncrasies of character, as in the episode of the man who can not for long be a good philosopher or a good German because he is not a good smoker.

But Borrow himself constantly obtrudes. And we would sacrifice something strange and fascinating if these parts, so imperfect and damaging to the structure of his work, were omitted. His opinions are out of line—a Tory in a land dominated by Liberals, hating or ignoring industrial progress; a frequenter of by-ways who attacked the straightness and direction of the main road; a man who saw but one side of a question, and frequently only one part of that—and violently expressed; they are the ideas of a narrow, sometimes crabbed, partisan mind. Yet a man's personality may compensate in an imperfect world for some artistic imperfections: the question becomes, eventually, not one of judgment by the critic but of acceptance by the reader.

Borrow's prose redeems in part his irregularities. It has the qualities of a clear mountain stream rushing cleanly and precipitously along, with jutting troublesome boulders in the shape of archaic phrasings and inordinate apostrophes to break the sweep and united strength of his writing. His models show the bent of his own mind: the Bible, the old Court trials, Bunyan, DeFoe, Swift, Cobbett, and Byron. Not subtlety but strength, not decoration but intrinsic richness, were the excellences in style he aimed at, and largely attained; but in a florid age his prose sounded hard and dry, so that one critic was misled into writing that he had no style. His work seemed, also, devoid of sentiment. Richness of style and sentiment there is, however, under the outer covering of spare dryness, for those to find who have an ear for words and sentences.

The highly personalized writer will always have a place, though rarely the highest place, in literature as long as men remain interested in vital personalities. Properly, work of this type is outside the scope of criticism, for it appeals directly to sympathies and prejudices and habits of thought. Although Borrow wrote no book which is strictly a novel, he made himself, virtually, the hero of autobiographical works that have the character of picaresque novels. That he succeeded in spite of his method may be the highest testimony to his style and to his validity as a person.

II

Almost all normal boys deify their fathers, believe that they can whip any man in the surrounding country. Few have reason for such justification; young George Borrow had. His father's one great distinction in life was that he had fought and conquered one of the great battlers of England, Big Ben Brain. Whatever the reasons for the combat, they had long since ceased to matter; the tradition of his father's physical prowess remained, and the boy was intensely proud of it. In his turn he became one of the most famous of England's amateur fighters, and never did he allow himself to forget that his father had once knocked out the heavy-weight champion of England.

Thomas Borrow was a Cornish gentleman in reduced circumstances, a proud man who could not go into trade. He was a soldier most of his life, yet never rose above the rank of captain. A good officer and fine disciplinarian, if we can trust his son's account, Captain Borrow lacked the money to purchase advancement according to the custom of his time, and lacked the good fortune, if such it may be called, of ever being allowed to prove his bravery in battle. His service was entirely in England and Ireland; he trained recruits, but he never fought against the French. It was the great tragedy of his life.

George's mother was Ann Perfrement, descendant of Huguenots who had emigrated to England after the Revocation of the Edict of Nantes. Looking back, the man recognized his devotion for her as something more than conventional, but confesses that he was a problem, a child difficult to understand and to deal with. The brother, three years older, seemed all that a growing boy should be: loving play, quick at his books, a pretty, clever boy who caused his parents little trouble.

The younger lad was different. Moody, timid, given to sitting for long periods in secluded corners or in his own room, he was a constant source of worry to his parents—a queer child roused from lethargy only by an unholy love for snakes. His mother he frightened by handling vipers, but, according to his story, though they hissed and struck at his mother and brother, they never bothered him. He hardly stayed long enough in one place to collect such pets, for almost from his birth at Dereham, July 5, 1803, George Henry Borrow was a wanderer. His father was constantly moving from one part of the country to another with his regiment; any continuity of home life was unknown to him.

Two things interested him: *Robinson Crusoe* and snakes. He read incessantly about Crusoe and Friday, imagining himself in their place; as the best substitute, he persuaded an old snake charmer to teach him how to charm and tame snakes. The budding adventurer, not yet in his teens, had become quite independent of his parents and his playmates. With an evil-looking viper coiled in his shirt bosom, he wandered through the woods in perfect safety.

This comparative freedom from danger was soon proved. When ten years of age, out hunting for more snakes to add to his collection, George blundered into a gypsy camp, and was in danger of his life. Apparently the tribe was not gifted with the fore-sight claimed by many of their fortune-tellers, for they saw in the boy only a meddlesome brat who had caught them making counterfeit money. A dangerous thing to do ... but the viper concealed in George's bosom lifted his head and hissed—and its owner was treated with respect, endowed with the name of sap-engro, "snake-master."

It was the most exciting episode in his boyhood. Though constantly moving from place to place, Captain Borrow kept his sons in school, if possible in a classical school, with *Lilly's Latin Grammar* as the foundation for all knowledge. Two years were spent in Scotland at Edinburgh, just north of the Tweed, but though he picked up the brogue and joined with the High Towners in their brawls with the Low Towners, Scotland made no lasting impression on him.

In 1815 his father's regiment was ordered to Clommel, Ireland. Napoleon was cooped at last in a rocky cage, and England had little use for soldiers. Only the Irish were troublesome, not to be trusted, and because of their pugnacious instinct George had a year's training at an Irish school—training of which he was very proud. Looking back, the arrogant old author was disposed to call all that had ever happened to him good: "I, having no duties to perform, was sent to school. I had been to English schools, and to the celebrated one at Edinburgh; but my education, at the present day, would not be what it is—perfect, had I never had the honor of being *alumnus* in an Irish seminary."

Most men might have said this with tongue in cheek. Not so Borrow; he was intensely proud of his learning, certain that the fields of knowledge he had taken to be his province had been, or could be, mastered more thoroughly by no other man. Scholars have sneered at his scholastic pretensions, even his admirers have unanimously agreed that his knowledge was spotty, at best broad rather than thorough; but these were points never conceded by Borrow.

At any rate, he began the study of languages early, and continued that study with an unflagging zeal throughout his life. The boy of twelve could read Latin and was studying Greek, but the old Irish language, spoken occasionally by his comrades, fascinated him. An older lad, Murtagh, agreed to teach him Irish as payment for a new pack of cards. As boy or man George Borrow had little use for cards; he was affected strangely little by any of the vices common to most men.

A year in Ireland, a smattering of Irish—then the regiment was ordered back to Norwich, England, and disbanded. Captain Borrow settled down on half-pay, and saw his elder son, by now a lieutenant, depart with his regiment for the West Indies. The lieutenant was a source of pride and satisfaction to the father; he gave promise of being all that the gallant captain had once hoped, and expected, to be. George remained a problem; tall, and strong for his age, he seemed to have a genius for choosing disreputable companions: snake charmers, gypsies, wild Irishmen and Scottish gangsters, racing touts, prize fighters—anyone and everyone save reputable boys and girls or older people with whom he might have associated with advantage to himself.

Once settled in Norwich, the fourteen year old boy began looking for new tongues to conquer. He could dismay the heathen by torrents of abuse in wild Irish, or by copious quotations from *Lilly's Latin Grammar*, but that seemed insufficient. Nor was he particularly interested in the ordinary games of his school-fellows, which seemed tame and childish; his early love for charming snakes had also worn thin.

In Norwich resided a banished priest, and from him George took French and Italian. Captain Borrow agreed only with much grumbling, and ominous forebodings of future ills. But his son was already headstrong, unwilling to listen to a parent's advice that he should prepare himself for the law, or study in order to take orders. George read French and Italian, conversed with the old priest, and deviled the poor man because he could give him only rudimentary instruction in Spanish.

Assuredly he was quick with strange tongues, proud of his new learning. That he became a capable linguist his translations, many of them made before he was twenty-one, attest; his great fault, in the cavilling eye of scholars, was that he called himself not a linguist but a philologist. Yet it seems fairly clear that Borrow was correct in his claim to such a title. The thing that has shifted is the meaning of the word philologist. In our specialized scientific age words have become technical, limited—and as a result our vocabulary has become more exact but far less expressive, far less grand and sonorous. A philologist today is one who picks words to pieces, who studies closely their derivatives, their cognates, all the little minutiae that in any way have any bearing on those words. Such a man is a scientific student of linguistics—and usually as far removed from the original meaning of the word as could be. Even Knapp, in 1899, looked superciliously on Borrow's claims to philological knowledge—but Dr. Knapp was strictly a philologist in the modern sense of the word.

When Borrow claimed to be a philologist our language had not become scientific and pauperized. The meaning of the word was plain, its derivation apparent—*phil* meaning love, *logos* meaning words. Such he was, a lover of words for their own sake—and sound; as such he felt himself entitled to use that word:

I much question whether philology, or the passion for languages, requires so little of an apology as the love for horses. It has been said, I believe, that the more languages a man speaks, the more a man is he; which is very true, provided he acquires languages as a medium for becoming acquainted with the thoughts and feelings of the various sections into which the human race is divided; but, in that case, he should rather be termed a philosopher than a philologist—between which two the difference is wide indeed. An individual may speak and read a dozen languages, and yet be an exceedingly poor creature, scarcely half a man; and the pursuit of tongues for their own sake, and the mere satisfaction of acquiring them, surely argues an intellect of a very low order; a mind disposed to be satisfied with mean and grovelling things, taking more pleasure in the trumpery casket than in the precious treasure it contains, in the pursuit of words, than in the acquisition of ideas.

I cannot help thinking that it was fortunate for myself, who am, to a certain extent, a philologist, that with me the pursuit of languages has been always modified by the love of horses. . . . I might, otherwise, have become a mere philologist; one of those beings who toil night and day in culling useless words for some *opus magnum* which Murray will never publish, and nobody ever read; beings without enthusiasm, who, having never mounted a generous steed, cannot detect a good point in Pegasus himself; like a certain philologist who, though acquainted with the exact value of every word in the Greek and Latin languages, could observe no particular beauty in one of the most glorious of Homer's rhapsodies. What knew he of Pegasus? he had never mounted a generous steed; the merest jockey, had the strain been interpreted to him, would have called it a brave song!

It is a just criticism of ninety per cent of our present-day philologists: men who cannot see the poem for the words. The mature Borrow saw and hated this specialization of linguistics; the boy knew nothing of such matters. He wanted to read and to talk foreign languages, and his first tutors were an Irish school boy with a love for gambling and a banished priest who had to make a living. Neither sufficed, though it is doubtful if he exhausted the knowledge of either.

Activities more natural to his age were riding, fishing, and boxing. Horses were not always available, but boxers were. For the boy, with the same genius for picking queer companions, had taken up with a sportsman and friend of bruisers, a man later executed for murder, John Thurtell. The captain approved, however—had not he in his day conquered Big Ben Brain, champion of all England? Thurtell taught the already skillful Borrow the science of boxing, and carried him to many famous prize-fights.

Hazlitt's "The Fight" has long been praised by literary critics for its gusto and its evermounting interest—but Hazlitt was merely a spectator watching his first fight. Borrow had witnessed hundreds, had himself fought many such battles with gentlemen as skilled in the art as the bruisers they patronized. When he wrote *Lavengro* prize-fighting had become unpopular and illegal; what we know today as Victorianism was then in the saddle. In this era of smug moral goodness George Borrow wrote of rascals and gypsies, of sportsmen and bruisers; he courted unpopularity with his matter and his attitude. But the self-assured fellow loved boxing, and glorified it in one of his most vivid chapters:

Let no one sneer at the bruisers of England—what were the gladiators of Rome, or the bull-fighters of Spain, in its palmiest day, compared to England's bruisers? Pity that ever corruption should have crept in amongst them—but of that I wish not to talk; let us hope that a spark of the old religion, of which they were the priests, still lingers in the breasts of Englishmen. There they come, the bruisers, from far London, or from wherever else they might chance to be at the time, to the great rendezvous in the old city; some came one way, some another; some of tip-top reputation came with peers in their chariots, for glory and fame are such fair things, that even peers are proud to have those invested therewith by their sides.

Once again he became friendly with the gypsies, and persuaded an old friend, Jasper Petulengro of the "Wind on the Heath" conversation, to teach him Rommany. (Strangely enough, though in the body of the book he spells it *Rommany*, when Borrow came to title the second part of his autobiography, the spelling became *Romany, The Romany*

Rye; either, however, is correct.) But he did not confine himself solely to the study of their language—"I went on studying the language, and at the same time the character and manners of these strange people. My rapid progress in the former astonished, while it delighted, Jasper. 'We'll no longer call you sap-engro (snake-master), brother,' said he, 'but rather Lavengro, which in the language of the gorgios meaneth Word Master.' 'Nay, brother,' said Tawno Chikno, with whom I had become very intimate, 'you had better call him Cooro-mengro, I have put on the gloves with him, and find him a pure fist master'."

A good father must watch over his children's material, as well as their spiritual, welfare. Captain Borrow, though he had long since given up the attempt to understand this wayward child, exerted every effort to be a good father. Now staid and respectable for all his prize-fighting youth, he observed his son's vagabondage with no little alarm. The life of scholar or tramp seemed almost equally disreputable, and he made haste to article his son to a firm of solicitors in Norwich.

The idyllic days were over, or should have been. Simpson and Rackham were capable lawyers, well fitted to train him for material success and legal renown. After this manner Borrow studied law:

I had adopted a profession, and—to keep up with my character, simultaneously with that profession—the study of a new language —I speedily became a proficient in the one, but ever remained a novice in the other: a novice at the law, but a perfect master in the Welsh tongue.

Yes! very pleasant times were those, when within the womb of a lofty deal desk, behind which I sat for some eight hours every day, transcribing (when I imagined eyes were upon me) documents of every description in every possible hand, Blackstone kept company with Ab Gwilym—the polished English lawyer of the last century, who wrote long and prosy chapters on the rights of things —with a certain wild Welshman, who for some four hundred years before that time indited immortal cowydds and odes to the wives of Cambrian chieftains—more particularly to one Morfydd, the wife of a certain hunchbacked dignitary called by the poet facetiously Bwa Bach—generally terminating with the modest request of a little private parlance beneath the greenwood bough, with no other witness than the eos, or nightingale, a request which, if the poet himself may be believed, rather a doubtful point, was seldom, very seldom, denied.

In dilettante fashion he flirted with the law for five years; his serious courtship he reserved for languages. Knapp, himself a well-known philologist, says that he had previously studied —"I do not say learned"—Latin, Greek, Irish, French, Italian, Spanish, and the broken jargon then current in England as Gypsy. While studying, or presumably studying, law, he began, at first secretly, then ostentatiously, a series of seven more languages: Welsh, Danish, German, Hebrew, Arabic, Gaelic, and Armenian. German he learned under the tutelage of "Godless Billy" Taylor, the man given credit by Lockhart for inspiring Sir Walter Scott's love for German literature. Taylor, however, was also a popularizer, a scholar whose learning sat lightly on him, and once again Borrow's knowledge was broad rather than deep. Indeed, one of the greatest tragedies in the life of the "word-master" was that academic and critical persons of rank considered his legitimate claims plain lying, his philological knowledge a spurious charlatanism.

The translation mania was upon him. He did not have an inventive mind; such a thing as a plot is almost foreign to his works. With the law as a shield he was assimilating new languages with scarcely more effort than a baby suckles its mother's breast; he was the proud, harum-scarum young friend and pupil of a famous, learned, and dissipated man, to whom he always referred with respect and affection. The great fault was that he knew a little of so many languages, knew no language thoroughly.

But at nineteen he felt a great pride in his knowledge. There was a day for making an inventory of himself—the same day on which his father made his will, leaving all his property to his wife. "What have I done already? I have learned Welsh, and have translated the *Songs of Ab Gwilym*, some ten thousand lines, into English rhyme. I have also learnt Danish, and have rendered the old book of Ballads into English metre. I have learned many other tongues, and have acquired some knowledge even of Hebrew and Arabic."

Such were the mental attainments of the young man, described in prose—and he was even less modest in verse. He had, somehow or other, developed into the ideal young man described in his poem, "Lines to Six-Foot-Three":

> A lad who twenty tongues can talk
> And sixty miles a day can walk;
> Drink at a draught a pint of rum,
> And then be neither sick nor dumb;
> Can tune a song and make a verse,
> And deeds of Northern kings rehearse;
> Who never will forsake his friend
> While he his bony fist can bend;
> And, though averse to brawl and strife,
> Will fight a Dutchman with a knife;
> O that is just the lad for me,
> And such is honest six-foot-three.

Never did the youthful Borrow's energies flag. His translations began to appear in the *Monthly*, the *New*

Monthly, the *Edinburgh*, and other magazines. According to Thomas Seccombe, it was an erroneous belief in the literary and marketable value of these "rococo English versions" of Welsh triads, Danish ballads, Hungarian folk-songs, and the like, that led him in 1824 to abandon the law and go to London. His father had just died; his mother's maintenance was provided for, and his articles of indenture had expired—leaving him with doubtfully sufficient legal knowledge to make a living. He entered on a career of hack writing with the feeling that he had at last mounted Parnassus.

Sir Richard Phillips, the publisher, gave him plenty of work to do: to write critical notices of new books for the *Monthly Magazine*, to compile six volumes of *Newgate Lives and Trials*, "each volume to contain by no manner of means less than one thousand pages, the remuneration which you will receive when the work is completed will be fifty pounds, which is likewise intended to cover any expenses you may incur in procuring books, papers, and manuscripts necessary for the compilation. Such will be one of your employments, sir—such the terms. In the second place, you will be expected to make yourself useful in the *Review*—generally useful, sir—doing whatever is required of you; for it is not customary, at least with me, to permit writers, especially young writers, to choose their subjects."

In addition, Phillips praised highly the young man's knowledge of German, and "I have determined that you shall translate my book of philosophy into German."

"Your book of philosophy into German, sir?"

"Yes, sir; my book of philosophy into German. I am not a drug, sir, in Germany, as Goethe is here, no more is my book; I intend to print the translation at Leipzig, sir; and if it turns out to be a profitable speculation, as I make no doubt it will, provided the translation be well executed, I will make you some remuneration. Sir, your remuneration will be determined by the success of your translation."

It is significant, however, that the famous publisher completely refused to publish any of Borrow's original verse or his translations.

Borrow did not like reviewing—"I did not read the reviewals of my colleagues; I did not read my own after they were printed"—but he was fascinated by the *Newgate Lives and Trials*, from which he said that he first learned to write genuine English. But he found himself unable to translate his employer's work on philosophy, much of it being scientific and based on physics—its exact title being *The Proximate Causes of the Material Phenomena of the Universe*. One suspects Borrow never understood it in English, and his knowledge of German was inadequate—he might have translated Goethe into English, and perhaps have made of it a fine piece of work, but he lacked the scientific knowledge and the scientific language to understand the book in English.

There is little need to analyze the criminal compilation Borrow made for Sir Richard Phillips. In *Lavengro* he alternately praises and hates, enthuses over and condemns, the *Newgate Lives and Trials*; but it is evident that working with this hard, spare English had disciplined his own style. The over-sensational material he handled in a factual manner, so that to a piece of hack work he gave at least a slight distinction.

The editor had done the work, and was dismissed summarily. His name did not appear on the title-page, but in the preface written by Sir Richard Phillips, he was referred to condescendingly. The fifty pounds had been exhausted before the volumes were published. "In the literary harvest there is never any lack of reapers"—and Borrow's services were not needed. Several times, in that period, he planned, or at the least threatened, to commit suicide.

Up to this point the author of *Lavengro* can be trusted almost implicitly. Only names and titles had been changed: for example, the substitution of the title *Newgate Lives and Trials* for the long, clumsy *Celebrated Trials and Remarkable Cases of Criminal Jurisprudence.* And that was not only pardonable, but reasonable; Borrow only substituted the sprightlier name first agreed upon between editor and publisher. Whatever money Borrow received was soon spent, and no one would risk publishing his ballads and translations.

Now occurred an event in his life that remains to this day veiled and obscure. In London, out of work, in bad health, he describes in *Lavengro* how he wrote a book called *The Life and Adventures of Joseph Sell, the Great Traveller*, and sold it to an unnamed London publisher for twenty pounds. With this sum he began the gypsy wanderings that constitute the most famous portion of *Lavengro.*

That sounds accurate enough. Unfortunately, collectors and Borrovian enthusiasts have never been able to find a book named *Joseph Sell*, or one resembling it. Two volumes of George Borrow's were published in 1825; first, before considering these, Borrow's own statements must be considered.

From the *Newgate Lives and Trials* he turned to fiction of a similar nature:

This Joseph Sell, dear reader, was a fictitious personage who had just come into my head. I had never heard of the name, but just at that moment it happened to come into my head; I would write an entirely fictitious narrative, called the *Life and Adventures of Joseph Sell, The Great Traveller.*

He wrote with great rapidity and zealous perseverance, husbanding his resources with greatest care. Unfortunately, again, however, he tells nothing of the internal structure of the book, and, except that it was suggested to him by the *Newgate Lives and Trials*, nothing of its contents. The manuscript completed, "I spent my last three-pence on a breakfast somewhat more luxurious than the preceding ones, for one penny of the sum was expended on the purchase of milk."

The first publisher accepted his manuscript, and offered him five pounds for it:

"Dear me," said he, "I should never have supposed that you would have made any objection to such an offer; I am quite sure that you would have been glad to take five pounds for either of the two huge manuscripts of songs and ballads that you brought me on a former occasion."

"Well," said I, "if you will engage to publish either of those two manuscripts, you shall have the present one for five pounds." "God forbid that I should make any such bargain," said the bookseller, "I would publish neither on any account; but with respect to this last book, I have really an inclination to print it, both for your sake and mine; suppose we say ten pounds."

Borrow held out for twenty-five pounds, but in the end compromised on twenty. Quite obviously the manuscript in question had no connection with any of the ballads and poems—those the publisher refused to consider as a gift, even a gift endowed with fifteen pounds bonus. Once before in *Lavengro*, he had referred to a translation of a German novel, and its refusal by a snuff-taking publisher.

Since no record of the apocryphal *Joseph Sell* could be found, many Borrovians concluded that this must be the work referred to: *Faustus: His Life, Death, and Descent Into Hell*, translated from the German of Friedrich von

Klinger by George Borrow, and published by W. Simpkin and R. Marshall, London, 1825. Klinger, the man whose play *Sturm und Drang* gave a name to an entire period of German literature, was very popular at the time, but on the title-page Borrow or the publisher does not even mention his name.

This book can hardly be fitted into the description given by Borrow. Yet it was published in 1825—a fact never mentioned in *Lavengro*. A translation, not an original piece of work, it could never have been suggested by the *Newgate Lives and Trials*. Yet, for lack of an authentic work that would answer the description, *Faustus* was accepted as *Joseph Sell* by Clement Shorter and a few others; most Borrovians believed the manuscript hopelessly lost.

W. I. Knapp refused to believe the work imaginary:

We now come to the crucial test. If all the rest of *Lavengro* is strictly true, why not this *Life of Joseph Sell*, and the nomadic episode that is the resultant? So far everything has been verified and the date fixed by reliable records. Only names have been distorted or substituted—the *Oxford Review*, the *Newgate Lives and Trials*, the *Publishers' Philosophy*; but they have been identified. Tredinnoch was put in for Trethinnick; Petrement for Perfrement, Philoh for Philo, Ardry for Arden, Taggart for Bartlett, Joey's for Charlie's, Isopel for Elizabeth, Jasper for Ambrose, etc.; but registers, newspapers, and the autograph MSS. correct them. There were *Sells* at Norwich; their great artist was John Sell Cotman. The fact that Mrs. Borrow rejected the work and episode with scorn is of no importance whatever. She knew nothing of her husband's *Sturm und Drang* period, for she never saw him till the end of 1832, and he kept his own counsel touching his early struggles. Witness the "Veiled Era." How many times, while *Lavengro* was on the stocks, did Richard Ford in his letters implore him to "lift the veil from over those seven years." That signified the unrevealed mystery lying *between*

1825 and 1833, exclusive of those years. Hence all that preceded and followed, from 1826 backward and 1832 forward, was known and acknowledged. Hence the gypsy tramp of May to August, 1825, was in the main authentic. Please to trust the present writer in the undocumented part, as you must trust him in the rest that is abundantly authenticated. In the end, when all the data lies before you, you will come to know the man. The only key to his methods, as well as to his heart, is sympathy.

Returning to the *Life of Joseph Sell*, a great deal has been said and written to prove that it was an imaginary, and apocryphal book. It has been sought for, but in vain, because it was not a book at all, and the author of it never said that it was. It is expressly stated to have been a tale in a collection or series of such, written by various authors—Christmas stories possibly—that may have been issued with an advanced date, as the *Bible in Spain* was—in this case, 1826. Mr. Borrow himself did not see the work, and did not know under what general title the "Collection" was published. He sold the MSS. and left town and did not return to London for more than a twelve-month.

Just such a collection of stories was discovered in 1921 by Mr. Walter Jerrold, and published in *The Complete Works of George Borrow*, London, 1924. *Tales of the Wild and Wonderful* was published in 1825. It contains five stories, two of which are original; one, "Der Freischutz," is translated from the German, and two of the stories, "The Yellow Dwarf" and "The Lord of the Maelstrom" are largely original, though based on Norse mythology. Of these stories "The Fortunes of De La Pole" most nearly resembles his *Celebrated Trials*.

The stories require little consideration from the literary point of view. All of them sound like translations: their chief literary merit is the vigor and the clarity of the prose. Borrow's preface is of more interest than any of the stories; it has the stamp of *Lavengro* written all over it:

I, moreover, designed to have given thee a little poetry for thy money, gentle reader, but the booksellers shook their heads when I mentioned my design, and told me it was out of fashion; so I returned my treasures in that way to my desk, there to remain, among many other excellent things, until it shall again be the taste in England; and, in the meantime, offer these Tales of *Diablerie* for your amusement.

Borrow was not highly interested in these tales of *diablerie*, however; to him they represented chiefly just so much hack work. He felt, though without much reason, that his real talent, his great literary accomplishment, lay in the ballad translations. More inexplicable is his lack of interest in the *Faustus* and *Tales of the Wild and Wonderful*. A highly ambitious young author, with one book of original stories and a long prose translation, might justifiably have felt that life was promising, London not altogether grim, forbidding, and unappreciative of genius.

But his health was bad, and that excuses all depths of pessimism. Moreover, Borrow felt that he had been cheated on all sides. Sir Richard Phillips had used him and cast him aside, a husk from which the grain had been gathered; he had compiled a huge work in six volumes, to be told that he had already used up all the money due him—in addition, his name was hardly mentioned in the collection. His prose work was accepted, but it was only fair stuff: one could not safely trust people of such poor judgment. And the critics, kind to Borrow only once in a long literary life-time—when the *Bible in Spain* appeared—attacked it virulently. *The Literary Gazette* (16th July 1825) in particular criticized it harshly as

another work to which no respectable publisher ought to have allowed his name to be put. The political allusions and metaphysics, which may have made it popular among a low class in Germany, do not season its lewd scenes and coarse descriptions for British palates. We have occasionally publications for the fireside—these are fit only for the fire.

To one accustomed to modern literature, or to Elizabethan, it must be confessed that *Faustus* seems tame and free from most of the taints of evil; the early Victorian conscience was beginning to flower, or perhaps better, rigorously to choke off all flowers that seemed vigorous enough ever to be in danger of becoming rank. Borrow was only one of many attacked, but from that date he had a keen horror of critics and reviewers. Two copies of the book were burned at Norwich, and, worst of all, his publishers could not pay him anything except a bill dated six months ahead—and thirty copies of his own work.

With these experiences as author in the background, Borrow left London for a life of roving adventure—bound nowhere, either from the standpoint of geography or destination in life. But what, in sober fact, started out to be no more than a walking tour without destination or time limit proved an escape from a literary Newgate to the dingle and the wind on the heath, to an adventurous life with the gypsies, the record of which comprises the second half of *Lavengro* and all of *Romany Rye*.

III

Years later, when in *Lavengro* Borrow described his earlier life, he wrote not in the fashion of a dry biographer but after the manner of a creative artist. A huge mass of material had lain in his mind, and in the selective process he worked always with one eye on the dramatic effect. Yet the record is singularly lucid and accurate, until his departure from London; from this point one can never be sure what in his narrative is fact and what fiction.   Certain it is that the portrait he painted of himself was intended to be flattering, romantic—the re-written version, by a man of fifty, of his "Lines to Six-Foot-Three."

He left London on foot, but, yet weak from illness, he was forced to go by coach to Amesbury, and from there walked to Salisbury.   His picture of a coachman, in striking contrast with the sentimentalized jehus of Dickens, is anything but flattering to that class—and Borrow, whenever he mentions coachmen at all, portrays them as mean-spirited and greedy, insolent to the poor but subservient to the wealthy —in general, toadies, bullies, and bruisers.

But twenty pounds will not last forever, even when one is vagabonding.   Borrow felt a definite need for some occupation, and for ten pounds five shillings he bought a tinker's outfit and his territory.   Jack Slingsby had been warned to leave the territory by "the Flaming Tinman," a half-gypsy who ruled the members of that craft, and who had expelled the tinker from the pseudo-union.   Borrow was fascinated by the possibility of danger, the chance of physical combat; he was even more delighted with the prospect of an independent, outdoor profession, for he declared,

What can be better than to be one's own master?   Now a tinker is his own master; a scholar is not.   Let us suppose the best of scholars, a schoolmaster, for example, for I suppose you will admit that no one can be higher in scholarship than a schoolmaster; do you call his a pleasant life?   I don't; we should call him a school-slave, rather than a schoolmaster.   Only conceive him in blessed weather like this, in his close school, teaching children to write in copy-books, "Evil communication corrupts good manners," or "You cannot touch pitch without defilement," or to spell out of Abedariums, or to read out of Jack Smith, or Sand-ford and Merton. Would you compare such a dog's life as that with your own—the happiest under heaven—true Eden life, as the Germans would say,—pitching your tent under the pleasant hedge-rows, listening to the song of the feathered tribes, collecting soldering and joining, earning your honest bread by the wholesome sweat of your brow—making ten holes—hey, what's this? What is the man crying for?

Borrow's magnificent hymn to the open road had roused all the tender emotions of the tinker, until he blubbered in self-pity at leaving so noble an occupation. To Borrow it represented something more; it was a release, a chance for forgetfulness. One must remember that at this time (May, 1825), he was only twenty-two years old: though widely travelled, the author of one book, translator of another, and editor of a third, he was then hardly more than a boy—the same age as the average college graduate. A youth given to dramatizing himself, one who had sublimated his energies, wrapped himself completely in literary ambitions. Sex had played little or no part in his life. If, when one of "Godless Billy" Taylor's harum-scarum young men he had experienced love, or bought sexual experience, he never records the fact, nor has anyone else.

With his newly-acquired tinker's outfit he started into the marches of Wales. It was the land of the gypsies, and on his rounds he met Mrs. Herne, the mother-in-law of his old friend, Jasper Petulengro. She had always hated Borrow, had never forgiven her son-in-law for initiating a gorgio (outsider) into gypsy ways and secrets, and for teaching him Rommany. The ways of a woman are dark and devious, he found; for no apparent reason, or at least Borrow gives none save her ancient jealousy, she sent him some poisoned cakes. He lay groaning by the side of the road, when a Welsh preacher and his wife heard him. Liberal doses of castor oil proved a fine antidote, leaving Borrow utterly exhausted but drained of all the poison.

However, he had met the gypsies, if under rather discouraging circumstances, and at first he decided to cast in his lot with them. But a dose of poison hardly encourages closer intimacy, and the tinker decided to seek safety in solitude. Girls began to trouble him for the first time. He had found Mrs. Herne's granddaughter very attractive —and, after attempting to poison him, the old lady proposed a marriage between the two. Borrow refused, and departed, more in her bad graces than ever.

The same man who had run Slingsby the tinker from his territory now menaced his successor. Borrow had planned to spend the night in a camping-ground called Mumper's Dingle. He found it occupied by the Flaming Tinman, and found that gentleman ready for battle. With him was his wife and a tall, beautiful girl, Isopel Berners. Many times Borrow described fights, but never more effectively than this, the greatest fight of his career. At first neither could gain an advantage—then,

And now the Flaming Tinman was once more ready, much more ready than myself. I, however, rose from my second's knee as well as my weakness would permit me; on he came, striking left and right, appearing almost as fresh as to wind and spirit as when he first commenced the combat, though his eyes were considerably swelled, and his nether lip was cut in two; on he came, striking left and right, and I did not like his blows at all, or even the wind of them, which was anything but agreeable, and I gave way before him. At last he aimed a blow, which, had it taken full effect, would have ended the battle, but, owing to his slipping, the fist only grazed my left shoulder, and came with terrific force against a tree, close to which I had been driven; before the tinman could recover himself, I collected all my strength, and struck him beneath the ear, and then fell to the ground completely exhausted, and it so happened that the blow which I struck the tinker was a right-handed blow.

"Hurrah for Long Melford!" I heard Belle exclaim. "There is nothing like Long Melford for shortness all the world over."

Borrow had won; the dingle and the territory belonged to him. But he had won even more—during the fight Isopel Berners had become his partisan, and when the Flaming Tinman departed, she remained with George Borrow. He describes her as "an exceedingly tall woman, or rather girl, for she could scarcely have been over eighteen; she was dressed in a tight bodice and a blue stuff gown; hat, bonnet, or cap she had none, and her hair, which was flaxen, hung down on her shoulders unconfined; her complexion was fair, and her features handsome, with a determined but open expression."

For three months George Borrow lived in the dingle with Isopel Berners. He never states explicitly, but the implication is that their relations were platonic, since he omits entirely any mention of other and more intimate relations. Because of this Saintsbury says that the couple took up their residence, "a joint residence of perfect propriety," in this dingle; that Borrow only taught her how to conjugate "I love" in Armenian when the tall girl wanted, not philology, but passion. Few people would agree with him; human beings are not so constructed. Here Saintsbury, with the astounding literalness common to so many scholars, never reads anything more than the words. Surely the overtones imply that here was a summer idyll, consummately complete.

There was a very good reason for Borrow's circumspection when he related the story of his life with Isopel Berners, a very good reason why the girls who must have figured in his life are never mentioned. In 1840 he had married a rich widow some eight years his senior, a woman jealous of his affections and ever doubtful of her hold upon them. Borrow loved and admired her, and was constantly attempting not to hurt her feelings—rarely with success. It was a happy marriage, in the sense that marriages contracted late in life usually are: congenial companionship took the place of passion. Certainly it did on the part of George Borrow. Heaven knows, his wife was a pleasant creature, but she would never forgive his boastfully describing a perfect love of his youth. And Victorian society would have been equally unrelenting.

Whatever the facts, the author of *Lavengro* felt this summer to be the happiest period of life. The dingle was pleasant, and it was indescribably good to have a beautiful woman to talk with, to do the cooking and similar chores, and to show plainly her devotion. Occasionally she left, on excursions of her own; occasionally the tinker must bestir himself, and make some money—even the dingle lacked some of the advantages of Eden.

The one disturbing element was Belle's restless craving to go to America, and he had serious thoughts of going with her, to people the forests of America with "an enormous progeny of lusty children." It seemed a peaceful and enviable time, marred however from Belle's point of view by the lessons in Armenian. So Borrow temporized and procrastinated—he went neither to America nor to Gretna Green, and his companion adventured to America. He had, finally, offered to marry her, but he "kept putting off and putting off," as she wrote in her note of departure, and though "when you did make it, I frankly tell you that I had half a mind to accept it; at last, however, after very much consideration, I thought it best to leave you forever, because, for some time past, I had become almost convinced, that though with a wonderful deal of learning, and exceedingly shrewd in some things, you were—pray don't be offended—at the root mad!"

At first he determined to follow her, but Borrow's thoughts soon turned back to his first and greatest love—literature. In later life the events of this summer were to furnish the mature author with his greatest subject.

Approximately the next seven years in Borrow's life remain obscure, "the veiled era" which he preferred to keep dark and mysterious. But his life from September of 1825 to December of 1832 was apparently unpleasant; possibly, also, it was mainly empty and aimless. He appeared sometimes on the surface of public life; in *The Bible in Spain* he casually refers to himself as having been, during these years, in France, in Spain, and in Southeastern Europe. Whether these years were empty or horrible or even pleasant, Borrow in later life treasured them romantically as a personal secret. Clearly he never intended to continue his autobiography through that period.

Fortunately, there are a fair number of definite facts that can be recorded, a few other facts that seem certainties.

After Isopel Berners deserted him, Borrow purchased a horse with money loaned him by Mr. Petulengro. He worked for a brief time at the Swan Inn, Stafford; sold the horse for a good profit at a fair, paid his debts, and returned to Norwich.

While at Norwich the young author arranged for the publication of a book made up of translations from the Danish and other languages that had appeared in *The Monthly Magazine* between October 1823 and December 1825. Two hundred copies were subscribed for in advance; an edition of five hundred copies was published. *Romantic*

Ballads proved a still-born child. Few additional copies were bought; critics and reviewers gave it no attention. At the suggestion of a friend, Allan Cunningham, Borrow sent one copy to Sir Walter Scott—but that busy and famous writer not only failed to praise the book publicly; he even failed to acknowledge the courtesy. From that day Borrow hated Scott; in the appendix to *The Romany Rye* he attacked him viciously.

Once the book was published Borrow grew tired of Norwich. Quite probably he felt mortified at the reception given his verses. Some months later he appeared in London. Years before the older brother, John Borrow, had studied under Benjamin Robert Haydon—now George wrote to him, apparently in response to a request from the painter:

Dear Sir,—I should feel extremely obliged if you would allow me to sit to you as soon as possible. I am going to the South of France, in little better than a fortnight, and I would sooner lose a thousand pounds than not have the honor of appearing in the picture—

No portrait of Borrow has ever been identified in a Haydon picture. Whether he was painted or not is unknown; probably he was. Equally doubtful is the date of his departure for France. In *The Bible in Spain* he casually speaks of the gypsies whom he knew while in the South of France; he had already said that "during my own wandering in Italy" gypsies had been more than kind. Too, he was at Paris, Madrid, Bayonne; then back in England, with a new translation ready to be published. In the years 1828–29 four small volumes of the *Memoirs of Vidocq* were published in England. In *The Zincali* Borrow praised the memoirs constantly, extolled them highly: there is small doubt that he translated the work entire. That master-rogue turned detective would fascinate Borrow, and apparently no story in a foreign language ever appealed to him without also forcing him to translate it.

Other plans were not lacking to his eager brain. One of his friends at "Godless Billy" Taylor's had been Dr. John Bowring. Borrow persuaded him that the two should collaborate on a translation of Scandinavian ballads. In December 1829 Borrow returned to London; he pushed the matter of the translations vigorously, assuring Dr. Bowring that he had enough translations at hand to fill one volume. The publication seemed definitely settled, for a prospectus appeared in the March (1830) *Monthly Review:*

Dr. Bowring and Mr. George Borrow are about to publish, dedicated to the King of Denmark, by His Majesty's permission, *The Songs of Scandinavia*, in 2 vols. 8vo., containing a selection of the most interesting of the Historical and Romantic Ballads of North-Western Europe, with specimens of the Danish and Norwegian poets down to the present day.

But *The Songs of Scandinavia* caused Borrow as much trouble as had the *Celebrated Trials*. Bowring was lukewarm, at best, and when no subscribers appeared, the project was allowed to drop, though only after seething fulminations on the part of Borrow.

At the same time he tried to secure a post with the British Museum; on the 9th of March, 1830, he wrote Dr. Bowring for assistance, but again he failed. Both literary and material success were to be denied to him. One final effort he made, however, before disappearing entirely for two years. This episode is best told in his own words, in the preface to a limited edition of *The Sleeping Bard*, published by John Murray in 1860:

The following translation of the 'Sleeping Bard' has long existed in manuscript. It was made by the writer of these lines in the

year 1830, at the request of a little Welsh bookseller of his acquaintance, who resided in the rather unfashionable neighborhood
of Smithfield, and who entertained an opinion that a translation
of the works of Elis Wyn would enjoy a great sale both in England
and Wales. On the eve of committing it to the press, however,
the Cambrian Briton felt his small heart give way within him:
'Were I to print it,' said he, 'I should be ruined; the terrible
descriptions of vice and torment would frighten the genteel part
of the British public out of its wits, and I should to a certainty be
prosecuted by Sir James Scarlett. I am much obliged to you,
for the trouble you have given yourself on my account,—but Myn
Diawl! I had no idea till I had him in English, that Elis Wyn had
been such a terrible fellow.'

Thanks for several months hard labor—*The Sleeping
Bard* runs to one hundred and fifty pages—but no money;
George Borrow had another manuscript to store in his
trunk. Evidently this last episode seemed too much. He
returned to Norwich, travelled in Europe, studied Persian
and other Oriental languages, and later said casually that he
had travelled in the countries of South-Western Asia.
Whatever he did, it was a period of loneliness, of obscurity,
and poverty—a period which he never talked about; indeed,
refused point-blank even to mention. He was "digging
holes in the sand, and filling them up again."

In December, 1832, Borrow again returned to Norwich.
Soon after he entered the employ of the Bible Society.
From that time Borrow described his life fully, first in letters
and then in books. The "veiled period" was over.

The British and Foreign Bible Society had been formed to
spread the gospel throughout the world. Its home evangelical work had been steady, and, in the eyes of its supporters,
valuable. But its foreign work had been intermittent.
One ambitious project had been started in 1821 when the
head of the Society, Dr. Pinkerton, had engaged Stepan

Lipóftsof to translate the entire New Testament into Manchu. Lipóftsof had studied Chinese and Manchu at the National College of Peking, and had lived in China for twenty years. After his return to Russia he was appointed head of the Board of Censors for books printed in the languages of the Far East.

Lipóftsof had begun his work of translation immediately, and in 1822 an edition of 550 copies of the Gospel of St. Matthew had been printed in St. Petersburg. Lipóftsof continued with his translation which was completed in 1826, when it was carefully stored away in the vaults of the Society. The Bible Society vaguely intended to publish it in the near future.

In 1832 one of the missionaries of the Society, on his way to Siberia, discovered in St. Petersburg a manuscript translation of the Old Testament in Manchu. With this discovery a revival of enthusiasm was experienced by the officials of the Bible Society, and they determined to publish the complete Bible in Manchu as soon as the necessary arrangements could be made.

For once in his life Borrow was fortunate. A friend and member, the Rev. Francis Cunningham, recommended him to the Society. He knew little or nothing about the work in hand, evidently, but felt that a man of Borrow's great linguistic talents should be of value to the organization, for in a letter he described Borrow as "a person without university education, but who has read the Bible in thirteen languages." Cunningham's recommendation carried weight, and Borrow was invited to come to London for an interview.

Not having money to pay for transportation to London, Borrow walked the entire distance of one hundred and twelve miles in twenty-seven hours. The trip cost him five pence half-penny, for a pint of ale, a half-pint of milk, a roll of bread, and two apples.

For a week the officials of the Bible Society examined him in Oriental languages—then inquired if he would undertake to learn Manchu. It is a difficult language to learn, one grammarian saying that in five or six years time one can acquire a passable knowledge of Manchu. But a boy who could speak twenty languages before he was twenty-one could not be judged by ordinary standards: Borrow confidently agreed to master the language in six months, working chiefly with a French-Manchu grammar and the Lipóftsof translation of the Gospel of St. Matthew. Within a month he was writing to the Society that, if they would only procure for him a Manchu grammar, he would "in a month's time be able to send them a Manchu translation of Jonah." After nineteen weeks of study, Borrow seemed even to the cautious and perhaps scholarly officials of the Bible Society a man who could be trusted with editing the work.

Although he had accomplished the work of five years in nineteen weeks, he had not been content with that. The Bible Society would not pay him for studying, but did for correcting press-work of the Gospel of St. Luke translated into Nahuatl, the common dialect of the Mexican Indians. His brother John, retired from the army and failing as an artist, had gone to Mexico; Borrow, with his indefatigable curiosity about languages, had requested information and books about the language. At some time during the "veiled period" he had studied the Nahuatl dialect, and mastered it well enough to be able to correct the proof on a 140 page book—a correction in which one man's guess would probably be as good as another, for the Mexican Indians spoke, not one dialect, but among the various tribes some forty or fifty dialects, and few of them could read.

There seems reason to believe that Borrow was totally uninterested in the practical side—whether the Society's labor was useful or valueless did not matter greatly to him.

His own assigned tasks he performed conscientiously, but he instructed his mother that if his brother John Borrow returned home, he was on no account to be allowed near the Bible Society: John had lived many years in Mexico, and might shake the faith of the Fathers in their work, or at least in the literary portion of it.

The Society had determined to print the Manchu Bible in St. Petersburg. No presses capable of the work could be found in London. On July 31st, 1833, he left London for St. Petersburg, confident as ever, happy chiefly because "my salary commences from the time I set out on my journey." He visited Hamburg and Bremen on the way, arriving in St. Petersburg on the thirteenth of August.

For the first time in years—since the summer with Isopel Berners in the dingle eight years before—George Borrow was contented and happy. He liked his work, liked St. Petersburg,

Petersburg is the finest city in the world, London, Paris, Madrid, and other capitals I have visited, are not worthy to hold a candle to it. There are hundreds of enormous palaces, streets miles in length, and as straight as an arrow. The Nefski perspective is nearly three miles long, and is floored with wood. In a word, I can do little else but look and wonder.

Borrow was popular in St. Petersburg; in addition to social courtesies, Baron Schilling, the foremost authority on Manchu and possessor of a magnificent private library which contained "all the best works which have issued from the Pekin press in Chinese, Mandchou and Mongolian," had placed all his resources at Borrow's disposal. It was an immense task he had before him. Published in Manchu, the Bible would be in eight bulky volumes; it was not a small undertaking, under any circumstances, merely to read and correct the proof.

His own share of the labor troubled him little, however. Lack of funds annoyed him most; while waiting for money, he employed his time in studying Manchu under a native tutor, and in social visits with his new friends. In June, 1834, full authorization to proceed with the work, and credit of 700 pounds, arrived. Work could begin.

Manchu printers and type-setters were unknown, and Russian printers could not be depended on. Besides, being Greek Catholics, they had too many holidays. A German printing shop set up an annex, with German compositors, that was to be devoted solely to the printing of the Manchu Bible. Unfortunately, not one of them understood the mysterious Tartar alphabet, with its strange symbols and almost identical letters. The director had to teach them how to set up the type and read the alphabet. He worked energetically, zealously, and he forced others to work with him. By September, 1835, the entire edition of one thousand volumes was ready for distribution.

A new factor now entered into the situation. The Russian government had never been over-cordial: only the fact that Lipóftsof, who translated the Bible, was head of the Board of Censors over books translated into the languages of the Far East had prevented any earlier disturbance. Borrow wanted to go as a distributing missionary overland to China, and the Society had accepted his offer— his pay to remain the same, 250 pounds a year. At this point the Russian government interfered. A passport was refused, in such a way that nothing more was to be said. The Czar feared anything that might incite trouble on his borders; he was taking no chances.

Every man must have some recreation; his avocation is often as important in his career as his vocation. The great passion of Borrow's life was rhymed translating from foreign languages, especially the Danish and the Russian. One huge advantage had accrued to him—he was the head of his own printing-house, virtually, though its name remained Schultze and Beneze. The wonder is that Borrow was so moderate; he was burningly eager for the world to see his *Songs of Scandinavia*. Had he used foresight, he might have had his own publishing house print them.

As it was, he published two volumes of translations in 1835, in editions limited to one hundred copies of each. The first was titled *Targum, or Metrical Translations from Thirty Languages and Dialects*. Targum is supposed to be a Chaldean word meaning interpretation. The chief point of interest about these forty-six poems is, as the title indicates, the number of languages from which they were translated. Even the kindest of Borrow's critics admit they have small literary merit—though in 1835 Dr. Hoke wrote to Borrow:

[William B.] Donne is greatly delighted with the *Targum*. He says the language and rhythm are vastly superior to Macaulay's *Lays of Ancient Rome*, which created such a sensation.

Perhaps they are as good—Macaulay's *Lays* seem fairly shoddy and artifical today; but Borrow's work seems even worse. In a single thin volume, however, he had translated poems from the following languages: Ancient British, Ancient Danish, Ancient Irish, Ancient Norse, Anglo-Saxon, Arabic, Cambrian British, Chinese, Danish, Dutch, Finnish, French, Gaelic, German, Greek, Hebrew, Irish, Italian, Latin, Malo-Russian, Manchu, Modern Greek, Persian, Polish, Portuguese, Provençal, Romany, Russian, Spanish, Suabian, Swedish, Tartar, Tibetan, Turkish, Welsh. If the translations lacked literary greatness, at least no other book of similar size would acquaint a reader with examples of the literatures of so many countries.

Three months later he published *The Talisman, From the Russian of Alexander Pushkin. With Other Pieces.* The volume contained seven poems in all; it is slim, with two poems translated from the Russian of Pushkin, "The Renegade" from the Polish of Mickiewicz, and four ancient Russian songs. Borrow had no more translations printed until 1860.

With his work completed to the satisfaction of everyone, and two volumes of translations published to the satisfaction of himself, Borrow departed from Russia. He returned to London, not certain that the Bible Society would keep him, but hopeful that he would be placed in charge of the distribution, this time by sea from London, of the Bibles in China. He wrote:

I hope the Bible Society will employ me upon something new, for I have of late led an active life, and dread the thought of having nothing to do, except studying as formerly, and I am by no means certain that I could sit down to study now. I can do anything if it is to turn to any account, but it is very hard to dig holes in the sand and fill them up again, as I used to do.

Although the Chinese expedition was abandoned, Borrow was in London less than a week. His new work was the distribution of Bibles in Spain and Portugal—surely one of the most quixotic undertakings any organization ever entered upon. All Spanish versions of the Bible, or any part of it, were forbidden in Spain by the *Index*—a direct challenge, of course, to the Society, and to George Borrow.

It is impossible to determine whether Borrow's abhorrence of popery and Catholicism dated from his experiences in Spain, or whether those experiences merely deepened his hatred. The latter is probably correct, but this hatred added a spur to his efforts, and in five years he distributed thirty thousand copies of the Bible. If any dent was made in the Catholic stronghold, it never became evident to any save the evangelical eye. Borrow reported to his Society, by letters, complete and unexpurgated (not in the usual sense, for he hardly mentions women) accounts of his exploits and adventures. They were published in the Society *Quarterly* and formed the ground work of *The Bible in Spain*.

Almost the first letter informed the Society that he considered Portugal a hot-bed of sin. He distributed Bibles all over Lisbon and the surrounding country. But he found it a thankless task, and soon informed the Society that he was going to Spain.

By this time Borrow had matured. He was a distinguished-looking man, very tall, well-built, with graying hair and cold blue eyes. He had walked with princes, but he had also walked with gypsies and with rogues—and in general found the latter more interesting. But he was not a placeable type: in Lisbon he met some Jews who thought him a rabbi; wandering gypsies took him for one of themselves; later, in Spain a Catholic priest took him for a fellow priest, and confided in him.

In fact, all of them confided in him. The vagabond explained why the gypsies are Egyptians, the priest explained the torturing doubts and difficulties that beset a member of the inquisition.

Although he made friends with all sorts and conditions of people in Spain, he could not gain the support of the Spanish government. The premier, Mendizabal, a Christianized Jew, insisted that the New Testament was a dangerous and subversive book, and he refused permission either to print or to distribute it. But Mendizabal died in March, 1836, and Borrow began disposing of his Bibles vigorously. He knew something was wrong with the Peninsula, and, though he had small faith in the practical efficacy of his work, he had a reformer's desire to change all such things. Besides, he meant to keep the good will of the Society.

In Seville, Cordoba, and Salamanca, Borrow received eager aid from the gypsies, who acted as his distributing agents. Then, to this impractical man came an idea worthy of an American industrialist: he advertised the Bible. In Salamanca a bookseller named Blanco, who had a printing-press, was first converted, and convinced that heaven was for him. Then he printed reams of advertisements that Borrow wrote, to the effect that The British and Foreign Bible Society was the only institution in the world dispensing the true gospel; the only ones who knew the will of heaven, and could with any degree of certainty guarantee an entrance into heaven. It was a scheme worthy of a Babbitt, but it worked, as all such schemes seem to do. The master-stroke, however, was that a Bible sold for a small sum—they were not distributed free, as before—and that for this mere pittance the recipient would achieve happiness in this world and salvation in the next.

Borrow travelled over most of Spain in his attempts to spread the gospel. One other agent, a Lieut. Graydon, was also employed in the same work. Graydon had a fanatical missionary spirit. Borrow did not. The two men never worked well together, and Borrow constantly suspected his fellow-worker of plotting against him.

The Spanish government had not forgotten him, and when Borrow sold Bibles openly on the streets of Madrid he was arrested and put in jail, on the first of May, 1838. A police officer had searched his rooms the day before, and caused him to be ejected from his private apartment—though only over Borrow's vigorous and unrestrained protests. He was charged with insulting an officer in the performance of his duty, and with selling a book (a gypsy translation of St. Luke) printed in Gibraltar and introduced into the country in contravention of the laws for the regulation of the press. The book was actually printed in Madrid, with the permission of the Spanish authorities, but that made small difference with the governor.

For eleven days George Borrow remained in jail, booked as an ordinary prisoner awaiting trial, though, as he could pay for anything he desired, he suffered far less than the usual run of prisoners. The English minister, Sir George Villiers, protested; at first to no avail, then more vigorously. The second protest, involving the rights of Englishmen, was effective. On the 11th of May, Borrow was released, and the British minister was informed that "the judicial authorities had approved putting Mr. Borrow immediately at liberty, and declaring that his honor was in no way affected. The police agent was punished by suspension for four months, and Mr. Borrow's expenses while in prison were paid." The minister further declared that Borrow's imprisonment was due to: "1st, his imprudent zeal; 2nd, from suspicions excited by the conduct of Mr. Graydon in attacking the Roman Catholic religion [a thing Borrow had carefully avoided]; and 3rd, from the proceedings of the British Methodist Society in establishing a school at Cadiz." With this school, or Society, Borrow had nothing to do; the Bible Society was non-denominational, and had no connection with the British Methodist Society.

Whether his arrest was justified or not, Borrow had earned his full share of fame, or notoriety. The *Affaire Borrow* made a sensation both in England and Spain. Also, it roused dissension in the Bible Society, and Graydon and Borrow, never friendly, became open enemies. They were cutting one another's throats, a much more interesting pastime than handing out Bibles. For a year the feud continued, with Borrow more and more disgusted and angry.

There was one way out. One of the prominent families of Norwich was the Skeppers of Oulton Hall. Mary Skepper was born in 1796, and in 1817 had married Lieutenant Henry Clarke, R. N. Within the year Clarke died of tuberculosis, leaving a posthumous daughter, Henrietta Maria. Despite the disparity in their ages, Borrow had paid frequent visits to the young widow after he reached maturity; she had introduced him to Cunningham and thus helped him in getting a place with the Bible Society; and from Russia and from Spain he corresponded with her.

In March, 1839, Mrs. Clarke wrote to him that she intended to settle for a short time in Seville, Borrow's headquarters. The reason was simple, though an explanation of it is involved. Her brother had died, and their joint estate was sold by the trustees for eleven thousand pounds. Then the trustees discovered they had made a poor bargain, and delayed proceedings; finally, in order that she should not be available to sign the documents, they advised her to take a European tour. She decided to visit Borrow.

That hardened campaigner had primitive notions of comfort; his directions to Mrs. Clarke are most amusing:

Houses in Spain are let by the day; and in a palace here you will find less furniture than in your cottage at Oulton. Were you to furnish a Spanish house in the style of cold, wintry England, you would be unable to breathe. A few chairs, tables, and mattresses are all that is required, with of course a good stock of bed-linen. . . .

Bring with you, therefore, your clothes, plenty of bed-linen, etc., half-a-dozen blankets, two dozen knives and forks, a mirror or two, twelve silver table spoons, and a large one for soup, tea things and urn (for the Spaniards never drink tea), a few books, but not many—and you will have occasion for nothing more, or, if you have, you can purchase it here as cheap as in England.

Their living together created no scandal in Seville, and Borrow simply informed the officials of the Society that two or three ladies were visiting him. Quite probably their conduct was conventional in everything save appearances. Surely no reason for scandal existed: they were mature persons, amply able to take care of themselves, and the world was little interested in them.

From Seville, Borrow and Mrs. Clarke went to the South of Spain, to San Lucas, Gibraltar, and on to Tangier. Afterwards he distributed Bibles in La Mancha, and to a practical eye his mission seemed little less hopeless and absurd than any of the famous expeditions of Don Quixote. Borrow was tired of the work; the Spanish government threatened to interfere actively again; and in April, 1840, embarked for England, with Mrs. Clarke accompanying him.

They were married in London, on the 23rd of April, and settled at Oulton. George Borrow had become, by marriage, an English country gentleman with an estate. But he had by no means renounced literary ambitions.

In addition to a wife-to-be, he brought back from Spain a completed book, and all the materials for a second book. *The Zincali, An Account of the Gypsies of Spain*, was published in April, 1841, in two volumes. Borrow's own account of its preparation is the best:

The greater part of it has been written under very peculiar circumstances, such as are not in general deemed at all favourable for literary composition: at considerable intervals, during a period of nearly five years passed in Spain—in moments snatched from more important pursuits—chiefly in ventas and posadas, whilst wandering through the country in the arduous and unthankful task of distributing the gospel among its children.

Dr. Knapp has pointed out that there is no such word as *Zincali*. It should be *Zincale:* "for, if there ever was such a word as *Zincali*, which I doubt, never having heard it used in Spain, it would signify a gypsy female. They always employ the term *calo* (black) for a gypsy man; *cali*, a gypsy woman; *cale* or *cales* for the plural."

The title was only one of many inaccuracies, but they are relatively unimportant. The book itself was a combination of three projected books, all worked together and printed as a unit: (1) translations of the Romany songs or rhymes that he had copied down when they were recited to him by his Gitano gypsy friends; to these he had added many others from the Spanish versions by Juan Bailly; (2) a Glossary, or Vocabulary of the Zincali; (3) a prose account of the Spanish writers on gypsy life and lore. Had he offered either of the first two projects separately, it would undoubtedly have been rejected, but the story of the gypsies was considered interesting enough to sell the book.

It was Borrow's first important work; appropriately enough, it dealt with gypsies. As literature it is not in any sense a great piece of work. Occasional prose passages are magnificent, but the vocabulary is spotty and the translations strained and ineffective.

Perhaps the most interesting thing about the book is Borrow's attitude toward the gypsies he loved so much and knew so well. He was essentially a realist in observation, but a romantic in point of view. He realized that the gypsies were cheats, vagabonds, rogues, liars, and thieves— but vagabonds and rogues had an irresistible fascination for him. Their dishonesty and knavery did not repel him, nor did their views on personal property: in their company Borrow the Tory ceased to exist, and Borrow the Romany Chal was born. For Borrow was essentially a primitive; he valued those things which the gypsies held most dear: loyalty to one's friends, regardless of danger; faithfulness; a chastity that consisted of devotion to one's mate. This was what he saw in the gypsies, and what he admired; it is also what he wrote in *The Zincali*. And, because all of us admire roguery and knavery, when it is combined with loyalty and faithfulness, that part of *The Zincali* is occasionally read and enjoyed today, in much the same fashion as picaresque novels are read.

Except for slight revision, *The Zincali* had been written in Spain. Borrow also brought back with him the materials for a greater and more famous book: *The Bible in Spain*. All his life he tried to be a great writer, and to win popular acclaim. Only once did he succeed, with this book. For *Lavengro*, popular as it afterward became, was but belatedly recognized during its author's life-time.

The book was a mosaic of the letters written from 1835 to 1840 to the officials of the Bible Society. Many are direct transcripts, few are changed much. John Murray published *The Bible in Spain* in 1843, and one morning Borrow awoke to find himself famous. Edition after edition was sold—seven editions in the first six weeks after publication. He was the literary lion of London. Critics praised the book highly. Perhaps, crowning irony that had as much of bitter as of sweet, the most remarkable incident connected with the sale of the book was that 30,000 copies were sold within a year in the United States; from these Borrow never received a penny.

But he had received a large sum of money from the book; he had an established position in English letters.

The fame he had yearned for so ardently as a young man had arrived, and life should have been sweet. In the past he could count a happy childhood, one happy summer in the dingle, and happy days in Russia and Spain. He was forty years old—and from that day he was wretchedly unhappy, discontented, satisfied with nothing. What the man had, he no longer wanted.

IV

When a man begins to live again in his youth, he has grown old. In the case of George Borrow, old age set in shortly after forty. Seemingly it was through no cause of his own; he struggled valiantly if fitfully against the insidious disease. But almost from the day he began his autobiography, he became a retrospective figure—so far as the world around him was concerned, a chimera running around in a vacuum. Yet the reason for writing an auto-biography was sound enough. Little of Borrow's life was known; that little, however, was romantic and adventurous enough to promise even more fascinating books about other periods of his life. The public was interested, seeking, as usual, every possible bit of information about the latest literary sensation. A quick, even if shoddy, autobiography published in 1844 or 1845 would have sold by the thousands.

One friend in particular was insistent that Borrow write the story of his life. Richard Ford had travelled for many years in Spain; returning to England, he spent ten years studying Spanish history, especially local histories. Then he returned to Spain, this time with an adequate back-ground. After sixteen years of patient reading and thor-ough travel, he wrote a *Hand-book for Travellers in Spain* (1845), and was, with the possible exception of Borrow him-self, the leading English authority on Spain. He had re-

viewed *The Bible in Spain* for the *Edinburgh Review;* before
the book's publication he had helped Borrow a great deal in
getting it ready for the press.   Now he wrote:

How I wish you had given us (in the Gypsies) more about yourself.   I shall give you a hint to publish your *whole* adventures for
the last twenty years.   Would you like me to furnish a few hints?
—What countries have you been in?   What languages do you
understand?   All this would excite public attention and curiosity,
and sell the future book.

Borrow required no great amount of urging; even before
The Bible was published he had written to John Murray
(Dec. 1, 1842): "I hope our book will be successful; if so,
I shall put another on the stocks.   Capital subject: early
life; studies and adventures; some account of my father,
William Taylor, Big Ben, etc., etc."
    Such was the genesis of *Lavengro*.   It was to be an auto-
biography; not precisely a factual biography, for on January
24th, 1844, Richard Ford wrote to a friend:

I am here on a visit to *El Gitano*; two 'rum' coves, in a queer
country . . . we defy the elements, and chat over *las cosas de
España*, and he tells me portions of his life, more strange even
than his book (*The Bible in Spain*) . . . [with] a zomarra (sheep-
skin coat) now before me, as I am in a sort of summer-house called
La Mesquita, in which El Gitano concocts his lucubrations, and
paints his pictures, for his object is to colour up and to poetize
his adventures.

Borrow worked intermittently on *Lavengro* from 1842 to
1851: the autobiography of the first twenty-two years of
his life required nine years of agonized writing.   On the
second of October, 1843, he wrote to his publisher, John
Murray:

I wish I had another *Bible* ready, but slow and sure is my maxim. The book which I am at present about will consist, if I live to finish it, of a series of Rembrandt pictures interspersed here and there with a Claude. I shall tell the world of my parentage, my early thoughts and habits; how I became a sap-engro, or viper-catcher; my wanderings with the regiment in England, Scotland, and Ireland. . . . Then a great deal about Norwich, Billy Taylor, Thurtell, etc.; how I took to study and became a lav-engro. What do you think of this as the bill of fare for the first Vol.? The second will consist of my adventures in London as an author in the year '23 [evidently a mis-date, as Borrow did not go to London until 1824], my adventures on the Big North Road in '24 [also incorrect—should read '25], Constantinople, etc. The third—but I shall tell you no more of my secrets.

To plan proved much easier than to do. Over and over he repeats that he wants this book to be the best work he can possibly write: he wanted it to be "full of grave fun and solemn laughter like the *Bible*." "I am writing to please myself, and am quite sure that if I can contrive to please myself, I shall please the public also."

For one thing, he had been too much the man of action. Now, for the first time in his life, he had money of his own in sufficient quantities to do as he pleased. In May, 1844, he went to Europe, and for seven months travelled through Hungary, Transylvania, Roumania, Wallachia, and on to Constantinople. Much of his time was spent with the gypsies, and he planned to write about them, but never did. From Constantinople he went to Asia Minor, then back through Thessaly and Albania to Rome, Paris and London. If he made any notes or left any records of this journey they have been destroyed. Probably it pleased him that there should be a second veiled period of seven months in his life, comparable to the earlier seven year period.

In 1845 Richard Ford's *Handbook for Travellers in Spain*

appeared: two thick volumes as the result of sixteen years of labor. Borrow was asked to review the *Handbook* for the *Quarterly Review;* he wrote and sent in a review that consisted almost entirely of a diatribe against Spanish officials and the Roman Catholic Church. The editor, J. G. Lockhart, wanted to introduce into the article quotations from the book, and give it more of the nature of a review, but Borrow refused to have his work tampered with. There was only one excuse for him: at the time Borrow was sick. Mrs. Borrow wrote to Lockhart:

With regard to the article, it must not be received as a specimen of what Mr. Borrow would have produced had he been well, but he considered his promise to Mr. Ford sacred—and it is only to be wished that it had appeared under more favourable circumstances. Borrow was ill at the time, having been very unwell for the last month, and particularly so lately. Shivering fits have been succeeded by burning fever, till his strength was much reduced; and he at present remains in a low, and weak state, and what is worse, we are by no means sure that the disease is subdued.

The review was never published, and Ford was hurt badly by Borrow's treatment. Borrow wrote several letters to magazines and newspapers, however, and the two men remained friends.

The illness, to which he usually referred as laziness but which was a recurrence of a fever contracted in Spain, retarded his own writing. In 1846 he felt better, and completed the first draft of *Lavengro;* but revision was needed, and he refused to prepare the manuscript hurriedly for his publisher. Apparently he was tired of writing, and wanted something else to do.

After trying to get an appointment as magistrate, and failing, Borrow applied for the Consulate at Canton. His early experience in Russia while publishing the Bible in Manchu undoubtedly seemed to him ample qualifications, but Borrow's application was never seriously considered. This might have been only a bitter routine disappointment, save for one thing: he had requested Dr. John Bowring's help, since his old friend and collaborator had dabbled in politics for years, and Bowring had promised to use his influence with Lord Palmerston in Borrow's cause. Instead, Bowring himself was appointed Consul at Canton.

From that moment George Borrow hated him. In the Appendix to *The Romany Rye* he crucified him with all the invective at his command, and charged Bowring with having passed the Manchu Bible that Borrow had edited as his own. "The Old Radical" is the name given Bowring there, and as portrayed by Borrow he is one of the most despicable creatures in literature. The truth seems to be that he was a selfish and self-seeking man, willing to help others when not at the expense of himself. Borrow saw only ingratitude and injustice— and he concludes the Appendix to *The Romany Rye* with his answer to Bowring headed

> This very dirty man, with his very dirty face
> Would do any dirty act, which would get him a place.

In 1848 John Murray announced on his List of Forthcoming Works: *Lavengro, an Autobiography.* By George Borrow, author of *The Bible in Spain*, etc. The same year he advertised the book in the *Athanaeum* and *Quarterly Review* under the name *Life: A Drama*, by George Borrow. The first volume went to the printer, but Borrow was too ill to finish his work of revision—and he obstinately refused to allow the book to be published in its existing state. Again in 1849 and in 1850 Murray announced the volume as in press, under the title of *Lavengro, An Autobiography*, but no book appeared. Borrow corrected every page of proof with painstaking care, though most of the time he was suffering severely from a feverish malady that gave him little ease. Much of his time was spent in bed.

Finally, in the *Athanaeum* (Dec, 1850) an announcement appeared:

Just Ready. *Lavengro;* The Scholar—The Gypsy—The Priest. By George Borrow, 3 vols. post 8vo. With Portrait. In that form *Lavengro* was published on the 7th of February, 1851, in an edition of three thousand copies—which lasted just twenty-one years.

Lavengro is so largely autobiographical that it leaves but slight room for criticism. The first volume was a record of his early life, the other two volumes of his London career and his gypsy wanderings. The final volume ended abruptly, when a postillion concluded a story he had been telling at the inn. The remaining matter was to be published immediately, in a fourth volume called *The Romany Rye*, advertised with *Lavengro*. Even the Isopel Berners episode hung fire; they were left living together in the dingle. The conclusion had all the elements of a section of a magazine serial.

Its reception was almost unanimously unfavorable. Dr. Bowring had previously contracted to review the book for the *Edinburgh Review*, but he himself received such uncomplimentary treatment that no review appeared. Not until *The Romany Rye* appeared six years later did the *Edinburgh Review* mention *Lavengro*, when it reviewed the two books. *The Quarterly Review*, no longer under the editorship of Lockhart, did the same thing, reviewing the two books under the heading, "Roving Life in England." The *Athanaeum* wrote that "few books have excited warmer expectations than this long-talked-of biography; and great is the disappointment which it will leave in the minds of those who expected anything beyond a collection of bold picaresque sketches." *Fraser's* said, "Mr. Borrow would choose that men should hold their breath at the mention of him. . . . He mystifies everybody, but nobody mystifies him. His universe seems to divide itself into two parts: George Borrow, active; the universe, minus George Borrow, passive. . . ."

All the old doubts about Borrow's philological learning and his general truthfulness were reviewed. His glorification of prize-fighting was reviled as uncivilized and immoral; his glorification of vagabondage considered a frontal assault on morality.

The book-buying public agreed with the critics. Victorian morality was outraged. It did not matter that he wrote superlatively well of gypsies and vagabonds, of bruisers and prize-fights. It was an age of gentility and refinement, when the legs of a piano were referred to as limbs, and in one home at least, draped with ruffled skirts. Borrow's ideal man must be ready to knock another man down if occasion required it. That his descriptions of fights are about the best written helped him not at all. A moral man outside the folds of the church is more dangerous than a sinner, the preachers say; he causes other people to wonder how such a man can be damned to eternal torment, and from that to doubt the value of the church—particularly if they compare the moral man with the usual run of the church members. People felt the same about Borrow's gypsies: he describes them as thieves, poisoners, cheats, blackguards, counterfeiters; he allows them only two virtues, chastity on the part of their women and loyalty and faithfulness to the tribe and all its members on the part of all of them. Yet he writes so well about gypsies, makes them and their way of life so attractive, that he was far more dangerous than a poorer, less powerful writer would have been.

To this flood of recrimination Borrow reacted somewhat after the manner of a wounded lion. He girded himself for combat; the lion could hardly have attacked more rapidly or more fiercely. There was a conspiracy against him; all the adverse criticism of the book that he had written with such care was caused by sheer vindictiveness and jealousy. He wrote to John Murray: "If ever a book experienced infamous and undeserved treatment, it was that book. I was attacked in every form that envy and malice could suggest."

He reached his peak in this polemical warfare in the Appendix to *The Romany Rye*, written between 1852 and 1854, though not published until 1857. In it he exhibits the critics, the pseudo-critics he labels them, "with blood and foam streaming from their jaws," and he is "proud of a book which has had the honour of being rancorously abused and execrated by every unmanly scoundrel, every sycophantic lacquey, and every political religious renegade in Britain." Invective and vocabulary mounted together: the critics had lacked the knowledge to detect some misspelling of foreign names; they had attacked only the true and valuable portions. His opinion of their personal habits and manhood he expressed in a paragraph worthy of Swift:

In the first place he wishes to dispose of certain individuals who call themselves men of wit and fashion—about town—who he is told have abused his book 'vaustly'—their own word. These people paint their cheeks, wear white kid gloves, and dabble in literature, or what they conceive to be literature. For abuse from such people the writer was prepared. Does anyone imagine that the writer was not well aware, before he published his book, that, whenever he gave it to the world, he should be attacked by every literary coxcomb in England who had influence enough to procure the insertion of a scurrilous article in a magazine or newspaper! He has been in Spain, and has seen how invariably the mule attacks the horse; now, why does the mule attack the horse. Why, because the latter carries about with him that which the envious hermaphrodite does not possess.

After such fashion did Borrow receive his punishment for giving, not a straight narrative of events, but a rich, strange mixture of fact and dream, a philological compound too potent for the people of his time. For two years he occupied himself exclusively with completing the sequel to *Lavengro*, and in writing the appendix to that volume. Never once did he doubt that his book was worthy: he had written a great book, and its critics were fools. However, he did not confine himself to the critics alone. Sir Walter Scott came in for some glancing blows because he favored the Stuarts and wrote "Scotch-gentility nonsense"—though some of his novels and poems Borrow thought very fine. The Roman Catholic Church, and the priestcraft which in *Lavengro* he had portrayed so virulently in "the man in black,"was again and in even more vigorous language pictured as the greatest danger to freedom, and especially to religious liberty, in England. The refinement and pseudo-gentility that had been offended by the bruisers and gypsies he considered unhealthy, since it consisted of sham, false modesty, and tawdry glitter. The man was angry, and it was the natural man who spoke, in his own right, without benefit of art, but with a devastating directness.

One episode occurred in this period that must have delighted his sense for the personally dramatic. All his life he dramatized himself; once he was acclaimed a hero by the nation. Mr. and Mrs. Borrow had spent the summer of

1853 at Yarmouth, resting and fishing. The local newspaper reported, in its careful English way—

Intrepidity—Yarmouth jetty presented an extraordinary and
thrilling spectacle on Thursday the 8th inst., about one o'clock.
The sea raged frantically, and a ship's boat, endeavoring to land
for water, was upset, and the men were engulfed in a wave some
thirty feet high, and struggling with it in vain.   The moment was
an awful one, when George Borrow, the well-known author of
Lavengro and *The Bible In Spain*, dashed into the surf and saved
one life, and through his instrumentality the others were saved.
We ourselves have known this gifted man for years, and, daring
as was this deed, we have known him more than once to risk his
life for others.   We are happy to add that he has sustained no
material injury.

Papers throughout the country headlined the "Gallant
Conduct of George Borrow," and that much maligned
author must have felt considerable satisfaction at receiving
praise for his personal conduct when his books were being
vilified.

Though finished in 1854, *The Romany Rye* was not published until 1857.   John Murray received the manuscript
late in 1854, but he had been burnt once, and he hesitated
to start another conflagration.   He delayed, and wrote
about *conditions* of publishing.   Borrow was furious, and
did not hesitate to remind him of the success of *The Bible
in Spain*, and to demand the return of the manuscript, that
he might submit it to another publisher.   This threat
sufficed, though belatedly, and an edition of 1000 copies
was published in April, 1857.

It was more successful than *Lavengro*: perhaps because of
the Appendix, loaded with invective after the manner of
Pope or Swift.   That edition was exhausted within the year,
and a second edition of 750 copies was issued early in 1858.

Never, however, did it threaten to rival *The Bible in Spain* in popularity.

The critics were mellower and fairer, although all deplored the Appendix, calling it ill-advised and unjust. Most of them praised the narrative, however, and with it *Lavengro*: typical was the attitude of the *Quarterly Review*:

> Though we do not think Mr. Borrow is a good counsel in his own cause, we are yet strongly of opinion that Time in his case has some wrongs to repair, and that *Lavengro* has not obtained the fame that was its due.

Unfortunately, he had angered too many people. London and a literary atmosphere had no attraction for him. The family moved from Oulton to Norfolk, but the change brought with it no freshness of spirit. He spent much of his time in solitary walking tours, sometimes visiting old relatives in Cornwall who had discovered his existence when he rescued a Yarmouth sailor—they had never heard of his books. In the summer of 1854, he went on a sixteen weeks walking tour in Wales; in 1855, on a vacation to the Isle of Man. He kept note-books of these trips, and planned to write about them. Again in August, 1857, he visited Wales, tramping four and a half miles an hour with a huge green umbrella clutched in his hand. He had determined to write another book, this time about Wales.

A decision of this kind was inevitable. George Borrow was not a gregarious person; social life of any kind bored him. He had few intimate friends; since his estrangement from Richard Ford, only John Murray and Dr. Gordon Hoke remained—and many times his relations with Murray were strained. To this list could now be added Edward Fitzgerald, who had sent him a copy of his translations of Calderon, and consulted him about the Rubaiyat. They were totally unlike in temperament, in learning, and in style of writing—the fine rapier of the translator of Omar contrasts strangely with the huge fists of the bruiser of England.   But friends they were, and friends they remained.

His mother died at Oulton on the 16th of August, 1858. Borrow had loved her devotedly, and his sorrow was intense. The circle of his intimates was becoming ever more circumscribed.

For consolation he went on a long walking tour through the Highlands of Scotland.   On his return, tormented again by the desire to see his beloved translations in print, he sent *The Sleeping Bard* to John Murray.   That book, whose terrors had so frightened the little Welsh bookseller in 1830, had no attraction for the London publisher.   Though he refused to publish it himself, he allowed Borrow to use the Murray imprint on the book, and an edition of 250 copies was printed at Yarmouth in 1860.   The only review of it was by Borrow himself, worked into an article on *The Welsh and their Literature*, published anonymously in the *Quarterly Review* for January, 1861.   Borrow's venture was successful, however, and highly satisfactory to himself: the entire edition was sold within a month.

In the meantime he was working steadily on his book about Wales.   In 1860 the family moved from Norfolk to Brompton, and they lived even more quietly than before. Nothing save writing and walking, and the companionship of his wife, were left him.   She was invaluable to him, for she copied his scrawl in legible hand-writing and carried on his correspondence, as well as furnished him satisfactory companionship.   Sometimes the two of them, with her daughter, returned to Oulton.

In 1862 *Wild Wales* was published, in three volumes. The edition (1,000 copies) was soon exhausted, but even yet the critics had no use for Borrow. Few noticed the book; only one praised it, in the *Spectator*: "This is the first clever book we remember to have seen in which an honest attempt is made to do justice to Welsh literature." An analysis of the book follows, then "He likes the country and its language, and he is very hearty in his likes and dislikes. As it is, he has written the best book about Wales ever published."

In many ways, *Wild Wales* is about the last thing one would expect from the author of the Appendix to *The Romany Rye*. It reveals a chastened Borrow, older and wiser, who tramps through its pages at from four and a half to six miles an hour, satchel on shoulder and green umbrella in his hand, shouting Welsh and Scandinavian songs. He stays close to the subject: it is the record of his rambles through Wales in 1854, touched up with the added experience gained during his visit in 1857. He wrote in a more restrained, objective manner; there is nothing against the pope, and his animosity toward "gentility-nonsense" rarely shows itself. There were no bruisers, and no gypsies until almost the end of the book.

In their place was something of the atmosphere of Wales. The jealous clannishness of the Welsh, their clinging to their own language, the fact that Welsh poets are national poets, folk poets common to the mass and not for the few—these and the trivial incidents of travel, such as his blessing, in Latin, a group of Irish laborers who mistook him for a priest, give the book great charm. It is one of his major books, well qualified to rank with *The Bible in Spain* and *Lavengro*.

Soon after the publication of *Wild Wales*, Borrow dropped quietly from public notice. Occasionally he went on walking tours, but the man who had celebrated ale as a specific against indecision and spleen found it necessary to drink less ale and more water, and to shorten his journeys. A small but devoted circle of Borrovians began to collect around him, under the lead of Theodore Watts-Dunton; he saw himself gradually re-established in critical favor. This was pleasant enough, but it was slight compensation for his own increasing age, and none at all for the death of his wife in January, 1869. For the most part, in those days, he felt with Emerson:

> It is time to be old,
> To take in sail:—
> The god of bounds
> Who sets to seas a shore,
> Came to me in his fatal rounds,
> And said: 'No More!'

One brief period of activity was left for him. From 1872 to 1874 the old man worked over books that he had written years before. For one thing, the twenty-one year period was up, the three thousand copies of *Lavengro* were exhausted; a new edition was needed, and Borrow wrote a preface to the second edition:

Lavengro made its first appearance more than one-and-twenty years ago. It was treated in anything but a courteous manner. Indeed, abuse ran riot, and many said that the book was killed. If by killed was meant knocked down and stunned, which is the Irish acceptation of the word—there is a great deal about Ireland in the book—they were right enough. It was not dead, however, oh dear no! as is tolerably well shown by the present edition, which has been long called for.

The chief assailants of the book were the friends of Popery in England. They were enraged because the author stood up for the religion of his fathers, his country, and the Bible against the mythology of a foreign priest.

One more service Borrow performed for the Bible Society, re-working and reconstructing his translation of the Gypsy St. Luke gospel, first published at Madrid in 1837. It was published, or re-printed, in 1872.

Also, and much more important than either of these new editions, Borrow now found his gypsy supremacy threatened: an industrious group of imitators—or, to use a more just and polite word, emulators—had appeared. Borrow never considered them friends; they were jealous rivals to be envied.

One of these young men, Charles G. Leland, had written him in 1871, sending him translations of some gypsy ballads he had recently had published. Also, he intended to prepare a book on the language of the English gypsies. Leland admired the older author: "My dear Mr. Borrow, for all this you are entirely responsible. More than twenty years ago your books had an incredible influence on me, and now you see the results."

It was the result that aroused him. His had been a unique place, and it was not for him to share it with some pretentious upstart, no matter how friendly. Borrow prepared for the press the volume called *Romano Lavo-Lil: Word-Book of the Romany*. But he was growing old—a man of seventy cannot revise proof-sheets rapidly, and he had always been a slow, careful writer. Leland's book appeared first. Its author had asked to be allowed to dedicate the book to George Borrow, but never received an answer.

What Borrow presented to the world in 1874 was a vocabulary slightly enlarged over the notes he had made before 1843. The critics praised Borrow and his gypsy books, but criticized the *Lavo-Lil*. He had not kept up with the times. Scientific scholars, drudging pedants, had turned to the gypsy for a new field, and their work was very valuable as well as very thorough. Borrow's philological work was never definitive; it was valuable only as it added to the richness of his narrative prose, and called to the language the attention of less gifted but more painstaking men. His vocabulary consisted of fourteen hundred words; that same year a German professor, Dr. Miklosich, published the first part of a twelve-volume work, *On the Dialects and Migrations of the Gypsies In Europe.*

The second section of *Lavo-Lil,* made up of scattered translations of prose and verse from the Romany, received more praise. However, George Borrow was finished. His last public pronouncement had been given to the world, as he might have thrown a stray cur a bone—and the bone had been cautiously sniffed at before being accepted. He retired to Oulton to live in solitude. Sometimes he was seen stalking along the roads or plunging through the woods, carrying his green umbrella, and wearing a broad-brimmed black hat and a Spanish coat. He was a tragic, lonely figure. A hermit withdrawn from the world, almost forgotten.

On the 26th of July, 1881, George Borrow died. He was buried beside his wife in West Brompton Cemetery. The restless body and the restless spirit were at last quiet.

V

A few men have made a place for themselves by their idiosyncrasies. George Borrow was such a one. His philosophy was as vague as Charles Lamb's. He had no great depth of thought, no large message to give to the world. True, he had the gypsies and a general knowledge of many languages, but it is not as a philologist, or an antiquarian or folklorist, or a biblical missionary, or a great traveller, that he will live. He was a personal writer capable of interesting many readers in the things that interested him; he was the master of a splendidly simple, powerful, Defoe-like prose that re-created English roadside life and Rommany Chals and bruisers. His prose is as vigorously alive as he was.

By no stretch of the imagination can Borrow be fitted into that absurd classification we call major writers. His books are not great mountain peaks, such as *Tom Jones* or *Paradise Lost*, from which, once we have mounted to the summit, the panorama of human life can be viewed behind us with a new understanding and a finer perception of all life. *Lavengro* and *The Bible in Spain* are out-of-the-way, precipitous knolls covered with an unusual shrubbery: once we have gained the summit we have secured a new perception of only a personalized territory and of two persons: George Borrow, and through him, ourselves.

Since his death the Borrovian cult has grown steadily larger. As the world grows more and more standardized and commonplace, more people seek the individual and the unusual. In 1924 an edition of the *Complete Works of George Borrow* was issued. It contains all the miscellaneous matter that could be collected, except the *Celebrated Trials*. Forty-three years after his death *The Songs of Scandinavia* were published, in a sumptuous complete edition; throughout his life he had believed that they were his surest passport to fame. Dr. Bowring refused them, and so did John Murray. There is little likelihood that the world will be more interested today: as poetry they are romantically inartistic, and as translations frequently inaccurate.

It is just as well. The author of *The Vicar of Wakefield*

is as certain of immortality as the author of *Hamlet*. And Goldsmith's admirers are such sincerely, and because of personal taste; the weight of public opinion, the judgment of centuries, does not force the mind to an artificial liking. So it is with George Borrow. *The Bible in Spain*, *Lavengro*, and *Wild Wales* will be read as long as men admire fine prose and great personalities, but they will be read also because in them the reader has found a congenial spirit. That is enough for any man to achieve.

Record of First Publication

Index